Inclusive Online and Distance Education for Learners with Dis/abilities

The term *Inclusive Online Education* has generated great interest within and across educational levels and contexts, yet practical applications of it remain elusive in many institutional settings. Chapters in this book highlight, define and interrogate definitions of inclusion. The research studies reported here focus on moving the conversation about inclusive online education away from individual accommodations for which students must *qualify*, to models where learning experiences are designed for the success of all students and teachers—both technically and relationally.

While some authors do mention the need to know and understand the Universal Design for Learning (UDL), the authors in these chapters go beyond UDL to include understandings about historical challenges with inclusive education, emerging understandings about designing strong online instruction, and how placed-based thinking and social settings provide resources from which to draw in creating online learning environments and experiences that are not only humanized but *humane*. This book highlights research focused on moving the conversation about inclusion away from individual accommodations for which students must *qualify* to models where learning experiences are designed to address historical inequities and promote success for all students and teachers. Collectively, the chapters underscore the need to choose materials, design assessments, plan instruction, and engage with students in accordance with relational commitments to equity.

Inclusive Online and Distance Education for Learners with Dis/abilities will be a great resource for academics, researchers, and advanced students of Education, Education Policy, Educational Research, and Disability Studies in Education. The chapters included in this book were originally published as a special issue of *Distance Education*.

Mary F. Rice is an Associate Professor of Literacy for the College of Education and Human Sciences at the University of New Mexico, Albuquerque, USA. She is a former Classroom Teacher of English language arts, ESL, and reading support. She has been involved with K-12 distance, online, and blended learning since 2013 as a Researcher, Evaluator, Teacher, and Teacher Educator. Mary's research focuses on the relational aspects of designing, delivering, and doing of inclusive and accessible online learning among educators, parents, and students. Mary has worked with individuals in online learning in most U.S. states and several countries. She was named an Emerging Scholar by the Online Learning Consortium in 2018 and has been honored with awards from organizations such as the American Educational Research Association and the Initiative for Literacy in the 21st Century. Most recently, Mary was awarded the National Technology Leadership Initiative Award in 2023, which is given for innovative interdisciplinary research shared across multiple professional organizations. Mary is the Managing Editor of Online Learning, the Editor-in-Chief of the *Journal of Online Learning Research*, and an Editorial Board Member for academic journals including *Distance Education* and *Studying Teacher Education*.

Michael Dunn is an Associate Professor of Special Education and Literacy at Washington State University Vancouver, USA, and teaches undergraduate and graduate courses applicable to K-12 educators. His areas of research interest include writing strategy interventions, struggling writers, learning disabilities, multi-tiered systems of support (MTSS), inclusion strategies for students with disabilities, and general education teachers' referral criteria for students' possible special education classification and placement. Dr. Dunn's research accomplishments include 43 journal articles, 2 edited books, 9 book chapters, 62 conference presentations, and 7 funded external grants. He taught in Toronto (Ontario) area elementary/middle schools for 11 years. His student caseload included learning disabilities (reading, writing, and/or math) and other disability types. Dr. Michael Dunn's awards include the following: the 2022 Nichols-Mitchell Research Award from Washington State University in recognition of his research aims and accomplishments; the Organization of Teacher Educators in Reading (OTER, a group within the International Literacy Association) chose his 2011 published manuscript in their *Journal of Reading Education* as the 2012 Outstanding Article Award; and in 2012, the College of Education awarded Dr. Michael Dunn the Judy Nichols Mitchell Research Fellow Award, which provided $10,000 for his research in each academic year across 2012–2015.

Inclusive Online and Distance Education for Learners with Dis/abilities

Promoting Accessibility and Equity

Edited by
Mary F. Rice and Michael Dunn

LONDON AND NEW YORK

First published 2024
by Routledge
4 Park Square, Milton Park, Abingdon, Oxon, OX14 4RN

and by Routledge
605 Third Avenue, New York, NY 10158

Routledge is an imprint of the Taylor & Francis Group, an informa business

Chapters 1–4 and 6–8 © 2024 Open and Distance Learning Association of Australia, Inc.
Chapter 5 © 2022 Poppy Gibson, Rebecca Clarkson, and Mike Scott. Originally published as Open Access.

With the exception of Chapter 5, no part of this book may be reprinted or reproduced or utilised in any form or by any electronic, mechanical, or other means, now known or hereafter invented, including photocopying and recording, or in any information storage or retrieval system, without permission in writing from the publishers. For details on the rights for Chapter 5, please see the chapter's Open Access footnote.

Trademark notice: Product or corporate names may be trademarks or registered trademarks, and are used only for identification and explanation without intent to infringe.

British Library Cataloguing-in-Publication Data
A catalogue record for this book is available from the British Library

ISBN13: 978-1-032-53450-3 (hbk)
ISBN13: 978-1-032-53451-0 (pbk)
ISBN13: 978-1-003-41207-6 (ebk)

DOI: 10.4324/9781003412076

Typeset in Myriad Pro
by codeMantra

Publisher's Note
The publisher accepts responsibility for any inconsistencies that may have arisen during the conversion of this book from journal articles to book chapters, namely the inclusion of journal terminology.

Disclaimer
Every effort has been made to contact copyright holders for their permission to reprint material in this book. The publishers would be grateful to hear from any copyright holder who is not here acknowledged and will undertake to rectify any errors or omissions in future editions of this book.

Contents

	Citation Information	vi
	Notes on Contributors	viii
1	Inclusive online and distance education for learners with dis/abilities *Mary F. Rice and Michael Dunn*	1
2	Making the invisible, visible: disability in South African distance education *Paul Prinsloo and Chinaza Uleanya*	7
3	Students with mental health (dis)Abilities' storied experiences within distance education *Rose C. B. Singh and Judy E. MacDonald*	26
4	Advising college students with dis/abilities in online learning *José Israel Reyes and Julio Meneses*	44
5	Promoting potential through purposeful inclusive assessment for distance learners *Poppy Gibson, Rebecca Clarkson, and Mike Scott*	61
6	Identifying accessibility factors affecting learner inclusion in online university programs *Rita Fennelly-Atkinson, Kimberly N. LaPrairie, and Donggil Song*	74
7	Higher education leaders' perspectives of accessible and inclusive online learning *Amy Lomellini, Patrick R. Lowenthal, Chareen Snelson, and Jesús H. Trespalacios*	92
8	Serving students with disabilities in K-12 online learning: daily practices of special educators during the COVID-19 pandemic *Allison Starks*	114
	Index	139

Citation Information

The chapters in this book were originally published in the journal *Distance Education*, volume 43, issue 4 (2022). When citing this material, please use the original page numbering for each article, as follows:

Chapter 1
Inclusive online and distance education for learners with dis/abilities
Mary F. Rice and Michael Dunn
Distance Education, volume 43, issue 4 (2022) pp. 483–488

Chapter 2
Making the invisible, visible: disability in South African distance education
Paul Prinsloo and Chinaza Uleanya
Distance Education, volume 43, issue 4 (2022) pp. 489–507

Chapter 3
Students with mental health (dis)Abilities' storied experiences within distance education
Rose C. B. Singh and Judy E. MacDonald
Distance Education, volume 43, issue 4 (2022) pp. 508–525

Chapter 4
Advising college students with dis/abilities in online learning
José Israel Reyes and Julio Meneses
Distance Education, volume 43, issue 4 (2022) pp. 526–542

Chapter 5
Promoting potential through purposeful inclusive assessment for distance learners
Poppy Gibson, Rebecca Clarkson, and Mike Scott
Distance Education, volume 43, issue 4 (2022) pp. 543–555

Chapter 6
Identifying accessibility factors affecting learner inclusion in online university programs
Rita Fennelly-Atkinson, Kimberly N. LaPrairie, and Donggil Song
Distance Education, volume 43, issue 4 (2022) pp. 556–573

Chapter 7
Higher education leaders' perspectives of accessible and inclusive online learning
Amy Lomellini, Patrick R. Lowenthal, Chareen Snelson, and Jesús H. Trespalacios
Distance Education, volume 43, issue 4 (2022) pp. 574–595

Chapter 8
Serving students with disabilities in K-12 online learning: daily practices of special educators during the COVID-19 pandemic
Allison Starks
Distance Education, volume 43, issue 4 (2022) pp. 596–620

For any permission-related enquiries please visit:
http://www.tandfonline.com/page/help/permissions

Notes on Contributors

Rebecca Clarkson is a Senior Lecturer in Education at Anglia Ruskin University, UK. Rebecca teaches on the education undergraduate and postgraduate courses. Her main research interests are teaching and assessment practices in primary literacy.

Michael Dunn is an Associate Professor of Special Education and Literacy at Washington State University Vancouver, USA, and teaches undergraduate and graduate courses applicable to K-12 educators. His areas of research interest include writing strategy interventions, struggling writers, learning disabilities, multi-tiered systems of support (MTSS), inclusion strategies for students with disabilities, and general education teachers' referral criteria for students' possible special education classification and placement. Dr. Dunn's research accomplishments include 43 journal articles, 2 edited books, 9 book chapters, 62 conference presentations, and 7 funded external grants. He taught in Toronto (Ontario) area elementary/middle schools for 11 years. His student caseload included learning disabilities (reading, writing, and/or math) and other disability types. Dr. Michael Dunn's awards include the following: the 2022 Nichols-Mitchell Research Award from Washington State University in recognition of his research aims and accomplishments; the Organization of Teacher Educators in Reading (OTER, a group within the International Literacy Association) chose his 2011 published manuscript in their *Journal of Reading Education* as the 2012 Outstanding Article Award; and in 2012, the College of Education awarded Dr. Michael Dunn the Judy Nichols Mitchell Research Fellow Award, which provided $10,000 for his research in each academic year across 2012–2015.

Rita Fennelly-Atkinson is an Adjunct Professor at Sam Houston State University, Huntsville, USA, and the Director of Micro-credentials at Digital Promise. She identifies as disabled and has worked at the intersection of education and technology to create inclusive and accessible learning environments for learners for the past 20 years.

Poppy Gibson is a Senior Lecturer in Education at Anglia Ruskin University, UK; Primary Education Studies Accelerated Blended course Lead; and Senior Lecturer in Primary Education. Poppy's key research interests are around mental health and well-being.

Kimberly N. LaPrairie is the Director of the Instructional Systems Design and Technology doctoral program at Sam Houston State University, Huntsville, USA. She has over 20 years of education experience focusing on technology integration to improve educational and training systems in organizational settings, instructor effectiveness, and content accessibility.

Amy Lomellini is an Associate Director of Blended and Online Learning at Molloy University, USA, and a Doctoral Candidate at Boise State University, USA. She leads the design and implementation of quality blended and online learning initiatives. Her research focuses on accessible and inclusive online course design for higher education.

Patrick R. Lowenthal is a Professor in the Department of Educational Technology at Boise State University, USA. He specializes in designing and developing online learning environments. His research focuses on how people communicate using emerging technologies—with a specific focus on issues of presence, identity, and community—in online learning environments.

Judy E. MacDonald is a Professor and Director of the School of Social Work and the Assistant Dean of Equity and Inclusion in the Faculty of Health at Dalhousie University, Halifax, Canada. Judy's scholarship focuses on access and inclusion within postsecondary institutions for disabled students.

Julio Meneses is an Associate Professor of Research Methods at the Faculty of Psychology and Education Sciences at the Universitat Oberta de Catalunya, Barcelona, Spain; the Head of the Learning Analytics Unit (eLearning Innovation Center); and an Internet Interdisciplinary Institute Researcher.

Paul Prinsloo is a Research Professor in Open Distance Learning in the Department of Business Management at the University of South Africa, South Africa. His research focuses on student success in open and distributed learning environments, digital identities, learning analytics, and issues pertaining to student data privacy and ethics.

José Israel Reyes is a Doctoral Candidate at the Universitat Oberta de Catalunya, Barcelona, Spain. His research interests include the analysis of students with dis/abilities' experiences in online higher education in terms of socialization, collaboration, and interaction, as well as the improvement of the academic support to promote their academic success.

Mary F. Rice is an Associate Professor of Literacy for the College of Education and Human Sciences at the University of New Mexico, Albuquerque, USA. She is a former Classroom Teacher of English language arts, ESL, and reading support. She has been involved with K-12 distance, online, and blended learning since 2013 as a Researcher, Evaluator, Teacher, and Teacher Educator. Mary's research focuses on the relational aspects of designing, delivering, and doing of inclusive and accessible online learning among educators, parents, and students. Mary has worked with individuals in online learning in most U.S. states and several countries. She was named an Emerging Scholar by the Online Learning Consortium in 2018 and has been honored with awards from organizations such as the American Educational Research Association and the Initiative for Literacy in the 21st Century. Most recently, Mary was awarded the National Technology Leadership Initiative Award in 2023, which is given for innovative interdisciplinary research shared across multiple professional organizations. Mary is the Managing Editor of Online Learning, the Editor-in-Chief of the *Journal of Online Learning Research*, and an Editorial Board Member for academic journals including *Distance Education* and *Studying Teacher Education*.

Mike Scott is a Higher Education Study Skills Tutor and Mentor, working specifically with students with autism spectrum disorder. Mike is currently working toward a doctorate of education at Bournemouth University, UK.

Chareen Snelson is Associate Professor in the Department of Educational Technology at Boise State University, USA, with over 20 years of experience in online education. Her scholarly activity emphasizes scoping reviews in educational technology, video in online education, and teaching qualitative research methods courses online.

Rose C. B. Singh completed this research as part of their Master of Social Work degree at Dalhousie University, Halifax, Canada. Rose is currently a Sessional Lecturer at Dalhousie University, Halifax, Canada, and a PhD Student at Memorial University of Newfoundland and Labrador, St. John's, Canada.

Donggil Song is an Associate Professor of Engineering Technology and Industrial Distribution at the College of Engineering at Texas A&M University, USA. His research lab focuses on artificial intelligence engineering for human learning, human-centered artificial intelligence, and machine learning based mixed-reality artificial intelligence systems.

Allison Starks is a Mixed-Methods Researcher and Doctoral Candidate at the University of California-Irvine, USA. She studies digital spaces as contexts for child development and how to promote digital equity for youth.

Jesús H. Trespalacios is an Associate Professor in the Department of Educational Technology at Boise State University, USA. He teaches online graduate courses on instructional design, technology integration, and educational research. His scholarly activity includes instructional design education, communities in online environments, teachers' technology integration, and doctoral advising.

Chinaza Uleanya is a Post-doctoral Fellow in the Department of Business Management at the University of South Africa, Pretoria, South Africa. He is an Educationist and passionate about researching into fields capable of enhancing teaching and learning activities. His niche research area includes higher education, leadership education, and rural education and development.

Inclusive online and distance education for learners with dis/abilities

Mary F. Rice and Michael Dunn

When Mary's grandparents were children in the 1930s, they lived in a rural area in the Snake River Valley on the border between Oregon and Idaho in the United States of America. At the young age of 7, Mary's grandmother's brother Howard drank some machine oil for a farming implement. The quaff burnt his vocal cords and caused long-term damage. After the accident, other children at school made fun of his voice, and he got into fights. Educators in the local school recommended that he be sent to a state school in Idaho. From childhood until his death in 1979, Great Uncle Howard lived and worked at that school. Though it is difficult to locate and access records, there is a possibility that the school benefited from Howard's labor while school officials collected monetary government benefits, supposedly to manage his care.

Educational models where children with varying types of disabilities, exceptionalities, and injuries were sent away from their families to obtain a physically isolated education from their families and the rest of their peers largely fell out of fashion in the United States of America amid other efforts to address civil rights issues. Legislation such as the Americans with Disabilities Act (1990), the Individuals with Disabilities in Education Act (2004), and Section 504 of the Rehabilitation Act of 1973 guaranteed some legal protection in the United States of America for youth and adults as well as in education settings.

While Howard's injury caused him to be seen as problematic in his original school setting, he built a life the best he could under exclusionary circumstances; the information we have suggests that he taught children at the school where he had been a student. Instead of planning for what individuals can do in learning settings with access to people and the best supports available within a culture or social context, educational institutions often stigmatize learners with disabilities because of what they are unable to do without support. These deficit orientations persist despite cultural historically grounded research suggesting that what individuals can do with support is a more important indicator of learning than what they can do independently (Gallimore & Tharp, 1990; John-Steiner & Mahn, 1996). A turn away from an adoration for learner independence is also crucial for positioning learners as having something to contribute to one another, to a knowledge base, and even to a community (Bekiryazıcı, 2015).

While Howard did have a physical injury with implications for his learning, the reason he could not continue in school was because the social context was disabling (Goodley et al., 2019; Marks, 1999; Sinclair, 2013). To acknowledge the nuances of understanding about how learners might be perceived as *abled* or *disabled* depending on the supports available in their environments, terms such as *(dis)abled*, *dis/abled*, and *dis-abled* have emerged (Rausch et al., 2019). When a disrupted form of disabled is used, it calls attention to the socially constructed nature of disability rather articulating a condition that exists within a person. The term also implicates other identities that might bring additional injustices on a person, such as race (Schiek & Chege, 2009; Smith, 2016).

Thus, it is critical to consider shifts in thinking from disability to dis/ability where decision-makers in social contexts must acknowledge their role in disabling students with unsupportive programming. Currently, many learners are at risk of receiving a disabling education, and thus there was a "necessity and urgency" to provide learners with access to the inclusive contexts (UNESCO, 1994, p. viii). For years now, many nations have made public agreements to provide inclusive learning environments through declarations, such as the Salamanca Statement and Framework for Action on Special Needs Education (UNESCO, 1994), the rectification of the United Nations Convention on the Rights of Persons with Disabilities (United Nations, 2006), the Millennium Declaration (United Nations, 2000), and most recently, the United Nations (2016) Sustainable Development Goals. As a result of these global efforts, many countries have clarified and amended their respective laws to include access for all learners to educational opportunities at all levels.

While it seems a step in right direction to require inclusion, in theory, practical efforts have been fraught with complications. For example, Björnsdóttir and Traustadóttir (2010) conducted research in Iceland and found that inclusive efforts failed to account for identities other than the proscribed or assigned dis/ability. In another study, Pavenkov et al. (2015) compared the laws and practices around inclusion in Russia and India and found that both countries' needs for specially trained teachers and other educators was radically out of sync with the aspirations and requirements of their laws and policies. More recently, Mavropoulou et al. (2021) captured and described sharp divides between inclusive policy and inclusive practices in Australia. As far as we know, there is no country in the world that has been able to make a strong match between social goals for inclusion with practical outcomes in education. The overall outcome is ongoing efforts to dis/able students and frame them as deviant for not being able to be successful in environments that were not designed to be more than minimally supportive.

The increase in digital technologies and distance education practices might offer some promise in terms of increasing access to teachers and other professionals with specialized training. Think of what it might have meant to Howard, his immediate family, and the generations of family that followed if he could have accessed assistive technologies to help him communicate. If he had lived in a time when private individuals and schools had access to the Internet, Howard might have even benefitted from teletherapy for speech language services and/or social support for the bullying he was enduring. However, digital and distance learning are not magic solutions to inclusion. Leading up to and now moving through the COVID-19 pandemic, educational institutions at all levels were developing a greater awareness of learners with diverse physical, emotional, and learning challenges (de Bruin, 2019; Koçdar & Bozkurt, 2022; Sniatecki et al., 2015; Weedon & Riddell 2016). Despite the heightened awareness, educational opportunities for learners with dis/abilities have been lagging. For example, while enrollment in institutions of higher education in the United States of America is increasing, degree completion rates for students with dis/abilities has been lower than those of peers (Järkestig Berggren et al., 2016). What this means is that institutions are gathering tuition, fees, and other monies from students and then not providing sufficient access to documentation of their efforts (e.g., a diploma) or providing them with the means to build an opportunity structure.

The increased use of distance learning strategies and affordances during the COVID-19 pandemic for all students can be seen as both an affordance and a barrier for learners with dis/abilities. Students will not automatically succeed merely because they are learning online or in some type of distance setting, but they are in a much stronger position to do so in an accessible environment (Layne et al., 2013; Xu & Jaggars, 2014). For example, a review of literature from Kinash et al. (2004) found that attending to the accessibility needs of students with dis/abilities held strong promise for ensuring online education would be accessible for all students, regardless of disability identity or status. After almost 20 years, this promising finding still has not found its way into the growing use of technology in distance and online learning, although other scholars have made similar findings (e.g., Hromalik & Koszalka, 2018). Without vigilance, distance and online educational settings may solidify within an ableist framing as designers, instructors, and leaders give into social and political pressures to converge around some notion of normative learning and away from alternative, disruptive approaches. Further, while it is important to design spaces around sound cognitive practices, re-envisioning digital spaces to directly confront social inequities is also necessary for learning. With these ideas in mind, we conceptualized this special issue on inclusion. The papers we accepted demonstrated promise in building the practical conception of learners who need support not as deviant bodies or minds, or as disturbers of otherwise orderly educational spaces, but rather as individuals who deserve to be included and who make contributions to educational settings and other spaces.

In "Making the Invisible, Visible: Disability in South African Education," Paul Prinsloo and Chinaza Uleanya conducted a scoping review of online and distance education and inclusive practices for students with disabilities in South Africa. Their insight into a specific country as a context demonstrates the global problem of institutional statements of or claims to commitments to inclusion that ring hollow with students, who report feeling largely invisible and underserved. The authors offer not just recommendations but provocations for transformative action.

In "Students with Mental Health (dis)Abilities' Storied Experiences within Distance Education," Rose Singh conducted a narrative inquiry with students learning in a context where their mental health conditions were framed as barriers. Six participants from two Canadian universities narrated their experiences living alongside the researcher on a landscape that was set up to dis/able them rather than support them. Key tensions that emerged included the need not just to cope well enough to stay in the program but to successfully navigate the landscape together.

In "Advising Students with Disabilities in Online Learning," José Israel Reyes and Julio Meneses employed exploratory case study methods using semi-structured interviews with 14 university student advisers at an online university in Spain. Many of the advisers in this study who were working with students who have mental health issues and chronic health challenges in a system that devalues human differences expressed frustration and deficit orientations to students. However, promise for meaningful inclusion emerged through the understanding that advisers, faculty, and staff benefitted from stronger collaboration and better coordination in their work. Advisers' use of flexible and diverse communication methods with students also provided for better dialogue and success.

In "Promoting Potential through Purposeful Inclusive Assessment for Distance Learners," Poppy Gibson, Rebecca Clarkson, and Mike Scott, all scholars from the United Kingdom, completed a literature review about inclusive assessment practices in online higher education classes. Based on their findings, the authors suggested three strategies: (1) Students should be more involved in decisions about assessments; (2) Students should participate in online group work, even though this requires some special planning from instructors; and (3) Instructor feedback in various modes (e.g., audio, video) is essential to the opportunity for all students to learn. Their work highlights what initial efforts might be made by instructors, designers, and program leaders to increase inclusion.

In "Identifying Accessibility Factors in Affecting Learner Inclusion in Online University Programs," Rita Fennelly-Atkinson, Kimberly LaPrairie, and Donggil Song, all from from the United States of America, completed an exploratory mixed-methods study about universities' online course checklists. Specifically, they evaluated the degree to which these lists met accessibility criteria and which criteria are most or least represented using Web

Content Accessibility Guidelines criteria. University factors around enrollment were also examined. The authors found that online program enrollment was linked with universities' management of accessibility compliance and the training of faculty for students' online course accessibility. Thus, designing online spaces to be accessible supports enrollment and retention of students.

In "Higher Education Leaders' Perspectives of Accessible and Inclusive Online Learning," Amy Lomellini, Patrick Lowenthal, Chareen Snelson, and Jesus Trespalacios analyzed qualitative interviews from leaders in higher education institutions about accessibility and inclusion in online learning in the United States of America. The leaders contended that although there are improvements to be made, they perceived an increase interest among their colleagues in designing online educational experiences that are more inclusive and they acknowledged the critical role the instructional designers are positioned to play in making these improvements.

Finally, in "Serving Students with Disabilities in K-12 Online Learning: Daily Practices of Special Educators during the COVID-19 Pandemic," Allison Starks asked special education teachers in the United States of America to complete an online survey and participate in interviews about online and/or remote K-12 learning with the use of technology during the pandemic. The findings of this study offer ideas about how special education teachers' use of strategies to differentiate instruction in both hybrid content instruction as well as home-school partnerships can help support all learners.

Given the insights and findings from these contributions to this special issue, we make the following general recommendations for practice, research, and policy. For practice, the articles in this issue suggest that time spent communicating with learners about their needs for support is vital for providing inclusive opportunities. To us, this does not mean holding a focus group or giving a survey once, designing a course, and then continuing without further comment or revision. It means that every learner individually and every class collectively deserves to participate in designing their learning experience, and this must be more than the choice of whether to write a response or make a video of a spoken response. It means a constant evaluation and positioning of the best tools and the widest exposure to others as possible. Instead of language and literacy being the goals of learning, language and literacy are the tools for learning (Vygotsky, 1978).

Drawing on the position that learners deserve access to people and the best cultural tools for their work, research and development should be searching for these and collaborating with educational settings to provide the best opportunities for learning that can focus on what learners know and can do and what they want to be able to know and do. Learners who have been or are at risk for being dis/abled in educational settings should participate in tool development, testing, and evaluation, regardless of whether a tool is conceptualized as an assistive technology or not. In circularity: whatever all learners must use should be usable by all learners. We have enough research problematizing learners— we need more research that shows how environments can be re-envisioned as inclusive, supportive spaces (Mellard et al., 2020; Waitoller & Artiles, 2003).

Earlier in this editorial, we highlighted the many mismatches between intentions and actions regarding inclusive distance and online educational spaces (Björnsdóttir & Traustadóttir, 2010; Mavropoulou et al., 2021; Pavenkov et al., 2015). The articles in this special issue collectively stand as testimony to those previous findings. However, they also offer the potential for new thinking about how to enable the agencies of individuals in school spaces to have more time to communicate with students, learn from each other, try new tools and approaches, and have their own needs as human beings met. Policies about people in complex circumstances have little chance of changing procedures and outcomes unless they fully frame the entangled nature of people and their contexts (Rice, 2022; Rice & Smith, 2022).

References

Americans With Disabilities Act of 1990, 42 U.S.C. § 12101 et seq. (1990). https://www.ada.gov/pubs/adastatute08.htm

Bekiryazıcı, M. (2015). Teaching mixed-level classes with a Vygotskian perspective. *Procedia – Social and Behavioral Sciences*, *186*, 913–917. https://doi.org/10.1016/j.sbspro.2015.04.163

Björnsdóttir, K., & Traustadóttir, R. (2010). Stuck in the land of disability? The intersection of learning difficulties, class, gender and religion. *Disability & Society*, *25*(1), 49–62. https://doi.org/10.1080/09687590903363340

De Bruin, K. (2019). The impact of inclusive education reforms on students with disability: An international comparison. *International Journal of Inclusive Education*, *23*(7-8), 811–826. https://doi.org/10.1080/13603116.2019.1623327

Gallimore, R., & Tharp, R. (1990). Teaching mind in society: Teaching, schooling, and literate discourse. In L. Moll (Ed.), *Vygotsky and education: Instructional implications and applications of sociohistorical psychology* (pp. 175–205). Cambridge University Press.

Goodley, D., Lawthom, R., Liddiard, K., & Runswick-Cole, K. (2019). Provocations for critical disability studies. *Disability & Society*, *34*(6), 972–997. https://doi.org/10.1080/09687599.2019.1566889

Hromalik, C. D., & Koszalka, T. A. (2018). Self-regulation of the use of digital resources in an online language learning course improves learning outcomes. *Distance Education*, *39*(4), 528–547. https://doi.org/10.1080/01587919.2018.1520044

Individuals with Disabilities Education Act, 20 U.S.C. § 1400. (2004). https://sites.ed.gov/idea/statute-chapter-33/subchapter-i/1400

Järkestig Berggren, U., Rowan, D., Bergbäck, E., & Blomberg, B. (2016). Disabled students' experiences of higher education in Sweden, the Czech Republic, and the United States: A comparative institutional analysis. *Disability & Society*, *31*(3), 339–356. https://doi.org/10.1080/09687599.2016.1174103

John-Steiner, V., & Mahn, H. (1996). Sociocultural approaches to learning and development: A Vygotskian framework. *Educational Psychologist*, *31*(3-4), 191–206. https://doi.org/10.1080/00461520.1996.9653266

Kinash, S., Crichton, S., & Kim-Rupnow, W. S. (2004). A review of 2000-2003 literature at the intersection of online learning and disability. *American Journal of Distance Education*, *18*(1), 5–19. https://doi.org/10.1207/s15389286ajde1801_2

Koçdar S., Bozkurt A. (2022) Supporting learners with special needs in open, distance, and digital education. In O Zawacki-Richter & I. Jung (Eds.), *Handbook of open, distance and digital education* (pp. 2–13). https://doi.org/10.1007/978-981-19-0351-9_49-1

Layne, M., Boston, W. E., & Ice, P. (2013). A longitudinal study of online learners: Shoppers, swirlers, stoppers, and succeeders as a function of demographic characteristics. *Online Journal of Distance Learning Administration*, *16*(2), 1–12. https://ojdla.com/archive/summer162/layne_boston_ice162.pdf

Marks, D. (1999). Dimensions of oppression: Theorising the embodied subject. *Disability & Society*, *14*(5), 611–626. https://doi.org/10.1080/09687599925975

Mavropoulou, S., Mann, G., & Carrington, S. (2021). The divide between inclusive education policy and practice in Australia and the way forward. *Journal of Policy and Practice in Intellectual Disabilities*, *18*(1), 44–52. https://doi.org/10.1111/jppi.12373

Mellard, D., Rice, M., Ortiz, K., & Curry, T. (2020). *Strategic accommodation framework for students with disabilities in online environments*. Inclusive Digital Education Collaborative.

Pavenkov, O. V., Pavenkov, V. G., Rubtcova, M. V., & Narayanamurthy, H. (2015). Inclusive education in India and Russia: A comparative analysis of legal frameworks. *Rajagiri Journal of Social Development*, *7*(2), 123–136. http://journals.rajagiri.edu/index.php/rssJ/article/view/119/108

Rausch, A., Joseph, J., & Steed, E. (2019, December 21). Dis/ability critical race studies (DisCrit) for inclusion in early childhood education: Ethical considerations of implicit and explicit bias. Zero to Three. https://shorturl.at/cfnz7

Rehabilitation Act of 1973, Section 504 Regulations, 34 C.F.R. § 104.1 et seq. https://www2.ed.gov/policy/rights/reg/ocr/edlite-34cfr104.html

Rice, M. (2022). Special education teachers' use of technologies during the COVID-19 era (Spring 2020—Fall 2021). *Tech Trends*, *66*, 310–326. https://doi.org/10.1007/s11528-022-00700-5

Rice, M., & Smith, E. (2022). Special education teachers' entangled agencies, intersectional identities, and commitments to equity and inclusion. *Journal of Special Education Technology*. https://doi.org/10.1177/01626434221134260

Schiek, D., & Chege, V. (Eds.). (2009). *European Union non-discrimination law: Comparative perspectives on multidimensional equality law*. Routledge.

Sinclair, J. (2013). Why I dislike "person first" language. *Autonomy, the Critical Journal of Interdisciplinary Autism Studies*, *1*(2). http://www.larry-arnold.net/Autonomy/index.php/autonomy/article/view/OP1/html_1

Smith, B. (2016). Intersectional discrimination and substantive equality: a comparative and theoretical perspective. *The Equal Rights Review*, *16*(1), 73–102. https://shorturl.at/cdDHR

Sniatecki, J. L., Perry, H. B., & Snell, L. H. (2015). Faculty attitudes and knowledge regarding college students with disabilities. *Journal of Postsecondary Education and Disability*, *28*(3), 259–275. http://www.ahead-archive.org/uploads/publications/JPED/jped28_3/JPED28_3_Final.pdf

UNESCO. (1994). *The Salamanca Statement and Framework for Action on Special Needs Education*. https://unesdoc.unesco.org/ark:/48223/pf0000098427

United Nations. (2000). *Millennium Declaration*. https://www.un.org/en/development/devagenda/millennium.shtml

United Nations. (2006). *Convention on the Rights of Persons with Disabilities*. https://www.ohchr.org/en/resources/educators/human-rights-education-training/12-convention-rights-persons-disabilities-2006

United Nations. (2016). *Transforming our world: The 2030 Agenda for Sustainable Development*. https://sdgs.un.org/2030agenda

Vygotsky, L .S. (1978). *Mind in society: The development of higher psychological processes*. Harvard University Press.

Waitoller, F. R., & Artiles, A. J. (2013). A decade of professional development research for inclusive education: A critical review and notes for a research program. *Review of Educational Research*, *83*(3), 319–356. https://doi.org/10.3102/003465431348390

Weedon, E., & Riddell, S. (2016). Higher education in Europe: Widening participation. In M. Shah, A. Bennett, & E. Southgate (Eds.), *Widening higher education participation: A global perspective* (pp. 49–61). Chandos Publishing.

Xu, D., & Jaggars, S. S. (2014). Performance gaps between online and face-to-face courses: Differences across types of students and academic subject areas. *The Journal of Higher Education*, *85*(5), 633–659. https://doi.org/10.1080/00221546.2014.11777343

ORCID

Mary F. Rice http://orcid.org/0000-0002-8138-512X
Michael Dunn http://orcid.org/0000-0001-9420-3121

Making the invisible, visible: disability in South African distance education

Paul Prinsloo 🆔 and Chinaza Uleanya 🆔

ABSTRACT
Distance education celebrates its humanitarian mission of providing opportunities for disadvantaged and marginalized individuals who do not have access to traditional campus-based higher education. Large enrolments of students necessitate an industrialized approach in planning, design, and delivery informed by a normative assumption of ableism. In the context of post-apartheid South Africa, distance education fulfills a particular important role in ensuring access to education for all. This scoping review addressed two questions: "What is currently known, in the context of distance education in South Africa, about the educational experiences of SWDs?" and "How should we understand and respond to these experiences?" The scoping study shows, inter alia, that while there is an institutional commitment to providing equitable learning experiences, the lived experiences of students with disabilities provide evidence of their invisibility in the design, planning, and delivery of learning. The study concludes with some recommendations and provocations.

Introduction

> Disability marks the body in ambiguous ways — it appears and disappears, is noticed and is hidden — as we move through different physical and social spaces, and as we find ourselves in different political and historical moments. (McGuire, 2010, ¶3)

Distance education has always embraced its "humanitarian task of providing access for *all* learners, with special focus on those disadvantaged by distance, by precarious economic conditions, by belonging to discriminated minorities, or by being disabled" (Peters, 2010, p. 32). Distance education is also an important form of delivery for realizing Sustainable Development Goal 4 which emphasizes *equitable* access to education to all, regardless of their dis/abilities (UNESCO, n.d.).

In the context of post-apartheid South Africa, only 20% of students with disabilities (SWDs) who qualify to attend higher education actually registers at a higher education institution. It is therefore worthwhile to consider to what extent distance education in the context of South Africa provides *equitable* access to SWD.

Distance education has been characterized as an *industrialized* form of education provision (Peters, 1983, 1993) making affordable and quality education-at-scale possible through, inter alia, technologies, standardized processes and economies of scale, while balancing access, cost and quality referred to as an "iron triangle" (Daniel et al., 2009). Providing access to SWDs in distance education contexts therefore poses significant challenges due to, inter alia, the dominance of ableism as normative discourse, distance education as an industrialized form of educational provision, and the challenges of balancing access, cost, and quality.

The scoping review will unfold as follows: We will briefly locate our approach to disableism within the context of critical disability studies, before mapping distance education as industrialized form of delivery and the "iron triangle" (Daniel et al., 2009) and its impact on providing equitable access to SWDs. This is followed by our research design and methodology, analysis, and findings. We conclude this article suggesting moving beyond justice to an ethics of care.

Disablism and students with disabilities

There are different approaches to the study of disability (Pfeiffer & Kiger, 1995; Thomas, 2004), and we reject medicalized views of disability and embrace the study of disability (Pfeiffer & Kiger, 1995) as a transdisciplinary, relational, and intersectional space, opposing disablism as "a form of social oppression involving the social imposition of restrictions of activity on people with impairments and the socially engendered undermining of their psycho-emotional wellbeing" (Thomas, 2007, p. 73). Disability constitutes a "space from which to think through a host of political, theoretical and practical issues that are relevant to all" (Goodley, 2013, p. 632). Furthermore, we accept that "Having an impaired body does not equate with disability. In contrast, disability was [is] a problem of society" (Goodley, 2013, p. 634). As such, individuals with disabilities are "the ultimate intersectional subject, the universal image, the important modality through which we can understand exclusion and resistance" (Goodley, 2013).

In the specific context of South Africa, we cannot ignore the legacy of colonial and apartheid "epistemic, ontological and practical negligences" (Grech & Soldatic, 2015, p. 1) of disability. We are compelled to recognize disability as "a key site of colonial administrative power, a lived experience under colonial control, or a category of difference in place to maintain colonial legitimacy and control (overtly or covertly)" (Grech & Soldatic, 2015, p. 2). As such, we have to account for the violent materialities still shaping the lived experiences of individuals navigating and negotiating their disability in a colonial present (Meekosha, 2011).

Critical disability studies (e.g., Goodley, 2013) allow us to engage the "colonial logics" (Titchkosky & Aubrect, 2015, p. 69) still informing the materialities of the "convergence and divergence of multiple markers" (Goodley, 2013, p. 636). We furthermore have to be cognizant of how higher education, and distance education in particular, functions as relational systems of ableism, coming into contact with "racialised bodies, queer bodies, classed bodies, gendered bodies, bodies that already have been touched by other (and perhaps multiple) systems of oppression" (McGuire, 2010, ¶3).

Understanding distance education as context

Distance education as an industrialized form of educational delivery

Peters (1993) refers to distance education as an industrialized form of education that is "pre-planned, prepared and organised" combined with a division of labour, the "growing use of technical equipment to work with" and "formalised evaluations" (pp. 15–16).

Zawacki-Richter (2019) revisits the notion of distance education and points to how distance education as industrialized form of education arose from the need to address the "rising cost per student and limited teacher productivity" (p. 22), and as a result, economies of scale and division of labor became an integral part of distance education. Zawacki-Richter (2019) points to the following elements that are inherent in the theory of industrialization, namely (1) rationalization; (2) division of labor, whereby delivery of teaching is divided into smaller units, for example, design, the development of learning materials, production, and delivery to realize economies of scale; (3) mechanization and the use of technology as indispensable in the production of learning materials; (4) integrated systematic planning to guide the process; (5) scientific control methods, formalization, and standardization; and (6) concentration and centralization.

An integral part of this industrialized process that impacts directly on offering educational opportunities to SWDs is the notion of standardization (Farnes, 1993; Peters, 1983). Standardization was an integral element of distance education as industrialized form of educational delivery and, even moving to digital processes, "a sequential, mechanistic production line" (Farnes, 1993, p.15) continued to inform much of distance education practice. Standardization was furthermore integral to the cost of distance education provision and no deviation from using the "standard student" could be afforded. While Farnes (1993) points to greater flexibility in the design of learning experiences in post-Fordist modes, Teixeira et al. (2019) propose that "the industrialisation process emerges as an opportunity to scale fragmented content from unplanned and perfectly contextualized random links" (p. 11). (Also see Zawacki-Richter, 2019.)

In the context of this article, we have to ask how the very notion of distance education as industrialized system, with predesigned and produced standardized teaching resources embraces and sanctions ableism and the "average student" to the exclusion of the "other"—those who do not fit the mould of the "average student." How does understanding distance education as an industrialized system (and everything it refers to) allow SWDs and allies to resist, confront, but also assist distance education to provide equitable learning journeys, for all?

The notion of the iron triangle—Cost, quality, and access

Daniel et al. (2009) do not question the increasing massification of higher education and the role of distance education institutions to provide access, but rather ask "how they can do so rapidly and with reasonable quality" (p. 32). The three vectors in the iron triangle—cost, quality, and access—are interdependent, meaning that an increase in any of the three vectors inevitably impacts on the other two vectors. The vectors also have fixed-length parameters meaning "that one can only increase access to a given course under circumstances where one lowers its level of quality" (Power & Gould, 2011, p. 23). For example, providing access to an increasing number of enrolments may lower the costs of provision through economies of scale, but then also raise a number of challenges, such as ensuring the quality of teaching and learning. Kanuka and Brooks (2010) claim that it is impossible to balance the three vectors, and "distance education can achieve any two of the following: flexible access, quality learning experience and cost-effectiveness – *but not all three at once*" (p. 69; emphasis added).

Power and Morven-Gould (2011) analyze stakeholder views (management and administration, faculty, as well as students) on quality, access, and cost and suggest that the three vectors constitute perspectivesand are not fixed. They further propose changing costtocost-effectiveness "as being a more complete and significant indicator" and access to accessibilityas referring to "increasing access for students" (p. 25). They found that the three stakeholder groups have different views with management and administration considering cost-effectiveness as the most important, while faculty was concerned with quality and students with accessibility. (Also see Daniels, 2019; Lane, 2014.)

Let us assume, for now, that providing equitable access and support to good quality learning experiences will require *non*standardized designs, processes, and "products" that will (most probably) fall outside and require deviation from industrialized processes, with no potential of economies of scale; then, it follows that this would be possible only at have higher costs to the institution and/or students. Following from this, the question arises, to what extent does distance education in the context of South Africa provide *equitable* access to SWDs?

Methodology

Scoping reviews map key concepts which underpin research, while systematic reviews draw upon evidence from various study designs in order to proffer answers to a specific and/or series of related research questions guiding a study (Peters et al., 2015). Scoping reviews aid the identification and illustration of one or more research gaps in a subject, as well as reveal the absence of studies conducted within the context of specific territories, while a systematic review is used to identify and retrieve published evidence (Munn et al., 2018). Scoping reviews provide an overview of the existing evidence base regardless of the quality of methodologies (Peters et al., 2015) and summarize and disseminate research findings, and make recommendations for the future research (Tricco et al. 2016).

We adopted the framework (Stages 1 to 5) for scoping reviews as put forward by Arksey and O'Malley (2005) and as adopted by Uleanya (2022). We furthermore adhered to the guidelines of Cooper et al. (2021) with regard to providing evidence for every stage of this scoping review to ensure transparency and add to the trustworthiness of the scoping review.

Stage 1: Identifying the research question

In the first stage (Stage 1), we identified the research questions guiding the study, namely "What is currently known, in the context of distance education in South Africa, about the educational experiences of SWDs?" and "How should we understand and respond to these experiences?"

Stage 2: Identifying relevant studies phase

Arksey and O'Malley, (2005) highlight several sources by which relevant studies can be identified and retrieved: electronic databases, hand-searching of key journals, reference lists, conferences, as well as organizations. In this scoping review, we selected Scopus and Web of Science (all indices), being comprehensive bibliographic databases that cover peer-reviewed scholarly literature from various disciplines (Paperpile, 2022).

Following the selection of the databases, and in line with our research question, we decided on the following search terms: "students with disabilities" AND "South Africa" AND "distance education" OR "distance learning." However, an initial search using these search terms yielded a very limited number of potential documents. In line with the characteristics of scoping reviews, we added additional search terms to be included in the search, namely "e-learning" OR "elearning" OR "virtual learning" AND "higher education."

Stage 3: Study selection phase

For the purpose of this study, we included articles and conference proceedings in the specific context of South Africa in relation to the research focus and search terms. Articles which were not in the specific context of South Africa were excluded as well as books and book chapters due to the unavailability of access to complete digital texts.

Figure 1 provides an overview of the process followed from the initial search for the articles and conference proceedings to selecting the final corpus which was adopted for analyses.

Figure 1 shows that from the initial corpus on Web of Science and Scopus, 145 documents were identified ($n = 145$). Four documents were excluded for being duplicates (overlaps from the two databases).

Subsequently, the researchers exported the titles, authors, and abstracts of 141 documents to an Excel spreadsheet and excluded articles that did not discuss SWDs in the specific content of distance education (and alternative terms as indicated in the search terms above) and South Africa. The researchers individually coded the abstracts and compared codes to establish inter-rater reliability. Following Tricco et al. (2016),

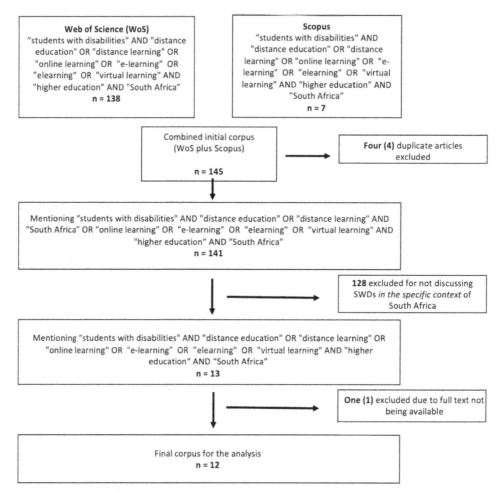

Figure 1. Flow diagram: Exclusion and inclusion process.

we aimed to achieve 75% agreement. Differences were discussed, and where the researchers were in doubt or could not agree about including or excluding a document, the document was *included*.

As such, we excluded 128 articles, resulting in a corpus of 13 documents. The researchers then downloaded the full articles. One article was subsequently excluded as the researchers could not get access to the document. The final corpus of literature considered for this study was 12 articles.

Stage 4: Charting the data phase

An inductive content analysis approach was adopted for this study (Hsieh & Shannon, 2005). The researchers both coded three documents and discussed the initial coding. A coding agenda was agreed upon with a mutual agreement to be open to emerging new codes (e.g., Saldana, 2016).

Following the initial coding, an Excel spreadsheet was used to indicate the codes retrieved from the analysed literature. Once the whole corpus was coded, the two researchers created categories from which themes were generated (see Table 3). The extracted data are reported in the next phase, Stage 5.

Stage 5: Collating, summarizing, and reporting the results phase

During this stage, the themes were collated, and a number of quotations were selected to illustrate the theme. The generated themes are:

1. The role and scope of design
2. Equity as principle
3. Usability
4. Training
5. Flexibility for diversity
6. Access
7. Going forward.

Each of the identified themes is explained in the discussion section of this article using subthemes where necessary. The seventh theme, Going forward, is discussed under the section "Discussion and pointers for going forward."

Analysis and findings

This section comprises two parts. In the first part, we provide a brief overview of:

- the authors, their affiliation, and the journals in which the articles were published
- the research method used, sampling design, and sample size
- how these documents understand disability
- how these publications understand distance education.

In the second part, we provide an overview of the themes.

Part 1: Analysis and findings

Authors, their affiliation, and journals

As can be seen in Table 1, Ngubane-Mokiwa as well as the collaboration between Maboe, Eloff, and Schoeman are responsible for four of the 12 documents in the corpus, with the outputs by Maboe et al. (2018, 2019) being in conference proceedings and Ngubane-Mokiwa collaborating with two co-authors in two journal articles (Ngubane-Mokiwa & Khoza, 2021; Ngubane-Mokiwa & Zongozzi, 2021). The articles in this corpus are scattered across a range of journals, with three articles published in specifically South African and African journals and two papers in South African conference proceedings. Interestingly, two articles were published in journals not dedicated to disability as were the two conference papers.

Table 1. Overview of authors, affiliations, and journal titles.

Authors	Affiliation	Journal titles
[1]Ngubane-Mokiwa, S. A., & [2]Zongozzi, J. N.	[1&2]University of South Africa, Pretoria, South Africa	Journal of Intellectual Disability - Diagnosis and Treatment
[1]Chiwandire, D., & [2]Vincent, L. Zongozzi, J. N.	[1&2]Rhodes University, South Africa University of South Africa, Pretoria, South Africa	African Journal of Disability International Journal of Disability, Development and Education
Ntombela, S.	University of South Africa, Pretoria, South Africa	Turkish Online Journal of Distance Education
[1]Van Jaarsveldt, D. E., & [2]Ndeya-Ndereya, C. N.	[1&2]University of the Free State, Bloemfontein, South Africa	Disability & Society
[1]Tekane R., & [2]Potgieter, M.	[1&2]University of Pretoria, Pretoria, South Africa	South African Journal of Science
[1]Subrayen, R., & [2]Dhunpath, R.	[1]University of KwaZulu-Natal, Durban, South Africa [2]University of KwaZulu-Natal, Durban, South Africa	African Journal of Disability
[1]Maboe, M. J., [2]Eloff, M., & [3]Schoeman, M.	[1&3]University of South Africa (Unisa) [2]School of Computing, University of South Africa (Unisa)	Annual Conference of the South African Institute of Computer Scientists and Information Technologists. (SAICSIT '19), September 17–18
[1]Maboe, M. J., [2]Eloff, M., & [3]Schoeman, M.	[1,2,3]University of South Africa (Unisa)	Annual Conference of the South African Institute of Computer Scientists and Information Technologists. (SAICSIT '18), September 26–28
Ndlovu, S.	University of Johannesburg, Johannesburg, South Africa	International Journal of Environmental Research and Public Health
[1]Ngubane-Mokiwa, S. A., & [2]Khoza, S. B.	[1]University of South Africa, Pretoria, South Africa [2]University of KwaZulu-Natal, Durban, South Africa	Education Sciences
Ntombela, S.	University of South Africa, Pretoria, South Africa	Disability & Society

Table 1 furthermore shows that all authors of the retrieved and reviewed literature are from institutions in South Africa. The table also shows that 7 of the authors are affiliated with the University of South Africa, with the rest of the authors affiliated with Rhodes University, the University of the Free State, the University of Pretoria, the University of KwaZulu-Natal, and the University of Johannesburg.

Research method used, sampling design, and sample size
Table 2 shows that while eight of the articles employed qualitative methods, one was literature review, and the three others were conceptual articles. Convenience and purposive sampling are the two main techniques adopted in the 13 articles.

How these publications understand disability
There is some evidence of understanding disability as relational and intersectional (e.g., the gender of an SWD is mentioned); however, intersectionality and the relational aspects of disability in the context of a particular ableist environment do not receive attention. The articles focus on the experiences of SWDs, and the imposition of restrictions through a lack of access or usability, or lack of appropriate student support and access to, for example, assistive technologies. Most of the articles (see the thematic

Table 2. Overview of sample size, research methodology, and types of disability.

Author & year of publication	Research method	Sampling	Sample size
van Jaarsveldt, D. E., & Ndeya-Ndereya, C. N. (2015)	Qualitative	Purposive	48
Subrayen, R., & Dhunpath, R. (2019)	Qualitative	Non-probability	2
Zongozzi, J. N. (2020)	Qualitative	Convenient	9
Maboe, M. J., Eloff, M., & Schoeman, M. (2019)	Qualitative	Purposive	20
Ngubane-Mokiwa, S. A., & Zongozzi, J. N. (2021)	Qualitative	Purposive	10
Chiwandire, D., & Vincent, L. (2019)	Qualitative (critical lLiterature review)	Not applicable	Not applicable
Tekane, R., & Potgieter, P. (2021)	Conceptual research	Not applicable	Not applicable
Ndlovu, S. (2021)	Qualitative	Purposive	6
Ntombela, S. (2022)	Conceptual research	Not applicable	Not applicable
Ntombela, S. (2020)	Conceptual research	Not applicable	Not applicable
Maboe, M. J., Eloff, M., & Schoeman, M. (2018)	Qualitative	Purposive	15
Ngubane-Mokiwa, S. A., & Khoza, S. B. (2021)	Literature review	Not applicable	Not applicable

analysis below) engaged with the challenges faced by SWDs on a very pragmatic level (e.g., access, use), without necessarily considering how the challenges faced by SWDs have been and continue to be shaped by broader political, and sociocritical understandings of ableism.

How these publications understand distance education

While all the articles focus on SWDs in South African distance education contexts, there was very little evidence of mapping the experiences of SWDs against a critical understanding of the evolution of distance education, and some of the main theories that have informed an understanding of the complexities of providing affordable and quality educational opportunities, at scale, to SWDs. Theories that do get a mention include, inter alia, the community of inquiry framework, the theory of transactional distance, and universal design for learning.

Part 2: Thematic analysis

The analysis identified seven themes and these are not presented, in no particular order. The seventh (7th) theme is discussed in the section Discussions and pointers for consideration and future research. Table 3 provides an overview of the codes, categories, and themes.

Theme 1: The role and scope of design

The analysed literature showed that the issue of design is an important consideration and refers to the design of physical spaces, the web and online learning interfaces, choice of technology, and ensuring inclusivity in the design of online learning. It is important to note that the design of spaces, whether physical, web interface, or online course sites, impacts on issues such as access and usability.

Table 3. Codes, categories, and themes from reviewed literature.

Codes	Categories	Themes
Design of space: Physical	The importance of design	The role and scope of design
Web and online interfaces		
Assistive technologies		
Ensuring inclusivity in the design of online learning		
Equitable learning experiences	Flexibility for diverse needs	Equity as principle
Diverse needs		
Usability	Usability	Usability
The need for training	Training	Training
Training - Assistive technologies		
Inclusivity: Nonmarginalization	Flexibility for diverse needs	Flexibility for diversity
Challenges of SWDs		
Access to the Internet	Access	Access
Access and availability - Assistive technologies		
Access: Labs		
Access - Online learning materials		
Designing learning experiences differently	Inclusivity	Going forward
Need for implementation of policies on granting access to and support for SWDs	The role of policy	

Subtheme 1.1: Physical. Interestingly, while an integral characteristic of distance education is the physical or geographic separation of students from the delivering institution, the design of physical spaces and their impact on SWDs are mentioned by a number of authors. For instance, Ntombela (2020) states that "poor infrastructural designs negatively affect these students in as far as access, equity" (p. 22, italics added). This is supported by Ngubane-Mokiwa and Zongozzi (2021), who quote one student: "The Labs are not designed to cater for students with disabilities! Since I am now quadriplegic, I must be lifted by people in order to get to the 2nd floor of the Programming Labs as they are only accessible through the stairs. Equally, if you are partially-sighted you won't be able to work in those labs as the instructions are in small print" (Female student with mobility disability) (p. 145).

Subtheme 1.2: Web and online Interfaces. The design and accessibility of institutional web and registration pages often exclude SWDs. Maboe et al. (2018) report that "the institutional websites must be designed in such a way [...] that people with disabilities will be able to use the technology properly" (p. 227). Institutional web and registration pages are, for many SWDs, the first contact with an institution, and the research in this corpus shows that these first encounters with institutional web pages impact negatively on SWDs and confirm their isolation and otherness.

Subtheme 1.3: Assistive technologies. It comes as no surprise that most of the articles mention or discuss the role of and access to assistive technologies. The range of assistive technologies include, but is not limited to "screen reading or voice recognition software and a foot mouse, that enable students with disabilities to be independent in their learning endeavours" (van Jaarsveldt & Ndeya-Ndereya, 2015, p. 204). Other assistive technologies mentioned by Ngubane-Mokiwa and Zongozzi (2021) are "NVda screen readers, Index Everest v5, Natiq Reader, Braille display, OCR software for

PDF reading, Text to speech software, and etc" (p. 146). Tekane and Potgieter (2021) refer to "Braille and tape-recorded readings, sign language interpreters, alternative assessments, and assistive technology such as Job Access With Speech (JAWS) software" (p. 2), and Chiwandire and Vincent (2019) highlight "laptops with specialist digital voice recording" (p. 7).

Subtheme 1.4: Ensuring inclusivity in the design of online learning. According to van Jaarsveldt and Ndeya-Ndereya (2015), "Amongst some of the important adjustments that need to be made are the design and implementation of e-learning spaces and learning materials that are accessible to all students, including those with physical, sensory and/or learning disabilities" (p. 200). This necessitates that "The learning and assessment design team should involve students with disabilities in testing learning platforms so as to avoid barriers in online learning" (Ngubane-Mokiwa & Zongozzi, 2021, p. 145).

Theme 2: Equity as principle
Subtheme 2.1: Equitable learning experiences. The reviewed literature shows how equitable learning experiences are not realized due to decreases in public funding (Chiwandire & Vincent, 2019), and "poor resourcing and poor infrastructural designs negatively affect these students in as far as access, equity and support are concerned" (Ntombela, 2020, p. 22). There is also the need to "incorporate concepts of universal design into faculty instruction and curricula that ultimately benefit all students in their learning process" (Zongozzi, 2020, p. 8). Interestingly, Zongozzi (2020) states "we are not accommodating students with disabilities because we are still using printouts and copies so obviously a student who is blind will not be able to use the material that we have at the moment" (p. 8).

Subtheme 2.2: Diverse needs. One of the most important findings of this scoping review is the (impact of) diverse needs of SWDs, according to a combination of their physical impairment with other factors such as gender, race (e.g., Ngubane-Mokiwa & Khoza, 2021; Tekane & Potgieter, 2021), as well as differences with regard to the severity of the impairments. While, for example, students with visual impairment may share the need for a particular type of assistive technology, the exact severity of the impairment, combined with other, intersectional characteristics and socio-structural factors, disrupts the notion of a one-size-fits-all approach.

Theme 3: Usability
Usability remains a major constraint for both SWDs and their instructors as reported in the analyzed literature (van Jaarsveldt & Ndeya-Ndereya, 2015). "There is a misconception that because a student has a disability, they know how to use assistive technologies" (Ngubane-Mokiwa & Zongozzi, 2021, p. 144). Other issues revolving around usability include lack of digital skills to use the technologies (Ngubane-Mokiwa & Zongozzi, 2021; van Jaarsveldt & Ndeya-Ndereya, 2015) and websites not being user-friendly (Maboe et al., 2019).

Theme 4: Training
Subtheme 4.1: The need for training. Maboe et al. (2018) report that "Students with disabilities should additionally be provided with ICT training to enhance their experiences in the use of websites in general as well as e-learning websites" (p. 228). Tekane and Potgieter (2021) state that "most of the visually impaired students ... did not receive mobility training" (p. 2). The need for training of SWDs is also pointed out by Maboe et al. (2019) referring to very basic computer skills, keyboard training, and navigating the web. Ndlovu (2021) states that "academic staff who are central in the practice of teaching and learning lack training and expertise to teach students with disabilities" (p. 14).

Subtheme 4.2: Training - Assistive technologies. This theme suggests that where assistive technologies are available, training on how to use such is needed. Ngubane-Mokiwa and Zongozzi (2021) state that "In order to ensure fair and inclusive access to higher education, SWDs ought to be provided adequate training on the use of assistive technologies during the orientation phase rather than retrospectively" (p. 144). Zongozzi (2020) also point to the fact that "Although assistive technology is partially available for use by lecturers ..., adequate training on these technologies is required to enable those lecturers who need them, yet without the knowledge necessary to enhance the quality of teaching SWDs" (p. 12).

Theme 5: Flexibility for diversity
Subtheme 5.1: Inclusivity - Nonmarginalization. Ngubane-Mokiwa and Zongozzi (2021) state that "the prevalence of inequitable practices, alienation and inequalities ... exclude SWDs" (p. 144). With regards to inclusivity in the language of instruction, these authors state that "For students with visual impairments, the medium of instruction presented further challenges as some of the content relied on visual interaction" (p. 141). This is an excellent example of how a specific impairment is entangled in broader socio-cultural, political, ideological factors. Ngubane-Mokiwa and Zongozzi (2021) also point to how "STEM fields [are] being meant for non-disabled students only" (p. 145).

Subtheme 5.2: Challenges of SWDs. According to Ngubane-Mokiwa and Zongozzi (2021), "most SWDs come from socioeconomically disadvantaged backgrounds, nature of disability as a hindrance, prevalence of inequitable practices, alienation and inequalities that exclude SWDs, and high internet costs" (p. 142). Zongozzi (2020) states that "inaccessible learning material for SWDs and lack of capacity by lecturers to support SWDs" (p. 2), and Ngubane-Mokiwa and Zongozzi (2021) point to "ICT related systemic challenges which ranged from inadequate hardware and software provisions, aesthetic design that takes no consideration of the needs of students with disabilities" (p. 143). Also, they report that "students with disabilities faced challenges such as: exclusion due to being digitally illiterate, lack of respect for human dignity, inadequate time to complete online summative assessment, systemic challenges, inability to access learning materials in different formats, lack of digital skills to use assistive technologies" (Ngubane-Mokiwa & Zongozzi, 2021, p. 145). SWDs also face "negative attitudes, teacher-centred teaching and learning processes, inflexible curriculum, inadequate assistive and instructional technologies" (p. 20).

Theme 6: Access
Interestingly, while access was found to be a dominant theme, the theme is linked to and overlaps with other themes, discussed earlier.

Subtheme 6.1: Access to the Internet. According to Maboe et al. (2019) "The Internet and ultimately websites should be accessible and usable so that they can provide timely and accurate information in an effective, efficient and satisfactory way" (p. 1). Ngubane-Mokiwa and Zongozzi (2021) refer to the high cost of access to the internet, which is also mentioned by van der Merwe (2012), who refer to statistics (in 2012) pointing to the vast disparities of access to the Internet and hardware.

Subtheme 6.2: Access and availability - Assistive technologies. Zongozzi (2021) states that "Although assistive technology is partially available for use by lecturers at Unisa, adequate training on these technologies is required to enable those lecturers who need them, yet without the knowledge necessary to enhance the quality of teaching SWDs" (p. 12). Ngubane-Mokiwa and Zongozzi (2021) report on a lack of access to assistive technologies by SWDs and how they have to borrow these technologies from the library. Ntombela (2020) confirms that the provision of assistive technologies is inadequate.

Subtheme 6.3: Access – Labs. We reported earlier on how the design of laboratories impact on SWDs' experiences and, importantly, access (see the example reported by Ngubane-Mokiwa & Zongozzi, 2021, earlier): "The Labs are not designed to cater for students with disabilities!" (p. 145). It is important to note how access is linked to design, and if (the needs of) SWDs are invisible to those designing spaces, the resultant design impacts directly on access, for all SWDs.

Subtheme 6.4: Access - Online learning materials. "Amongst some of the important adjustments that need to be made are the design and implementation of e-learning spaces and learning materials that are accessible to all students, including those with physical, sensory and/or learning disabilities" (van Jaarsveldt & Ndeya-Ndereya, 2015, p. 200). Zongozzi (2020) mentions that "quality higher education for SWDs at Unisa is hampered ... [because of] inaccessible learning material" (p. 2).

Discussion and pointers for going forward

The questions informing this scoping review were "What is currently known, in the context of distance education in South Africa, about the educational experiences of SWDs?" and "How should we understand and respond to these experiences?"

The above analysis and presentation of the different themes provide insights to the first question. The second question is more difficult to answer. To assist in answering the second question, we look back to insights gathered from understanding distance education as an industrialized system constantly negotiating how to address the three vectors or perspectives of cost-effectiveness, accessibility, and cost. Understanding distance education as an industrialized system with preplanned designs, processes, and products informed by a normative understanding of ableism, does not provide justification for the exclusion of SWDs, and the inequitable learning experiences, but it does provide some understanding for the exclusion. There is an important difference between understanding current exclusions and a justification of these exclusions. This scoping review does not provide a justification for the experiences of SWDs, to the contrary.

We started this article with a quote from McGuire (2010) referring to how disability marks bodies in "ambiguous ways" (¶3)—making these bodies appear, disappear, and move through physical and social spaces. As these bodies move through different political, historical, and institutional moments, we get glimpses of how normative ableism is and how it shapes educational delivery, and distance education in particular.

As indicated earlier, the thematic analysis found a 7th theme (Going forward) with two subthemes referring to the need for adjustments in designs and the role of policy.

Theme 7: Going forward
Subtheme 7.1: Designing learning experiences differently. "Amongst some of the important adjustments that need to be made are the design and implementation of e-learning spaces and learning materials that are accessible to all students, including those with physical, sensory and/or learning disabilities" (van Jaarsveldt & Ndeya-Ndereya, 2015, p. 200). The corpus is also very clear that in order for staff to design and operationalize equitable learning experiences, they need training—"it is necessary to provide opportunities for lecturers to enhance their knowledge about meeting the learning needs of students with disabilities and to become more skilful in their use of technology" (van Jaarsveldt & Ndeya-Ndereya, 2015, p. 208). Designing differently also means ensuring that SWDs receive adequate and appropriate training (Ngubane-Mokiwa & Zongozzi, 2021).

Subtheme 7.2: Need for implementation of policies on granting access to and support for SWDs. Zongozzi (2020) proposes that "it is important for […] disability policies to have a good theoretical back-up as it may not be possible to implement a policy that is defective in its theoretical conception. Thus, a good disability policy should have theoretical validity and must be formulated based on an appropriate theoretical basis" (p. 11). Policies should also involve all key decision-makers (including staff and SWDs) to ensure legitimacy and support for implementation. Interestingly, van Jaarsveldt and Ndeya-Ndereya (2015) state that "beyond legislation and institutional policies relating to students with disabilities, lecturers should accept responsibility for and have an understanding of accessibility and the establishment of inclusive learning environments" (p. 210).

Ntombela (2020) points to the fact that although higher education, and distance education in particular, claim to provide and support SWDs with access and support,

Table 4. Overview of main findings.

Issue	Finding
Authors and affiliation	With Unisa being the largest distance education provider in South Africa it comes as no surprise that most of the authors in this scoping review are affiliated with the University of South Africa.
Research methods, sampling design, and sampling size	The majority ($n = 8$) of articles employed a qualitative design with purposive and convenience sampling as the main sampling methods.
Understanding disability	There is, in general, a lack of appreciation of disability as intersectional and personal experiences emerging from and located in intergenerational forms of exclusion and discrimination. Most of the research focuses on challenges SWDs face in distance education contexts.
Understanding distance education	There is very little, if any consideration of ableism as normative discourse in the design and delivery of distance education. SWDs are, to a large extent, invisible in the design and implementation of distance education.
Design, flexibility, and usability	Ensuring equitable learning experiences for SWDs start with the design of spaces (whether physical or online), flexible usability and catering for the diverse needs of SWDs.
Training	Training should be provided to staff and students in the use of (assistive) technologies.
Access	Providing equitable access encompasses designing equitable learning experiences, access to physical and online spaces and access to assistive technologies.

"the lives of these students have not changed much in spite of all that the Constitution and democratic policies promise" (p. 24).

Overview of the main findings

Table 4 provides an overview of the main findings of this scoping review.

As acknowledged earlier in the rationale for choosing a scoping review as well as recognizing its limitations (e.g., Munn et al., 2018), we found a paucity of evidence on SWDs in higher education and distance education contexts. As such, this scoping review points to significant research gaps (e.g., Tricco et al., 2016) in understanding the materialities and lived experiences of SWDS in South African distance education.

(In)conclusions

In the context of post-apartheid South Africa, providing educational opportunities to thousands who were previously marginalized and who did not have access to higher education, is entangled in the intergenerational legacy of colonialism and apartheid resulting in vast structural and intersectional inequalities. *Bodies* and the classification of bodies based on gender, race, religion, and culture informed much of the colonial and apartheid systems of resource allocation and opportunity. Disability still marks SWDs' bodies in ambiguous ways—"it appears and disappears, is noticed and is hidden—as we move through different physical and social spaces, and as we find ourselves in different political and historical moments" (McGuire, 2010, ¶3). Twenty-eight years into democracy, disability may have become visible in legislation and policies, but SWDs still remain invisible and unaccounted for in distance education.

Acknowledging the inherent characteristics of distance education as an industrialized form of educational delivery, and the constant negotiation between considering access, cost, and quality, this scoping review highlights some of the complexities of delivering equitable learning to all students, including SWDs.

While SWDs have an enforceable legal right to equitable learning experiences, distance education, in line with its humanitarian vision, should move beyond justice, to an ethics of care (Prinsloo, 2015).

Limitations

The findings of scoping reviews point to gaps in published research evidence and are, essentially, a scoping exercise. We acknowledge that the selection of the two databases, Web of Science and Scopus, as well as our search terms, may have limited the number of articles in the final analyzed corpus. This scoping review therefore does not provide a comprehensive state of the field of SWDs in distance education in the context of South Africa.

Acknowledgments

The authors would like to acknowledge the input and guidance received from the reviewers and editorial team.

Disclosure statement

No potential conflict of interest was declared by the author(s).

Funding

Funding for this research was received from the Project: Reconfigurations of Educational in/equality in a Digital world (RED). Initiative: Global Issues – Integrating Different Perspectives on Social Inequality. The authors would like to acknowledge and appreciate the project sponsor: Volkswagen Stiftung. The Grant Application Number for the application is: A130885.

ORCID

Paul Prinsloo http://orcid.org/0000-0002-1838-540X
Chinaza Uleanya http://orcid.org/0000-0002-7732-0905

References

Arksey, H., & O'Malley, L. (2005). Scoping studies: towards a methodological framework. *International Journal of Social Research Methodology, 8*(1), 19–32. https://doi.org/10.1080/1364557032000119616

Chiwandire, D., & Vincent, L. (2019), Funding and inclusion in higher education institutions for students with disabilities. *African Journal of Disability, 8*, Article 336. https://doi.org/10.4102/ajod.v8i0.336

Cooper, S., Cant, R., Kelly, M., Levett-Jones, T., McKenna, L., Seaton, P., & Bogossian, F. (2021). An evidence-based checklist for improving scoping review quality. *Clinical Nursing Research, 30*(3), 230–240. https://doi.org/10.1177/1054773819846024

Daniel, J. (2019). Open universities: Old concepts and contemporary challenges. *The International Review of Research in Open and Distributed Learning, 20*(4), 195–211. https://doi.org/10.19173/irrodl.v20i3.4035

Daniel, J., Kanwar, A., & Uvalić-Trumbić, S. (2009). Breaking higher education's iron triangle: Access, cost, and quality. *Change: The Magazine of Higher Learning, 41*(2), 30–35. https://doi.org/10.3200/CHNG.41.2.30-35

Farnes, N. (1993). Modes of production: Fordism and distance education. *Open Learning: The Journal of Open, Distance and e-Learning, 8*(1), 10–20. https://doi.org/10.1080/0268051930080103

Goodley, D. (2013). Dis/entangling critical disability studies. *Disability & Society, 28*(5), 631–644. https://doi.org/10.1080/09687599.2012.717884

Grech, S., & Soldatic, K. (2015). Disability and colonialism: (Dis)encounters and anxious intersectionalities. *Social Identities, 21*(1), 1–5. https://doi.org/10.1080/13504630.2014.995394

Hsieh, H., & Shannon, S. E. (2005). Three approaches to qualitative content analysis. *Qualitative Health Research, 15*, 1277–1288. https://doi.org/10.1177/1049732305276687

Kanuka, H., & Brooks, C. (2010). Distance education in a post-Fordist time: Negotiating difference. In M. F. Cleveland-Innes & D. R. Garrison (Eds.), *An introduction to distance education: Understanding teaching and learning in a new era* (pp. 69–90). Routledge.

Lane, A. (2014). Placing students at the heart of the iron triangle and the interaction equivalence theorem models. *Journal of Interactive Media in Education, 2014*(2). https://doi.org/10.5334/jime.ac

Maboe, M. J., Eloff, M., & Schoeman, M. (2018). The role of accessibility and usability in bridging the digital divide for students with disabilities in an e-learning environment. In E. Petratos (Ed.), *SAICSIT '18—Proceedings of the Annual Conference of the South African Institute of Computer Scientists and Information Technologists* (pp. 222–228). Association for Computing Machinery. https://doi.org/10.1145/3278681.3278708

Maboe, M. J., Eloff, M., & Schoeman, M. (2019). Analysis of students with and without disabilities in an e-learning setting. In C. de Villiers (Ed.), *SAICSIT'19—Proceedings of the Conference of the South African Institute of Computer Scientists and Information Technologists* (pp. 1–7). Association for Computing Machinery. https://doi.org/10.1145/3351108.3351138

Meekosha, H. (2011). Decolonising disability: Thinking and acting globally. *Disability & Society, 26*(6), 667–682. https://doi.org/10.1080/09687599.2011.602860

McGuire, A. (2010). Disability, non-disability and the politics of mourning: Re-conceiving the 'we'. *Disability Studies Quarterly, 30*(3/4). https://doi.org/10.18061/dsq.v30i3/4.1282

Munn, Z., Peters, M. D. J., Stern, C., Tufanaru, C., McArthur, A., & Aromataris, E. (2018). Systematic review or scoping review? Guidance for authors when choosing between a systematic or scoping review approach. *BMC Medical Research Methodology, 18*, 143–150. https://doi.org/10.1186/s12874-018-0611-x

Ndlovu, S. (2021). Provision of assistive technology for students with disabilities in South African higher education. *International Journal of Environmental Research and Public Health, 18*, 3892, 1–19. https://doi.org/10.3390/ijerph18083892

Ngubane-Mokiwa, S. A., & Khoza, S. B. (2021). Using community of inquiry (CoI) to facilitate the design of a holistic e-learning experience for students with visual impairments. *Education Sciences, 11*, 152–164. https://doi.org/10.3390/educsci11040152

Ngubane-Mokiwa, S. A., & Zongozzi, J. N. (2021). Exclusion reloaded: The chronicles of COVID-19 on students with disabilities in a South African open distance learning context. *Journal of Intellectual Disability-Diagnosis and Treatment*, 9(1), 137–147. https://doi.org/10.6000/2292-2598.2021.09.01.17

Ntombela, S. (2020). Teaching and learning support for students with disabilities: Issues and perspectives in open distance e-learning. *Turkish Online Journal of Distance Education*, 21(3), 18–26. https://doi.org/10.17718/tojde.761919

Ntombela, S. (2022). Reimagining South African higher education in response to Covid-19 and ongoing exclusion of students with disabilities. *Disability & Society*, 37(3), 534–539. https://doi.org/10.1080/09687599.2021.2004880

Paperpile. (2022). *The top list of academic research databases*. https://paperpile.com/g/academic-research-databases/

Peters, O. (1983). Distance education and industrial production: A comparative interpretation in outline. In D. Stewart, D. Keegan, & B. Holmberg (Eds.), *Distance education: International perspectives* (pp. 95–113). Croom Helm Routledge.

Peters, O. (1993). Understanding distance education. In K. Harry, J. Magnus, & D. Keegan (Eds.), *Distance education: New perspectives* (pp. 10–19). Routledge.

Peters, O. (2010). *Distance education in transition: Developments and issues*. BIS-Verlag der Carl-von-Ossietzky-University.

Peters, M. D., Godfrey, C. M., Khalil, H., McInerney, P., Parker, D., & Soares, C. B. (2015). Guidance for conducting systematic scoping reviews. *JBI Evidence Implementation*, 13(3), 141–146. https://doi.org/10.1097/XEB.0000000000000050

Pfeiffer, D., & Kiger, G. (1995). Introduction. Disability studies and the study of disability. *Journal of Health and Human Services Administration*, 17(4), 381–390.

Power, T. M., & Morven-Gould, A. (2011). Head of gold, feet of clay: The online learning paradox. *The International Review of Research in Open and Distributed Learning*, 12(2), 19–39. https://doi.org/10.19173/irrodl.v12i2.916

Prinsloo, P. (2015). The impact of an ethics of care on the iron triangle in ODL. In A. M. Teixeira, A. Szücs, & I. Mázár, I. (Eds.), *Expanding learning scenarios: Opening out the educational landscape—Proceedings of the European Distance and E-Learning Network Annual Conference* (pp. 55–63). European Distance and E-Learning Network. https://www.eden-online.org/proc-2485/index.php/PROC/article/view/1345/1053

Saldana, J. (2016). *The coding manual for qualitative researchers*. Sage.

Subrayen, R., & Dhunpath, R. (2019). A snapshot of the chalkboard writing experiences of Bachelor of Education students with visual disabilities in South Africa. *African Journal of Disability*, 8, Article 523. https://doi.org/10.4102/ajod.v8i0.523

Tekane R., & Potgieter, M. (2021). Insights from training a blind student in biological sciences. *South African Journal of Science*, 117(5/6), 1–7. https://doi.org/10.1080/13504630.2014.995394

Teixeira, A. M., Bates, T., & Mota, J. (2019). What future(s) for distance education universities? Towards an open network based approach. *RIED. Revista Iberoamericana de Educación a Distancia*, 22(1). https://www.redalyc.org/journal/3314/331459398006/331459398006.pdf

Thomas, C. (2004) How is disability understood? An examination of sociological approaches, *Disability & Society*, 19(6), 569–583. https://doi.org/10.1080/0968759042000252506

Thomas, C. (2007). *Sociologies of disability and illness: Contested ideas in disability studies and medical sociology*. Bloomsbury.

Titchkosky, T., & Aubrecht, K. (2015). WHO's MIND, whose future? Mental health projects as colonial logics. *Social Identities*, 21(1), 69–84. https://doi.org/10.1080/13504630.2014.996994

Tricco, A. C., Lillie, E., Zarin, W., O'Brien, K., Colquhoun, H., Kastner, M., Levac, D., Ng, C., Pearson Sharpe, J., Wilson, K., Kenny, M., Warren, R., Wilson, C., Stelfox, H. T., & Straus, S. E. (2016). A scoping review on the conduct and reporting of scoping reviews. *BMC Medical Research Methodology*, 16(1), 1–10. https://doi.org/10.1186/s12874-016-0116-4

Uleanya, C. (2022). Scholarly discourse of the Fourth Industrial Revolution (4IR) and education in Botswana: A scoping review. *Education and Information Technologies*. https://doi.org/10.1007/s10639-022-11298-9

UNESCO. (n.d.). *Unpacking Sustainable Development Goal 4: Education 2030*. https://docs.campaignforeducation.org/post2015/SDG4.pdf

Van Der Merwe, M. (2017, August 15). Students with disabilities disadvantaged at higher education level. *Daily & Maverick*. https://www.dailymaverick.co.za/article/2017-08-15-students-with-disabilities-disadvantaged-at-higher-education-level/

van Jaarsveldt, D.E., & Ndeya-Ndereya, C.N. (2015). 'It's not my problem': Exploring lecturers' distancing behaviour towards students with disabilities. *Disability & Society*, *30*(2), 199–212. https://doi.org/10.1080/09687599.2014.994701

Zawacki-Richter, O. (2019). The industrialization theory of distance education revisited. In I. Jung (Ed.), *Open and distance education theory revisited* (pp. 21–29). SpringerLink. https://doi.org/10.1007/978-981-13-7740-2_3

Zongozzi, J.N. (2020). Accessible quality higher education for students with disabilities in a South African open distance and e-learning institution: Challenges. *International Journal of Disability, Development and Education*, 1645–1657. https://doi.org/10.1080/1034912X.2020.1822518

Students with mental health (dis)Abilities' storied experiences within distance education

Rose C. B. Singh and Judy E. MacDonald

ABSTRACT
Distance education gives a diverse group of social work students access to further education. Research addressing the overall experiences of Canadian distance education social work students is limited, and even more so for distance education social work students with mental health (dis)Abilities. By means of a qualitative research project using narrative inquiry, I listened to the stories of social work students with mental health (dis)Abilities studying online as they each shared points of access and barriers within their distance education. Six study participants from two Canadian universities narrated multifaceted storied experiences of adapting, coping, and navigating through their distance courses and programs, highlighting attitudinal and institutional changes that would be supportive of their learning. Using narrative autoethnography, I also integrated my own experiences into the research. Through participants' storied experiences, I conceptualized recommendations for social work distance education programs.

Introduction

Distance education social work students are often mature learners, may live in rural or remote communities, representative of underrepresented groups within the profession and balancing employment, family, caregiving, and their studies (Afrouz & Crisp, 2021; Reamer, 2013). Many of these distance social work students already work in potentially stressful human services positions and juggle the multiple roles and responsibilities they have in their lives. Others might also identify as having existing mental health (dis)Abilities and bring these lived experiences to their distance studies and practice.

Despite increases in distance social work courses and program offerings (Kurzman, 2019; Regan, 2016), research centering student voices and lived experiences is limited, particularly in Canada and for students with mental health (dis)Abilities. Using narrative inquiry, a qualitative research study was designed (Singh, 2016) to invite social work students with mental health (dis)Abilities stories to be shared on their experiences within distance education.

This research was grounded in anti-oppressive and first voice perspectives. Anti-oppressive approaches strive for equity and the inclusion of underrepresented or excluded persons and groups, including people with mental health (dis)Abilities (Larson, 2016) and seek to elevate first voice perspectives (MacDonald, 2008) and center the expertise of the participants in the research (Moosa-Mitha, 2015). These perspectives determined the language and terminology utilized for this study; that is, *mental health (dis)Ability* was used as an all-encompassing term, including the many ways people define and describe their mental health lived experiences. The writing of (dis)Ability was informed by the definition from MacDonald and Friars (2009) with "'(dis)' to respect the person's social and physical connection with disability, and 'Ability' to highlight the creative and innovative ways of dealing with societal barriers" (p. 140). Capitalizing "Ability" emphasizes people's capabilities instead of a deficit view while acknowledging the oppressive structures and systems disabled persons navigate (MacDonald & Cooper, 2019; MacDonald & Friars, 2009).

Literature review

The personal struggles coupled with societal barriers experienced by those living with mental health (dis)Abilities have received greater acknowledgment publicly and within higher education. Understanding current perspectives on students with mental health (dis)Abilities is crucial to setting the context for this research. Specifically, the literature related to students with mental health (dis)Abilities was explored within three key areas: postsecondary student mental health, distance student mental health, and social work student mental health.

Postsecondary student mental health

Awareness and attention to postsecondary student mental health have been increasing (Linden et al., 2021; MacKean, 2011). More students with mental health (dis)Abilities are attending higher education, and more of these students are seeking support from their institutions (Condra et al., 2015; MacKean, 2011) with increasing severity of the mental health issues they are experiencing (Brown, 2018; Porter, 2019). Mental health literacy (Wiens et al., 2020), the age of onset of mental health concerns in conjunction with life, social, and academic stress that comes with attending higher education (Cunningham & Duffy, 2019; Duffy et al., 2019; Linden et al., 2021) are contributing factors to the greater prevalence of postsecondary student mental health challenges and reflect the need for mental health services and support among postsecondary students. In North America, the American College Health Association (2021) provides research survey results from its National College Health Assessment that capture the prevalence of mental health concerns among its postsecondary student respondents. Results from the fall 2021 survey (during the COVID-19 pandemic), which included 33,204 postsecondary student respondents from 41 schools across the United States of America, indicated that 50.8% of students reported moderate psychological distress and 22% reported serious psychological distress (American College Health Association, 2022, p. 12). The Canadian results from the spring 2019 survey (before the COVID-19 pandemic) that included 55,284 postsecondary student respondents from 58 schools across the country indicated that at any time during the 12 months prior, 68.9% of students experienced overwhelming anxiety and 51.6% had difficulty functioning due to feeling depressed (American College Health Association, 2019, p. 14). A cross-sectional trend analysis completed by Linden et al. (2021) of the American College Health Association-National College Health Assessment (2013, 2016, 2019) Canadian survey data shows that over this time frame, significantly more postsecondary students reported psychological distress, having mental health diagnoses, as well as seeking and receiving support for their mental health. While not specific to distance students, literature related to postsecondary student mental health and the American College Health Association-National College Health Assessment results reveal the overall challenges postsecondary students are generally experiencing related to their mental health.

Distance student mental health

Difficulties distance education students experience have been well documented in the literature and include continuing their postsecondary studies in conjunction with employment, family and caregiving responsibilities (Kahu et al., 2014), financial burdens (Qayyum et al., 2019), technology and internet connectivity issues (Milakovich & Wise, 2019), limited access to student support services (Tait, 2014), learning in isolation (Rath et al., 2019), challenges with the online learning environment (Bothma & Monteith, 2004) as well as attrition (Woodley & Simpson, 2014). Specific to student mental health, research has typically centered on postsecondary students in on-campus contexts.

However, distance student mental health has been the focus of several studies. In their study through the Open University in the United Kingdom, Richardson (2015) revealed how distance students with mental health (dis)Abilities, compared to distance students without mental health (dis)Abilities, had lower rates of completion, passing, and lower grades. Through their qualitative study within an Australian institution, McManus et al. (2017) showed the difficulties of distance learning experienced by students with mental health (dis)Abilities, which were related to the effects of their (dis)Abilities, personal situations, and the online environment. Three additional studies through the Open University in the United Kingdom also emphasized distance student mental health. Lister et al. (2021) explored "barriers and enablers" to mental health in distance education, presenting the interrelationship between these in their taxonomic wheel (pp. 10–11). Di Malta et al. (2022) highlighted the associations between distance student mental health, distance student academic performance, and increased opportunities for connection as a protective factor for distance student mental health. Waterhouse et al. (2020) brought awareness to the school, work, family role conflicts, and the consequential negative impact on distance students' mental health.

Social work student mental health

The prevalence of mental health (dis)Abilities among Canadian social work students, let alone distance education social work students, remains unknown. Legislation and laws exist with the intention to protect against discrimination and ensure accommodations are granted; however, social work students with mental health (dis)Abilities share experiences of stigmatization (Thompson-Ebanks, 2014) and sanism (Reid & Poole, 2013). Prejudice and discrimination against persons with mental health (dis)Abilities is referred to as sanism (Perlin, 2003), with awareness and action needed to reduce sanism within social work education, the profession, and beyond (Poole et al., 2012).

Equity and inclusion are central to social work education (Canadian Association for Social Work Education, 2022) and professional practice (Canadian Association of Social Workers, 2005). Yet, this is not always reflected in the social work literature and research on social work students with mental health (dis)Abilities, with these students sometimes described as complex or challenging (GlenMaye & Bolin, 2007; Reid & Poole, 2013). Students may encounter their own mental health concerns during their social work studies (Todd et al., 2019), field placements (Baird, 2021), or future practice (Kundra & Salzer, 2019), or they may have entered the profession with lived experiences of mental health (dis)Abilities (Goldberg, 2014). Often unaddressed is how many social work students are likely impacted, given the prevalence of mental health (dis)Abilities among postsecondary students and the stress these students encounter (Gair & Baglow, 2018). Social work students with mental health (dis)Abilities are currently in and will continue to enroll in distance social work programs, thus highlighting the need for their stories and suggestions to be shared.

Methodology

The voices of persons living with mental health (dis)Abilities are often silenced. Persons identifying with mental health (dis)Abilities need to be considered "active participants and experts on their own state of being" (Cohen, 2008, p. xi). Anti-oppressive social work, the theoretical lens informing this research, invites the voices of marginalized persons forward in the deconstruction of dominant discourses that have framed privileged positions within our institutions and social order (MacDonald, 2008). This aligns with narrative inquiry, which encourages participants to give voice to their experiences through storytelling (Riessman, 2008). Narratives are central to understanding our identities, experiences, and the world around us (Creswell, 2013). As Atkinson (1998) affirmed, "for it is through story that we gain context and recognize meaning" (p. 7). Narrative inquiry highlights how knowledge and multiple perspectives can be constructed and produced through interactions and communication. Further, narrative auto-ethnography was applied to this study whereby my lived experiences of a mental health (dis)Ability and studying within postsecondary education by distance helped inform the research topic and facilitated meaningful and genuine connection with the participants. Connelly and Clandinin (2006) noted, "Inquirers are always in an inquiry relationship with participants' lives" (p. 480). I also engaged in reflexivity throughout the research process, bringing an added layer of introspection and transparency to all stages of the research process (Wells, 2011).

Inviting stories

The considerations to "search" and "re-search" (Clandinin & Connelly, 2000, p. 124) emerged out of an iterative process informed by the literature, dialogue, and lived experiences. Conversations with participants from two Canadian universities who were studying social work through distance education and identified as students with mental health (dis)Abilities flowed from the following key areas:

- an exploration of their experiences within distance social work education
- storied experiences of the struggles or limitations related to distance education, along with storied experiences of the benefits or positive aspects of learning through distance education
- dialogue on the ways to improve distance social work education for students with mental health (dis)Abilities.

These considerations were explored through the utilization of seven open-ended questions to engage student participants in a relational conversation.

Participants

Ethical approval was received from Dalhousie University's Research Ethics Board prior to beginning the study. Criterion sampling was utilized whereby participants had to be from one of two selected Canadian universities, be a current distance education student in social work (either Bachelor or Master of Social Work) or had graduated from those programs within the past two years, and self-identify with mental health (dis)Abilities. Self-identification honors participants' lived experiences and their own definitions and perspectives of mental health (dis)Abilities (Boxall & Beresford, 2013; Price, 2013). Recruitment was sought through student groups and listservs within the selected programs.

Listening and hearing stories

Six participants shared their stories for this research. Information sharing meetings were held first with each participant, focusing on introductions, review of consent, and an opportunity to ask questions, as well as testing the selected audiovisual platforms used to meet. All six remained as participants and continued with the storying phase, engaging in conversation virtually from the comfort of their own homes or locations of choice. This also meant I could reach participants from various geographical locations, on a limited budget. Virtual meetings were possible due to participants' familiarity and comfort with technology, with the option of Skype or FaceTime as the platform. Online meetings were audio-recorded, with a mean time of 53 minutes.

All participants identified as women, all were mature students with partners, and five of the six participants had children. All had caregiving responsibilities. They were all helping professionals with experience in human services. Four of the participants shared they had mental health (dis)Abilities all their life, while two identified the onset during their teen years.

After the online conversation was completed and the recording ended, the participants and I had an opportunity to debrief and discuss the next steps. This included the transcript verification process and that I would be emailing the debriefing protocol, which outlined information on resources for mental health support, distress lines, crisis services, and counseling as needed.

Learning from stories

I transcribed all conversations, providing a two-channel approach to connecting with the participant's words – listening auditorily and reading visually. Narrative inquiry requires a close connection with the stories (Clandinin, 2016) involving reading and rereading the transcripts. Further, I created a transcription protocol, identifying numerous indicators to listen for so that distinct nuances of what was being shared would be captured. I checked the transcripts against the auto-recording three times before sending them to the participants for verification. Narrative inquiry demands attention to detail, hearing not only what is being said but where the silent voids emerge and what is not being said, detailing nonverbal communication through gestures, sighs (Riessman, 2002). The Lieblich et al. (1998) matrix of four cells related to holistic, categorical, content, and form was used for the narrative analysis, with specific attention on holistic-content and categorical-content. Holistic-content views the narrative as a whole, whereas categorical-content compares and contrasts the content of the narratives across all participants (Lieblich et al., 1998). For the narrative analysis, I followed detailed steps, including color-coding key themes and tracking themes through each narrative, while identifying contradictory or divergent themes.

Narrative inquiry is not meant to produce generalizability, for according to Riessman (2013), "the approach does not assume objectivity; rather, it privileges positionality and subjectivity" (p. 169). The goal of narrative inquiry is to "describe, understand, and interpret" (Lichtman, 2013, p. 139). Stories of students with mental health (dis)Abilities studying social work through distance education shared insights pertaining to the struggles and benefits of online learning for students with mental health (dis)Abilities, along with suggestions for how to create a supportive learning environment.

Telling and retelling stories

Five dominant themes emerged from the stories: flexibility and the (im)Balancing act, inaccessible accessibility services, misunderstanding mental health (dis)Abilities, intersection of (dis)Ability and distance education, and building connections and community.

Flexibility and the (im)Balancing act

Distance education was recognized as a way to create access to postsecondary education for the participants. None of the participants could have attended an on-campus program due to their full lives. In the words of one participant:

> Just the sheer flexibility of being able to, ... not go to class, not do a posting if I don't want to, or ... if I'm not up for it that night, ... instead do it the next night or do it three hours later. That made [it] much more, MUCH eas[ier] for me to balance life.

Students have complex lives, working full-time or part-time while studying, raising children, dealing with extended family responsibilities, let alone managing life with a mental health (dis)Ability. As one participant shared, "That has made it a ... great deal easier for me to manage my mental health." The flexibility provided by distance education allowed participants the opportunity to attend medical appointments and take care of their mental health needs; if they were not feeling well one day, they could choose to complete course work the next day. Living with a (dis)Ability requires adaptability for (dis)Abilities are fluid (Carter et al., 2017). Participants found learning by distance education afforded them the grace to be able to balance course work with aspects of their lives and their mental health (dis)Ability. As explained by one participant:

> A distance ed program made all the difference, ... because it meant that I could work at my own pace, at home, that I didn't have to be juggling family and work and driving a commute. Or you know, showing up for classes at a particular schedule ... So it really took an enormous amount of pressure off, ah, in terms of the stress of, of going back to school.

Another participant shared, "I was suffering from a lot of anxiety. And, I mean, just enormous fear, and agoraphobia, I didn't want to leave the house, um. And, so, it was great to be in front of a computer."

Distance education provided a level of flexibility that supported participants around managing their mental health (dis)Abilities. They could take breaks when needed and pace themselves with how they were feeling. One participant, however, identified they missed the structure of on-campus classes, as they tended to keep them motivated and on track. For most participants, flexibility helped create balance and opportunities for better mental health, noting it as the most beneficial and positive aspect of distance education. In completing their field placements, this same flexibility was not evident, as participants viewed field placements as being rigid and inflexible as they had to be completed within specific schedules and hours.

Inaccessible accessibility services

Only one of the six participants registered with the university accessibility services, due in part to the stigma of mental health (dis)Abilities, the struggle in coming to accept one's own identity as a (dis)Abled person, and priority given to on-campus services. Participants identified isolation and a disconnection from their programs and universities as creating further alienation. If someone had reached out, the participant likely would have used accommodations, but having to be the one to initiate contact was a challenge given her specific mental health (dis)Ability. The invisibility of mental health (dis)Abilities also contributed to participants not connecting with accessibility services, as one participant acknowledged, "when I grew up a (dis)Ability was something physical ... Mental illness was something on its own separate spectrum." Many participants thought they were not eligible for services due to their (dis)Ability being related to mental health or because they were distance education students. Outreach to distance education students pertaining to their eligibility for services was lacking. According to McManus et al. (2017), the lack of face-to-face interaction through distance education adds to the physical displacement of students, distancing them from the services from which they might otherwise benefit. Students with mental health (dis)Abilities are less likely to reach out to student services (Thompson-Ebanks, 2014), making it imperative that the institution initiates contact. Further, institutions need to specifically design services for distance education students, including mental health supports. Accessibility services requiring students with invisible (dis)Abilities to obtain medical documentation to prove their (dis)Ability denies their self-identification and presents an additional barrier to receiving support.

Participants primarily relied on their own informal support, as one participant noted, "You have to build up your own support, where you are, like at home ... as you go along in the program." Working participants utilized their Employee Assistant Programs, others saw counselors in their own community, received guidance and medication management through their family physicians, or in a crisis sought out emergency services at their local hospitals. Most significantly, participants' networks of family and friends were their primary source of support.

Misunderstanding mental health (dis)Abilities

Misunderstandings and misinformation about mental health (dis)Abilities were experienced by all participants from their classmates during group assignments or online discussion posts. One participant who was on medical leave from work related to stress had classmates view her situation as "having it easy" in comparison to their own situation of having to work full time while studying. The struggles of living with mental health (dis)Abilities were not acknowledged. Participants did not feel safe in sharing their own lived experiences:

> I didn't feel as though there was enough safety within the online community with the students to discuss, um ... discuss our own sort of issues around mental health, our own mental health, and how we are having difficulty or, you know, are being challenged by the distance education format and our anxiety.

Whether it was the stigma associated with mental health (dis)Abilities coming from their classmates, or the structure of distance courses where the sharing of personal information through a text-based discussion board seemed too risky, disclosures ended up being a cautious endeavor. Berger et al. (2009) noted that distance education poses more risk associated with "stereotyping and misunderstandings because of loss of capturing of nuances in non-verbal communication" (p. 477). When participants did risk sharing, the response was mixed: some received positive replies, while others received limited to no responses.

Participants recognized the emotional and mental energy required to disclose mental health (dis)Abilities with their instructors, particularly in not knowing how the instructor would respond. When sharing their lived experiences in their assignments, sometimes the sharing was not acknowledged, while other times they received supportive feedback. In all cases, disclosure required a great deal of thought, weighing the risks versus the potential benefits. The constant assessment and reassessment related to potentially sharing lived experiences of mental health (dis)Abilities was exhausting. Half of the participants were worried about being judged if they shared any aspect of living with a mental health (dis)Ability. They felt discouraged and vulnerable to the stereotypes and stigma associated with sanism. Understanding the implications of sanism within a distance classroom setting facilitates safer sharing of lived experiences from students with mental health (dis)Abilities from which all students learn.

Intersection of (dis)Ability and distance education

Participants shared that their mental health (dis)Abilities were challenging to manage during high stress times such as beginning the program or entering field placements. Trying new treatments, adjusting to medications while dealing with side effects that impacted their concentration and energy levels, and adjusting to learning online were difficult. Another struggle was being triggered by social work course content as it is not uncommon for students to encounter triggers when something they themselves have experienced is a topic being studied. However, given distance education's flexibility a student might be studying late at night with no way to debrief afterwards. Talking about the possibility of being triggered ahead of delivering the content and then offering support are important steps for instructors to consider. Participants also noted that their course work aided in their recovery. One participant had an assignment requiring her to write about her lived experiences; while challenging to write, it ended up being the most rewarding and beneficial assignment in her educational journey. Another participant described how success in her studies increased her self-worth and self-esteem at a time when she was struggling. As I shared in my researcher's voice comment, "successes in my online social work courses and programs were major personal accomplishments; proving it was possible to battle and overcome many barriers." Postsecondary education can impact how (dis)Ability is understood by dismantling attitudinal and structural barriers, while providing accessible curriculum that highlights the strengths of people with (dis)Abilities including students with mental health (dis)Abilities.

One of the most significant findings of this research is that none of the participants reached out to their schools to receive support related to their mental health (dis)Abilities. Rather, they would struggle through their assignments in times when they were unwell, silently suffering while their work failed to represent their full capacities. When possible, managing their school workloads was critical to maintaining balance with their mental health. Programs and courses need to have assignments distributed throughout the semester so as not to have high stress times when everything is due at once, along with exploring ways to invite students with mental health (dis)Abilities to come forward so that accommodations can be provided in an effort to support their learning journey.

Building connections and community

Disconnection and isolation was the primary negative aspect of distance education for participants. And, while many distance education students feel isolated (Angelaki & Mavroidis, 2013), it was further complicated for participants in this study as it impacted their mental health (dis)Abilities. The impersonal nature of distance education made it harder for one participant to explain her (dis)Ability to others. For another participant, the lack of connection with classmates and instructors compounded the isolation she was feeling due to agoraphobia. Fifty percent of the participants felt disconnected from their programs entirely.

Participants also shared positive and supportive experiences of connecting with fellow classmates or their professors. One participant connected with others in her distance program who were living in the same geographical area. They would meet in person as a study group, sharing ideas and perspectives related to course content as well as offering support to one another. Another participant connected with classmates during a face-to-face component of their program, and those friendships then carried over into the online environment. Angelaki and Mavroidis (2013) and Kahu et al. (2015) wrote about the importance of distance education programs building opportunities for students to meet and form collaborative relationships, as this breaks down the sense of isolation and promotes student well-being. Instructor engagement was also noted as being a central component of rich and meaningful distance education. The instructors, who were actively engaged in the course, made themselves available to students, and demonstrated a passion for teaching, which made it easier for participants to connect with them. Connections with classmates, instructors, and staff were critical to offset the disconnection and isolation they experienced as both distance education learners and students with mental health (dis)Abilities.

The five main themes framing the stories shared serve as a template for the participants' and my recommendations.

Storied lessons learned

While this research was completed prior to the COVID-19 pandemic, the participants' recommendations apply to and transcend these times in higher education, highlighting areas from attitudinal to institutional changes that would better support distance education students with mental health (dis)Abilities. Participants shared their recommendations through their narratives and were also asked their ideas for improvements. Six key categories emerged from conversations with participants: further education and professional development, financial assistance, technological support, improved accessibility and accommodations, and additional support. I also integrated my suggestions and supporting literature.

Further education and professional development

The need for further education and professional development on mental health (dis)Abilities was highlighted by four participants. Some felt such initiatives should focus on faculty, while others emphasized this for staff and/or students. Addressing the misunderstandings around mental health (dis)Abilities could be aided through further education offered to faculty, staff, and students. Professional development targeted toward professors around mental health as well as how to respond to and support students with mental health (dis)Abilities was recommended by some participants and is echoed by DiPlacito-DeRango (2016). Initiatives encouraging instructor mental health were also suggested. University-wide mental health promotion was emphasized as a way to welcome and initiate conversations around mental health for students, staff, and faculty alike, and is a component of the American College Health Association's (2020) healthy campus framework.

Financial assistance

Limited funding, scholarships, and bursaries exist for distance education students, those enrolled part-time, as well as for students with mental health (dis)Abilities. While this varies across jurisdictions, eligibility criteria for government student loans often exclude part-time and working students. Financial issues are also documented as a barrier (Brockerhoff-Macdonald & Sckopke, 2021) and a source of attrition (Qayyum et al., 2019). The overall lack of financial assistance available to distance education social work students with mental health (dis)Abilities was noted, suggesting more scholarships and bursaries be offered to students with this lived experience.

Technological support

Distance education requires students to possess technological skills. Learning the technical aspects of distance education may be challenging for students with or without mental health (dis)Abilities. Students new to distance education may not be fully aware of the technical requirements and skills needed to succeed, as outlined by Rath et al. (2019). Many distance education social work students are employed during regular business hours, leaving the evenings and weekends for their studies. Others live in time zones completely different from their institutions. Extra technical support was suggested, especially after hours when most students are online and completing their course work or assignments. Technical support available to distance students encountering issues after hours is central in successfully accessing and completing their studies (Britto & Rush, 2013; Milman et al., 2015).

Improved accessibility and accommodations

Several participants recommended relevant and available accessibility services for distance education students instead of accessibility services tailored solely for on-campus students. An example provided was extended and after-hours support for distance education students, who often work full-time during typical hours of operation or live in other time zones. Since distance students with mental health (dis)Abilities may be hesitant to disclose, register with accessibility services, or encounter barriers in this process, as evident in this study, incorporating universal design for learning principles (CAST, 2018) in course design and delivery planning may increase accessibility for these and other students who would benefit from this approach (Sherwood & Kattari, 2021; Smith-Carrier et al., 2021).

Improved accommodation processes were also suggested, such as forming the accessibility service provision policy around self-identification. Distance students with mental health (dis)Abilities may not have timely access to medical documentation due to the availability of physicians, specialists, and other medical staff in their home communities, which may be a deterrent to seeking accommodations when needed. Open communication, understanding, and flexibility from professors were viewed by participants as central to the accommodations process.

Additional supports

As programs expand to include more online offerings, careful consideration must be given to the services and supports available to students studying at a distance to ensure mental health and wellness are prioritized, as reiterated by Barr (2014). Recommendations from this research included online counseling and online support groups available for distance students, in addition to resources for self-care, such as tool kits, workbooks, and other interactive activities available virtually. For distance education students with mental health (dis)Abilities, being assigned an advocate was suggested by participants. This advocate would be a consistent support staff person for the duration of their distance studies, who would know the issues the student is facing, reduce the need for them to repeatedly explain their situation, facilitate communication, and reach out to them if they seem absent from their studies, and provide linkages to institutional services and supports.

The student health and wellness programming that exists at universities for on-campus students has not been available to distance students in the same ways. Even though the COVID-19 pandemic brought forward tremendous awareness, need, and resources to shift online, there have not been consistent offerings of student health and wellness services and support virtually. Patterson et al. (2021) also highlighted the importance of responding to student mental health needs in such a critical time. The concern remains whether distance students and online considerations will stay prioritized in the uncertainty of the COVID-19 pandemic and the possibility of returning to a version that would center again on on-campus operations.

Implications for distance education in social work

Through this study, we learned much from the stories and suggestions of the participants. Summarized in the Appendix are the experiences and recommendations of the distance education social work students with mental health (dis)Abilities who were part of this research. Both the participants and I emphasized the significance of challenging stigma and sanism within social work distance education and the profession. Shifting perspectives away from judgments and stereotypes, such as the preconceived notion that students with mental health (dis)Abilities are time-consuming and problematic, toward actions centered on respect and inclusion whereby the voices and experiences of students with mental health (dis)Abilities are acknowledged for their contributions. Supporting students with mental health (dis)Abilities during their distance education fosters the potential of having future social work practitioners who challenge stigma and sanism (Poole et al., 2012), diminish divisions between service users and service providers (Wilson & Beresford, 2000), bring forward insights and expertise from their lived experiences to improve social service delivery and programs (Collins, 2006), and integrate diverse perspectives into the profession (Gilbert & Stickley, 2012).

Acknowledgments

The authors wish to thank the participants who generously offered their time and stories for this research. The authors would also like to thank the two participating Schools of Social Work for their support and involvement in the study.

Disclosure statement

The authors report there are no competing interests to declare.

ORCID

Rose C. B. Singh http://orcid.org/0000-0002-8162-9497
Judy E. MacDonald http://orcid.org/0000-0002-9454-1179

Data availability statement

Due to the nature of this research, participants of this study did not agree for their data to be shared publicly, so supporting data is not available.

References

Afrouz, R., & Crisp, B. R. (2021). Online education in social work, effectiveness, benefits, and challenges: A scoping review. *Australian Social Work*, *74*(1), 55–67. https://doi.org/10.1080/0312407X.2020.1808030

American College Health Association. (2019). *Canadian Reference Group: Executive Summary: Spring 2019*. https://www.acha.org/documents/ncha/NCHA-II_SPRING_2019_CANADIAN_REFERENCE_GROUP_EXECUTIVE_SUMMARY.pdf

American College Health Association. (2020). *The healthy campus framework*. https://www.acha.org/App_Themes/HC2020/documents/The_Healthy_Campus_Framework.pdf

American College Health Association. (2021). *Survey data*. https://www.acha.org/ACHA/Resources/Survey_Data.aspx

American College Health Association. (2022). *Reference Group Executive Summary: Fall 2021*. https://www.acha.org/documents/ncha/NCHA-III_FALL_2021_REFERENCE_GROUP_EXECUTIVE_SUMMARY.pdf

Angelaki, C., & Mavroidis, I. (2013). Communication and social presence: The impact on adult learners' emotions in distance learning. *European Journal of Open, Distance and e-Learning*, *16*(1), 78–93. https://old.eurodl.org/materials/contrib/2013/Angelaki_Mavroidis.pdf

Atkinson, R. (1998). *The life story interview. Qualitative research methods series 44*. SAGE Publications. https://doi.org/10.4135/9781412986205

Baird, S. L. (2021). Understanding and responding to the complexities of student anxiety. In R. Csiernik & S. Hillock (Eds.), *Teaching social work: Reflections on pedagogy and practice* (pp. 231–247). University of Toronto Press.

Barr, B. (2014). Identifying and addressing the mental health needs of online students in higher education. *Online Journal of Distance Learning Administration*, *17*(2). https://ojdla.com/archive/summer172/barr172.pdf

Berger, R., Stein, L., & Mullin, J. B. (2009). Videoconferencing: A viable teaching strategy for social work education? *Social Work Education: The International Journal*, *28*(5), 476–487. https://doi.org/10.1080/02615470802308625

Bothma, F., & Monteith, J. L. dK. (2004). Self-regulated learning as a prerequisite for successful distance learning. *South African Journal of Education*, *24*(2), 141–147. https://www.ajol.info/index.php/saje/article/view/24979

Boxall, K., & Beresford, P. (2013). Service user research in social work and disability studies in the United Kingdom. *Disability & Society*, *28*(5), 587–600. https://doi.org/10.1080/09687599.2012.717876

Britto, M., & Rush, S. (2013). Developing and implementing comprehensive student support services for online students. *Online Learning*, *17*(1). https://doi.org/10.24059/olj.v17i1.313

Brockerhoff-Macdonald, B., & Sckopke, C. (2021). Identifying and removing barriers influencing new students' decision to enroll in an online course. *Online Journal of Distance Learning Administration*, *24*(1). https://ojdla.com/articles/identifying-and-removing-barriers-influencing-new-students-decision-to-enroll-in-an-online-course

Brown, J. S. L. (2018). Student mental health: Some answers and more questions. *Journal of Mental Health*, *27*(3), 193–196. https://doi.org/10.1080/09638237.2018.1470319

Canadian Association for Social Work Education. (2022). *About us*. https://caswe-acfts.ca/about-us/

Canadian Association of Social Workers. (2005). *Guidelines for ethical practice*. https://www.casw-acts.ca/en/Code-of-Ethics%20and%20Scope%20of%20Practice

Carter, I., Hanes, R., & MacDonald, J. (2017). Beyond the social model of disability: Engaging in anti-oppressive social work practice. In D. Baines (Ed.), *Doing anti-oppressive practice: Social justice social work* (3rd ed., pp. 153–171). Fernwood Publishing.

CAST. (2018). *Universal design for learning guidelines version 2.2*. http://udlguidelines.cast.org/

Clandinin, D. J. (2016). *Engaging in narrative inquiry*. Routledge. https://doi.org/10.4324/9781315429618

Clandinin, D. J., & Connelly, F. M. (2000). *Narrative inquiry: Experience and story in qualitative research* (1st ed.). Jossey-Bass Publishers.

Cohen, B. M. Z. (2008). *Mental health user narratives: New perspectives on illness and recovery*. Palgrave Macmillan. https://doi.org/10.1057/9780230593961

Collins, S. (2006). Mental health difficulties and the support needs of social work students: Dilemmas, tensions and contradictions. *Social Work Education: The International Journal*, *25*(5), 446–460. https://doi.org/10.1080/02615470600738809

Condra, M., Dineen, M., Gauthier, S., Gills, H., & Jack-Davies, A., & Condra, E. (2015). Academic accommodations for post-secondary students with mental health disabilities in Ontario, Canada: A review of the literature and reflections on emerging issues. *Journal of Postsecondary Education and Disability*, *28*(3), 277–291. http://www.ahead-archive.org/uploads/publications/JPED/jped28_3/JPED28_3_Final.pdf

Connelly, F. M., & Clandinin, D. J. (2006). Narrative inquiry. In J. L. Green, G. Camilli, & P. B. Elmore (Eds.), *Handbook of complementary methods in education research* (3rd ed., pp. 477–487). Lawrence Erlbaum/Routledge.

Creswell, J. W. (2013). *Qualitative inquiry and research design: Choosing among five approaches* (3rd ed.). SAGE Publications.

Cunningham, S., & Duffy, A. (2019). Investing in our future: Importance of postsecondary student mental health research. *Canadian Journal of Psychiatry*, *64*(2), 79–81. https://doi.org/10.1177/0706743718819491

Di Malta, G., Bond, J., Conroy, D., Smith, K., & Moller, N. (2022). Distance education students' mental health, connectedness and academic performance during COVID-19: A mixed-methods study. *Distance Education*, *43*(1), 97–118. https://doi.org/10.1080/01587919.2022.2029352

DiPlacito-DeRango, M. L. (2016). Acknowledge the barriers to better the practices: Support for student mental health in higher education. *The Canadian Journal for the Scholarship of Teaching and Learning*, *7*(2). https://doi.org/10.5206/cjsotl-rcacea.2016.2.2

Duffy, A., Saunders, K. E. A., Malhi, G. S., Patten, S., Cipriani, A., McNevin, S. H., MacDonald, E., & Geddes, J. (2019). Mental health care for university students: A way forward? *The Lancet, Psychiatry*, *6*(11), 885–887. https://doi.org/10.1016/S2215-0366(19)30275-5

Gair, S., & Baglow, L. (2018). "We barely survived": Social work students' mental health vulnerabilities and implications for educators, universities and the workforce. *Aotearoa New Zealand Social Work*, *30*(1), 32–44. https://doi.org/10.3316/informit.655929245237877

GlenMaye, L. F., & Bolin, B. (2007). Students with psychiatric disabilities: An exploratory study of program practices. *Journal of Social Work Education*, *43*(1), 117–131. https://doi.org/10.5175/JSWE.2007.200404112

Gilbert, P., & Stickley, T. (2012). "Wounded Healers": The role of lived-experience in mental health education and practice. *Journal of Mental Health Training, Education and Practice*, *7*(1), 33–41. https://doi.org/10.1108/17556221211230570

Goldberg, M., Hadas-Lidor, N., & Karnieli-Miller, O. (2014). From patient to therapatient: Social work students coping with mental illness. *Qualitative Health Research*, 1–12. https://doi.org/10.1177/1049732314553990

Kahu, E. R., Stephens, C., Leach, L., & Zepke, N. (2015). Linking academic emotions and student engagement: Mature-aged distance students' transition to university. *Journal of Further and Higher Education*, *39*(4), 481–497. https://doi.org/10.1080/0309877X.2014.895305

Kahu, E. R., Stephens, C., Zepke, N., & Leach, L. (2014). Space and time to engage: Mature-aged distance students learn to fit study into their lives. *International Journal of Lifelong Education*, *33*(4), 523–540. https://doi.org/10.1080/02601370.2014.884177

Kundra, L. B., & Salzer, M. S. (2019). Out of the shadows: Supporting social workers with a mental illness. *Social Work in Mental Health*, *17*(4), 462–478. https://doi.org/10.1080/15332985.2019.1576155

Kurzman, P. A. (2019). The current status of social work online and distance education. *Journal of Teaching in Social Work*, *39*(4-5), 286–292. https://doi.org/10.1080/08841233.2019.1660117

Larson, G. (2016). Mental health disability: The forgotten terrain. In J. Robertson & G. Larson (Eds.), *Disability and social change: A progressive Canadian approach* (pp. 188–204). Fernwood Publishing.

Lichtman, M. (2013). *Qualitative research in education: A user's guide* (3rd ed.). SAGE Publications.

Lieblich, A., Tuval-Mashiach, R., & Zilber, T. (1998). *Narrative research: Reading, analysis, and interpretation*. SAGE Publications.

Linden, B., Boyes, R., & Stuart, H. (2021). Cross-sectional trend analysis of the NCHA II survey data on Canadian post-secondary student mental health and wellbeing from 2013 to 2019. *BMC Public Health*, *21*(1), 590–590. https://doi.org/10.1186/s12889-021-10622-1

Lister, K., Seale, J., & Douce, C. (2021). Mental health in distance learning: A taxonomy of barriers and enablers to student mental wellbeing. *Open Learning: The Journal of Open, Distance and e-Learning*. https://doi.org/10.1080/02680513.2021.1899907

MacDonald, J. E. (2008). Anti-oppressive practices with chronic pain sufferers. *Social Work in Health Care*, *47*(2), 135–156. https://doi.org/10.1080/00981380801970285

MacDonald, J. E., & Cooper, S. (2019). (dis)Ability policy: A tangled web of complexity. In R. Harding & D. Jeyapal (Eds.), *Canadian social policy for social workers* (pp. 179–200). Oxford University Press.

MacDonald, J. E., & Friars, G. (2009). Structural social work from a (dis)Ability perspective. In S. Hick, H. Peters, & T. Corner (Eds.), *Structural social work in action* (pp. 138–156). Canadian Scholars.

MacKean, G. (2011). *Mental health and well-being in post-secondary education settings: A literature and environmental scan to support planning and action in Canada*. Canadian Association of College and University Student Services.

McManus, D., Dryer, R., & Henning, M. (2017). Barriers to learning online experienced by students with a mental health disability. *Distance Education, 38*(3), 336–352. https://doi.org/10.1080/01587919.2017.1369348

Milakovich, M. E., & Wise, J.-M. (2019). *Digital learning: The challenges of borderless education*. Elgar. https://doi.org/10.4337/9781788979467

Milman, N., Posey, L., Pintz, C., Wright, K., & Zhou, P. (2015). Online master's students' perceptions of institutional supports and resources: Initial survey results. *Online Learning Journal, 19*(4). https://olj.onlinelearningconsortium.org/index.php/olj/article/view/549 https://doi.org/10.24059/olj.v19i4.549

Moosa-Mitha, M. (2015). Situating anti-oppressive theories within critical and difference-centred perspectives. In L. Brown & S. Strega (Eds.), *Research as resistance: Revisiting critical, Indigenous, and anti-oppressive approaches* (2nd ed., pp. 65–94). Canadian Scholars.

Patterson, Z. R., Gabrys, R. L., Prowse, R. K., Abizaid, A. B., Hellemans, K. G. C., & McQuaid, R. J. (2021). The influence of COVID-19 on stress, substance use, and mental health among postsecondary students. *Journal of Interpersonal Violence, 9*(5), 536–556. https://doi.org/10.1177/0886260513505217

Perlin, M. L. (2003). "Things have changed": Looking at non-institutional mental disability law through the sanism filter. *New York Law School Journal of International and Comparative Law, 22*(1-2), 535–545. https://digitalcommons.nyls.edu/cgi/viewcontent.cgi?article=1046&context=fac_articles_chapters

Poole, J., Jivraj, T., Arslanian, A., Bellows, K., Chiasson, S., Hakimy, H., Pasini, J., & Reid, J. (2012). Sanism, 'mental health' and social work/education: A review and call to action. *Intersectionalities: A Global Journal of Social Work Analysis, Research, Polity, and Practice, 1*, 20–36. https://journals.library.mun.ca/ojs/index.php/ij/article/view/348

Porter, S. (2019). A descriptive study of post-secondary student mental health crises. *College Quarterly, 22*(1). http://collegequarterly.ca/2019-vol22-num01-winter/descriptive-study-of-post-secondary-student-mental-health-crises.html

Price, M. (2013). Defining mental disability. In L. J. Davis (Ed.), *Disability studies reader* (4th ed., pp. 298–307). Routledge.

Qayyum, A., Zipf, S., Gungor, R., & Dillon, J. M. (2019). Financial aid and student persistence in online education in the United States. *Distance Education, 40*(1), 20–31. https://doi.org/10.1080/01587919.2018.1553561

Rath, L., Olmstead, K., Zhang, J., & Beach, P. (2019). Hearing students' voices: Understanding student perspectives of online learning. *Online Journal of Distance Learning Administration, 22*(4). https://ojdla.com/archive/winter224/rathbeacholmsteadzhang224.pdf

Reamer, F. G. (2013). Distance and online social work education: Novel ethical challenges. *Journal of Teaching in Social Work, 33*(4-5), 369–384. https://doi.org/10.1080/08841233.2013.828669

Regan, J. C. (2016). Innovators and early adopters of distance education in social work. *Advances in Social Work, 17*(1), 113–115. https://doi.org/10.18060/21091

Reid, J., & Poole, J. (2013). Mad students in the social work classroom? Notes from the beginnings of an inquiry. *Journal of Progressive Human Services, 24*(3), 209–222. https://doi.org/10.1080/10428232.2013.835185

Richardson, J. T. E. (2015). Academic attainment in students with mental health difficulties in distance education. *International Journal of Mental Health, 44*(3), 231–240. https://doi.org/10.1080/00207411.2015.1035084

Riessman, C. K. (2002). Narrative analysis. In A. M. Huberman & M. B. Miles (Eds.), *The qualitative researcher's companion* (pp. 217–270). SAGE Publications. https://doi.org/10.4135/9781412986274.n10

Riessman, C. K. (2008). *Narrative methods for the human sciences*. SAGE Publications.

Riessman, C. K. (2013). Analysis of personal narratives. In A. E. Fortune, W. J. Reid, & R. L. Miller (Eds.), *Qualitative research in social work* (2nd ed., pp. 168–191). Columbia University Press.

Sherwood, K. L., & Kattari, S. K. (2021). Reducing ableism in social work education through universal design for learning and policy. *Journal of Social Work Education*, 1–14. https://doi.org/10.1080/10437797.2021.1997686

Singh, R. (2016). *Experiences of Canadian distance education social work students with mental health (dis)Abilities* [Master's thesis, Dalhousie University]. DalSpace. http://hdl.handle.net/10222/71617

Smith-Carrier, T., Goulden, A., & Singh, R. (2021). Implementing universal design for learning in social work education: A strengths perspective. In F. Fovet (Ed.), *Handbook of research on applying universal design for learning across disciplines: Concepts, case studies, and practical implementation* (pp. 149–171). IGI Global. https://doi.org/10.4018/978-1-7998-7106-4.ch008

Tait, A. (2014). From place to virtual space: Reconfiguring student support for distance and e-learning in the digital age. *Open Praxis*, *6*(1), 5–16.

Thompson-Ebanks, V. (2014). Disability disclosure among college students with psychiatric disabilities in professional majors: Risks and implication for rural communities. *Professional Development: The International Journal of Continuing Social Work Education*, *17*(2), 18–28.

Todd, S., Asakura, K., Morris, B., Eagle, B., & Park, G. (2019). Responding to student mental health concerns in social work education: Reflective questions for social work educators. *Social Work Education*, *38*(6), 779–796. https://doi.org/10.1080/02615479.2018.1563591

Waterhouse, P., Samra, R., & Lucassen, M. (2020). Mental distress and its relationship to distance education students' work and family roles. *Distance Education*, *41*(4), 540–558. https://doi.org/10.1080/01587919.2020.1821606

Wells, K. (2011). *Narrative inquiry*. Oxford University Press.

Wiens, K., Bhattarai, A., Dores, A., Pedram, P., Williams, J. V. A., Bulloch, A. G. M., & Patten, S. B. (2020). Mental health among Canadian postsecondary students: A mental health crisis? *The Canadian Journal of Psychiatry*, *65*(1), 30–35. https://doi.org/10.1177/0706743719874178

Wilson, A., & Beresford, P. (2000). 'Anti-oppressive practice': Emancipation or appropriation? *British Journal of Social Work*, *30*(5), 553–573. https://doi.org/10.1093/bjsw/30.5.553

Woodley, A., & Simpson, O. (2014). Student dropout: The elephant in the room. In O. Zawacki-Richter & T. Anderson (Eds.), *Online distance education: Towards a research agenda* (pp. 469–483). Athabasca University Press. https://www.aupress.ca/app/uploads/120233_99Z_Zawacki-Richter_Anderson_2014-Online_Distance_Education.pdf

Appendix. Storied lessons shared and learned

Experiences	Recommendations
Flexibility of distance education and the (im)Balancing act • Multiple roles and responsibilities (i.e., work, family) plus distance studies, potentially leading to negative impacts on mental health • Complete course work when feeling well • Attend mental health related appointments or services around online studies • Create balance and opportunities for better mental health	• Creative, flexible accommodations processes, not requiring extensive medical certifications or paperwork • Improve financial assistance for distance social work students with mental health (dis)Abilities • Make distance course content or modules available ahead of time, so students may work ahead • Online self-care courses and resources
Misunderstanding mental health (dis)Abilities • Lack of understanding and knowledge around mental health (dis)Abilities from classmates, staff, and faculty • Reluctant disclosures • Professional identity	• Mental health promotion, education and professional development for all • Progressive mental health courses and content deconstructing dominant discourses • Challenge stigma and sanism within social work education and profession
Mental health (dis)Abilities intersecting with distance education studies • Initial challenges when starting the program • Mental health impacted by school workloads and triggers from course content • Field placement challenges (i.e., lack of support from school, experiencing triggers) • Course work as part of recovery, using assignments to explore mental health related topics and own journey	• Orientations introducing supports and services available • After-hours supports and services • Universal design for learning, in courses and programs • Field placement accommodations and ongoing support • Social work courses, content, and assignments promoting first voice perspectives and valuing lived experiences
Inaccessible accessibility services and lack of mental health services or supports by distance, resulting in utilizing own supports	• Increased awareness and promotion around accessibility and mental health services and supports for distance education students with mental health (dis)Abilities • Application process support • Improved hours of operation, across times zones • Virtual counseling • Advocates
Disconnection and isolation, combined with mental health (dis)Ability	• Create connections and community online, with welcoming, open conversations about mental health and wellness as well as through outreach and online groups

Advising college students with dis/abilities in online learning

José Israel Reyes and Julio Meneses

ABSTRACT
Most distance universities have adopted advising practices traditionally employed in on-campus institutions. Nonetheless, little is known about the role of academic advisers while guiding students with dis/abilities to engage and achieve success in online higher education. This study aimed to explore and analyze advisers' perspectives related to supporting the diversity of these students in a fully online university. We followed the methodology of a case study based on semi-structured interviews in which 14 advisers participated. Our findings show that even though advisers face challenges when advising online students with dis/abilities, they attempt to support them proactively by offering personalized tracking. A paradigm shift from a reactive to a proactive approach by adopting inclusive practices would greatly improve the inclusion of all learners. Online institutions could better support learners with dis/abilities by framing all processes in the universal design principles and promoting collaborative and coordinated work among advisers, faculty, and staff.

Introduction

Most distance institutions have adopted advising practices traditionally employed in on-campus universities to support learners (Argüello & Méndez, 2019; Pardy, 2016). But advising and supporting students in online learning environments entail a change of paradigm (Kember et al., 2022; Snow & Coker, 2020; Tait, 2014), especially when it concerns the attention of those with dis/abilities (Kocdar & Bozkurt, 2022). Although online advising shares similarities with in-person advising, online learners face extra challenges in comparison with students in on-campus settings, including loneliness, anxiety, and technological issues (Argüello & Méndez, 2019; LaPadula, 2003). These challenges could have a higher impact when students are dealing with mental and physical conditions; hence, online advisers are required to develop new strategies aimed at supporting these learners to cope with such adversities.

Academic advising for online learners should stress key components such as communication, problem-solving, relationship management, learning and psycho-emotional support, and administrative processing (Warren & Schwitzer, 2018). Online institutions should also enable academic advisers to work with other stakeholders such as staff and faculty members to support students adequately (Rimbau-Gilabert et al., 2011). Coordinating actions to support learners among support services, advisers, administrative staff, and faculty positively affects their academic success (Kocdar & Bozkurt, 2022; Simpson, 2013; Thorpe, 2002).

The literature is solid in that academic advising in higher education, either in-person or online, is associated with students' persistence and success (Drake, 2011; Tippetts et al., 2020; Young-Jones et al., 2013). Most studies conducted in the last 2 decades have shown that students who receive effective advising from their first days at university are more likely to persist in their studies (Tippetts et al., 2020; Young-Jones et al., 2013). Recent investigations have also suggested that effective advising makes online students feel adapted and integrated into their programs of study as well as in the institution in general, which enhances their emotional well-being and academic performance (Argüello & Méndez, 2019).

One of the strongest components of advising is communication. Currently, online advisers contact students through different digital or electronic media, of which the most common is email (Argüello & Méndez, 2019). Communication by email is advantageous for advisers and advisees not only because it overcomes the time and distance barriers but because it allows both parties to have a record of their interactions (Argüello & Méndez, 2019; Rimbau-Gilabert et al., 2011). But it can also be challenging because, in some cases, students need immediate responses or closer human touch to cope with their study-related issues. Hence, several studies have suggested the use of online meetings by videoconferencing, which has proven efficient (Argüello & Méndez, 2019; Pardy, 2016), especially after the COVID-19 pandemic (Bornschlegl & Caltabiano, 2022).

Academic advising is employed for all students irrespective of their circumstances, which is positive for promoting inclusion. However, the literature unveils some challenges when advising online learners with dis/abilities because many practices are focused on arranging accommodations or offering personalized support upon students' request (Bornschlegl & Caltabiano, 2022; Kilpatrick et al., 2017). This advising approach based on reacting to students' demands has proven insufficient to address the needs of all learners (Kilpatrick et al., 2017; Reyes et al., 2022). For instance, there is solid evidence that some students do not disclose their condition to their advisers, instructors, or support services (Melián & Meneses, 2022; Tongsookdee, 2020), which means that they do not receive any support if courses, services, or processes are inaccessible.

The universal design (UD) approach applied in educational environments is highly effective to promote the inclusion of online learners with a wider range of profiles (Burgstahler, 2016; Rao et al., 2021). There are different frameworks of UD for educational purposes, such as universal design for instruction (UDI) and universal design for learning (UDL). UDI focuses on the entire system by designing learning environments and resources suitable to all learners (Scott et al., 2003); UDL focuses on promoting students' learning by considering inclusive course design, teaching, and assessment (Rao et al., 2021). In this regard, adopting these frameworks into advising practices may become very useful to enhance online learners' retention and success.

Advising strategies focused on UD in a fully online learning environment include, among others, enhancing the readability of textual information by writing short sentences, giving access to summaries of procedures (i.e., through infographics), and making sure that the information is understandable and meaningful to all learners (Lowenthal et al., 2020). Most importantly, all textual information must be offered in audiovisual formats, either through subtitled podcasts and short videos or images with descriptive texts (Burgstahler, 2016). Additionally, effective advising practices should incorporate diverse strategies such as seminars, workshops, writing courses, service and community-based learning, collaborative projects, and community building (Tait, 2014). All these strategies must be designed and carried out following UD principles.

Little is known about the application of UD frameworks when it concerns online advising, but the literature suggests some directions. As such, designing inclusive online courses, as well as advising and teaching, entails stronger efforts in terms of time and resources (Xie & Rice, 2021), but the results of doing so clearly contribute to enhancing online students' learning, persistence, and success (Catalano, 2014; Rao et al., 2021). The evidence indicates that advisers in on-campus universities face some challenges while advising learners with dis/abilities because of the lack of preparedness in addressing disability issues (Kilpatrick et al., 2017; Tongsookdee, 2020). This situation appears to be similar when it comes to distance learning. Therefore, advising online students by applying inclusive approaches based on UD principles could lead advisers to enhance their strategies while supporting all learners irrespective of their circumstances.

Online advisers' role should also focus on creating a supportive environment, so that learners have a reference person in the university to rely on (Debenham et al., 1999; Warren & Schwitzer, 2018). Strengthening the relationships at the beginning of all students' academic trajectories is a useful strategy to promote this bond with advisers (Bornschlegl & Caltabiano, 2022; Warren & Schwitzer, 2018), so that they have someone in the university to communicate any need or difficulty. Encouraging online learners to engage in social media networks to mutually support each other on study-related difficulties has also been proved an effective strategy to improve their chances of success (Argüello & Méndez, 2019).

Analyzing online advisers' experiences, perceptions, and reflections about their advising practices to support learners with dis/abilities in a fully online university would help to understand in which areas online universities could concentrate their efforts to improve the inclusion of these students. Such knowledge may be also useful for faculty and staff members to include the advisers' perspectives when planning or designing courses, as well as for the academic authorities responsible for setting effective policies to address learners' needs.

Methods

This study aimed to explore and understand what the academic advisers' role is in supporting learners with dis/abilities in a fully online learning environment, as well as analyze their reflections on how to make online advising more suitable for these students. The following research questions guided our analysis:

- What is the experience of academic advisers while advising students with dis/abilities in a fully online university?
- How do academic advisers support students with dis/abilities in a fully online university?
- How could a fully online university improve the advising practices addressed to support students with dis/abilities according to the advisers' experiences and reflections?

Research design

This investigation was based on the methodology of a case study (Yin, 2009, 2012). Given that the structure and organization of a fully online university itself were the unit of analysis, our design is consistent with an intrinsic case study. The main purpose of this study was to develop a better understanding of participants' subjective experiences on how inclusion may be possible in the learning environment being researched, and this research design enabled us to do so (Miles et al., 2014; Yin, 2009). Thus, we sought common patterns in the participants' testimonies, so that we can reflect on the lesson learned from their perspective, as Yin (2009, 2012) suggests, under a social constructivist approach.

Context

This study was carried out in a fully online university, grounded on an open entry policy, and based on asynchronous text-based interaction. The university reported having 87,500 students enrolled in its more than 100 undergraduate and graduate programs for the academic year 2021–2022. Of them, 1,944 students reported having a certified disability (Melián & Meneses, 2022). There are three academic and administrative figures to support students in this university: instructors, who accompany students with their learning acquisition; Student Services staff, who channel students' technical and administrative issues; and academic advisers, who support students alongside their academic trajectory with organizational, administrative, and decision-making processes. Each adviser supports a cohort of more than 100 students (the vast majority without a disability) and their role is based on addressing all students' general affairs rather than supporting those with specific issues, so they do not have any special expertise in disability. The communication among all these stakeholders and students takes place both via the university's virtual campus and by email. Instructors and advisers who directly attend to students have their main job in other institutions, so they reconcile their work in the university with their regular journey.

Procedures

Ethical considerations and participants' recruitment

The university's Ethical Committee approved the project and recommended the directives to adopt when contacting, selecting, and interviewing participants. Following these standards, both we and the participants signed an ethical protocol about the process of collecting, storing, and processing the information as well as guaranteeing the interviewees' confidentiality and anonymity. There was no relationship—either professional or personal—between the participants and us before the investigation.

The participants were selected through a purposive sampling in which we considered two selection criteria: participants' experience in advising students with dis/abilities in the university and the department to which they belonged, selecting two of them from each department. Next, in coordination with Student Services, we sent an invitation by email to participate in the study to the most experienced advisers, explaining the objectives of the study, how it would be conducted, and their rights as participants. The advisers interested in participating voluntarily contacted us, and we gave them more information about the study.

Data collection

We conducted semi-structured interviews by videoconferencing with 14 advisers (Table 1) for 45 to 70 minutes, with an average of 1 hour. The fieldwork was carried out from April 2021 to November 2021. The interview guide comprised five blocks of open questions: participants' trajectory as advisers, communication strategies to interact with students, strategies to advise and support learners, challenges and needs

Table 1. Participants' information.

Participant	Program	Profile	Experience as adviser
P1	Arts	EOL (adviser) and EDI	7 years
P2	Geography and Art History	EOL (adviser)	3 years
P3	Psychology	EOL (adviser)	5 years
P4	Law	EOL (adviser)	5 years
P5	Computer Engineering	EOL (former student, adviser, and instructor) and EDI	18 years
P6	Digital and Multimedia Interaction	EOL (adviser)	12 years
P7	Communication	EOL (former student, adviser, and instructor) and EDI	15 years
P8	International relations	EOL (adviser)	3 years
P9	Law	EOL (former student and adviser)	3 years
P10	Business administration and management	EOL (adviser)	20 years
P11	Communication	EOL (adviser and instructor)	12 years
P12	Speech Therapy	EOL (former student, adviser, and instructor) and EDI	3 years
P13	Employment and Labour Relations	EOL (adviser)	20 years
P14	Speech Therapy	EOL (adviser) and EDI	3 years

Note. EOL = Experience in online learning; EDI = Experience in disability issues.

while advising students with dis/abilities, and reflections. The interviews were recorded under participants' consent and then stored in a protected folder to be transcribed later.

Data analysis

We followed the six-phase approach of thematic analysis (Braun et al., 2015; Braun & Clarke, 2006) to analyze the participants' experiences, points of view, and practices employed aimed at promoting inclusion. Thematic analysis offered us enough flexibility to connect our interview-based information with our research design, as well as the assurance of the study's trustworthiness by coding and analyzing data systematically and iteratively. In this regard, we "got familiar" with the data while reading the corpus several times, highlighting the excerpts that fit our research questions, taking notes, and creating memos about the consensus of the participants. Next, we carried out an iterative coding process using Atlas.ti, through which we defined the themes that better matched the participants' experiences, perceptions, and reflections with our research questions.

Results

We have organized the participants' testimonies into three themes. First, we analyze the advisers' experiences while advising students with dis/abilities in a fully online learning environment, including how their profiles facilitate their role, as well as their challenges and needs. The second theme summarizes the main strategies employed by advisers to attend to these students in the university including communication and intervention (advising and support) strategies. Finally, we analyze the advisers' reflection on what measures a fully online university should incorporate as a priority to enhance advising practices toward inclusion.

Advisers' experience attending different types of disabilities

Advisers' profiles

Most respondents had extensive experience in online learning, either as former students, advisers, or instructors. But almost none had any experience in or knowledge of disability issues. Despite the lack of knowledge, these advisers attempted to support learners with dis/abilities from their experience in online learning. Those who self-identified as former students in the university described their experience as follows: "I (without a dis/ability) experienced successful and not successful moments as an online student, so I empathize with these students giving them emotional support" (Participant [P] 5). Another participant commented: "It motivates me to promote the access to education as a human right ... I am trying not to fail where I found my advisers failed" (P9).

Some advisers had experience in disability issues because they work or have worked in external contexts with people with dis/abilities. For them, supporting students living with any dis/ability is effortless since they recognize some patterns that suggest how to intervene. "Once I realized that I had this student [with multiple dis/

abilities] I started to revive everything; I contacted the person responsible for attending to these issues to communicate the student's situation and how to support her/him" (P5). Likewise, those with experience as both instructors and advisers face fewer difficulties in supporting these students as they address any issue by coordinating strategies with other university stakeholders such as faculty and staff. "Because I'm also an instructor, my coworkers see professors as part of the team; it facilitates working collaboratively" (P12). Other participants described themselves as "passionate about advising or teaching" (P7; P8), which guided them to support students proactively.

Attending different types of disabilities

The types of disabilities most challenging to attend to for the participants included mental health conditions and chronic illnesses. For instance, the advisers highlighted their difficulties while advising students who usually experience emotional changes. "This student emails me and says: 'I will abandon the studies, but 15 minutes or half-hour later comes back and says: 'I get back the studies', and this episode has happened many times" (P1). The adviser also expressed that students living with mental health conditions often do not take into consideration their advice, especially in decision-making processes such as the number of courses to enroll in. Many times, advisers feel overwhelmed as they do not know how to support them. "This student never listens to me. Trouble is that I am not an expert, and I don't know how to address his issues adequately" (P4).

According to the participants, advising students with chronic illnesses such as fibromyalgia, hypersensitivity to chemical products or electronic devices, and students dealing with cancer also turn out to be challenging. Advising students with severe or multiple dis/abilities also demands more intense and personalized support. "If I have many students like this one, it would be hard to attend them adequately because it requires three or four times the time I invest for other students without disabilities" (P2).

Limited guidelines and coordination

Our results showed that no clear guidelines on supporting learners with dis/abilities exist in the university. Hence, it causes the entire system to rely on reacting to students' requests, which may exclude those who do not feel comfortable disclosing their condition. According to advisers' testimonies, some students do not disclose their situation, or they do it just when they are in big trouble. Sometimes, these students even drop out of their studies. This issue is even harder to manage for advisers because they do not receive these students' information from anyone else. "I accessed these students' enrolment information, and they had a discount for disability issues incorporated ... But I haven't received any communication from the university" (P13). Internal communication is essential to attend to these students effectively and avoiding misunderstandings, as some advisers have experienced. "I have a student with Asperger's syndrome. In the beginning, I didn't understand why they asked the same thing several times until I realized their situation" (P2).

The advisers also perceive that, due to the nature of distance learning, information and guidelines among faculty and staff are missing when advising learners with dis/abilities: "I don't have a clear instruction on how to attend to these students; it's on my own initiative or empathy that I get involved" (P11). Regardless, it is evident that an institutional policy with clearer guidelines on supporting learners with different profiles from an inclusive frame is needed in this university. For instance, advisers often mediate between students and faculty to request or supervise curricular accommodations but, according to the participants, every instructor decides whether to grant or deny the petition. "There are instructors with a high readiness to support these students, but other ones are more reluctant … It is hard to get accommodation from them" (P4).

Advisers also experienced isolation issues while advising online students. The participants consider that such loneliness causes a significant scarcity of coordination and collaboration with university staff and faculty. As Figure 1 shows, according to advisers' experiences, communication and support processes when addressing learners' needs and demands in the university are not as fluid as they would like.

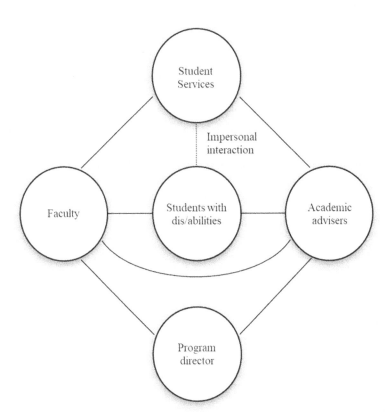

Figure 1. Institutional connections developed in the university to support students with dis/abilities.

Advisers' strategies to advise learners with dis/abilities

Communication strategies

All the participants communicated asynchronously both with students and other university stakeholders. They used two channels to communicate with students: the virtual campus to disseminate general information and email to advise students privately. Most advisers are aware that asynchronous communication is very convenient both for them and the students. Even though most advisers attempted to advise students with dis/abilities under the same terms as everyone to avoid segregation and stigmatization, some of them personalized the messages once they knew about the students' condition, so that students could access the information effortlessly. "When students are dealing with disorders such as hypersensitivity, I send them brief messages; something simple and readable" (P1). Additionally, some advisers were willing to address these students' demands as soon as possible, considering that their pace of work is slower than others without a disability. So, immediate responses are crucial for them to complete their learning and assessment activities in time.

Several respondents expressed they use alternative communication strategies, even synchronous such as phone calls, videoconferencing, or face-to-face meetings, to advise learners with dis/abilities. Face-to-face meetings—either by videoconferencing or in-person—usually happened at the beginning of students' trajectory because these learners needed accurate information about the university's procedures as well as wanting to express their situation. According to several participants, students who requested synchronous meetings have several physical or sensory disabilities. These advisers consider that such meetings positively influenced these students' adaptation given that they had a broader landscape of the university and felt more accompanied.

Advisers also employed communication strategies such as phone calls or voice notes by email throughout students' academic trajectory. Most of these strategies were addressed to students with learning dis/abilities or mental health conditions for whom text-based communication causes accessibility and emotional challenges. "I send the information by email first, but if I see they have trouble, we use WhatsApp (text message or Facetime) ... With students with dyslexia or autism we do videoconference by Google Meet" (P9). A few advisers also commented that they use phone calls with several students to address the most salient issues, even with those without a disability.

Intervention strategies

Advisers' strategies to support learners with dis/abilities included mediation between them and instructors or the Student Services staff, advising and counseling practices, and providing emotional and instrumental support. Some advisers directly contacted the Student Services and faculty members to request accommodations on behalf of students, even though they usually just mediate conflicting situations where students feel unsatisfied with the accommodation received in the courses. The advising and counseling strategies focused on offering personalized monitoring and guiding students with the processes of requesting accommodations for teaching and final exams. "Apart from the faculty, we, as advisers, remind the students of all the processes; this is so useful for students with special educational needs" (P12).

The advisers also offer these learners the human touch they usually do not get in any other structure of the university. This kind of affection includes moral and emotional support, which is essential for students who deal with several adversities. "When they see a person who is supporting them, who is monitoring their progress, they feel grateful." The advisers attempted to motivate students by sending them encouraging messages or supporting them through positive reinforcement "focused always on their success" (P5). Emotional support is often accompanied by instrumental support. While advisers provide students with motivational messages, they also suggest techniques to overcome the issues that students are dealing with. Some advisers go beyond and offer personalized support by phone and videoconferencing or adapt some textual contents that students find hard to access. One participant shared:

> One student with dyslexia was calling me almost daily ... one call was for emotional unloading and the next one was to address her issues ... I explained to her the learning contents that way ... I also have other students who shared with me some dense textual learning resources and I highlighted the most important parts, but I did it voluntarily. (P11)

Although most students disclose their condition to advisers with the aim of requesting specific support, some of them just do it to express that they do not want any special treatment. Advisers such as P7, P9, and P13 commented on experiences in which students communicated their condition just to inform them. "The student explained his situation to me, I offered him the special support provided by the university's Student Services, but he refused it" (P7).

The advisers in one department have developed a strategy to evaluate the interventions they employed with these students by having a record book in which they annotate every accommodation needed by each learner and its effectiveness. Thus, the advisers share such information with faculties for new courses in which these students enroll to coordinate the accommodations at least 2 months before the course starts. Advisers in other departments, such as P5 and P9, used similar strategies to track the effectiveness of their advising on these students' performance, but they did not share them with anyone else in the university.

Advisers' reflection on improving online advising for students with dis/abilities

Collaboration between university stakeholders

The participants reflected on aspects on which the university should work to improve advising for students with dis/abilities. One of the most salient themes was the collaboration between them and other stakeholders involved in supporting students, such as faculty and Student Services staff. "Better coordination is essential and critical" (P7).

The advisers' role in the university is generic, which makes it challenging to support those with specific needs. Hence, guiding advisers in addressing the needs of all learners under an inclusive framing is a necessity. Additionally, most of the participants do not know the university's staff who manage the accommodations or the faculties. "It would be great having available a space for advisers in which they [the university] accompany us, or at least that they tell us about the services offered to students" (P8).

The respondents have experienced difficulties while addressing students' disability-related issues because of the scarce preparedness along with limited information, guidelines, and knowledge. Even though the university does have a team within Student Services to coordinate the accommodations, several participants considered that having a team of advisers with expertise in disability would represent a great step forward toward the inclusion of learners with dis/abilities in a fully online university. Therefore, the advisers' testimonies reveal that a significant distance separates them from other stakeholders responsible for supporting students. Figure 2 represents a model of coordination and support based on the participants' points of view that may be useful to address advisers' isolation and coordination issues when supporting students with dis/abilities.

Advisers also stated that, if the university provides them with clear guidelines and learning opportunities on disability issues, it would improve their ability to attend to these learners. More than half of the respondents preferred to have a team—either as an "elite unit" within advisers or as an external group (which is already available)—that coordinates all the institutional strategies addressed to attend to these students. P5 reflected on that matter as follows:

> I think it would be better to have a team that works with these students directly. Someone who masters that knowledge so that can channel it through the program director and the faculties to agree on the type of support that would be offered to students according to their needs.

Many participants agreed with that idea, arguing that sometimes they manage issues out of their competence. "I can accompany students to some extent, but there are issues very sensitive to address and, perhaps, you're getting into something that's not your business" (P7).

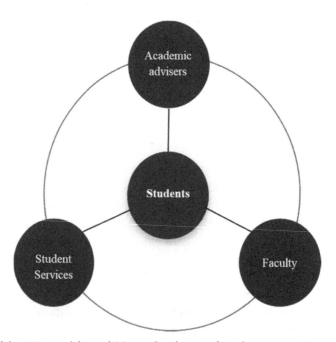

Figure 2. A collaborative model to advising online learners based on a proactive approach.

Shifting toward an inclusive approach

Some learners, especially those with mental health conditions, do not feel comfortable explaining their situation to every faculty and staff member. They prefer "someone else does it confidentially because they do not want to disclose their situation straightaway" (P2). But rather than waiting for students to communicate their condition, online universities are urged to adopt inclusive practices, so that all learners can access resources and services by default: "The university will be inclusive when all students with any dis/ability can participate with no limitation and be successful ... I mean, providing learners with accessible media and resources to enable them to have equitable opportunities" (P5). This entails a paradigm shift in which neither learners need to request accommodations nor faculties and advisers need to accommodate resources at the last minute. P1 questioned himself on this matter:

> If learners have universal access to information about paperwork it would be helpful ... I send this information through a PDF file and perhaps some students do not read it because it's inaccessible for them ... this is an issue that needs to be addressed.

Advisers' reflections showed that accessibility is an issue on which improvements should focus in all areas. "Many times, what these students find hard is not the course contents but accessing some tools and resources" (P6). The respondents also commented on the accessibility and usability faced by learners with dis/abilities with administrative procedures. In this regard, enabling universal access to procedures and resources is essential to guarantee all learners' inclusion in a fully online university. "It's mandatory making all the administrative processes accessible, usable, and more systematic" (P3).

Redesigning communication strategies

Several advisers agreed that asynchronous communication by email is very convenient for students, especially for those with severe and multiple disabilities, given that it enables them to interact flexibly with faculty and staff. Nonetheless, more than half of respondents also agreed that synchronous communication with learners is needed to reduce or eliminate some difficulties such as bureaucracy, misunderstandings, time-wasting, and even anxiety or stress. "If the fluency and exchange of information were faster, it would greatly facilitate everything because, sometimes, the students write an email, and they receive the answer from the Student Services staff 4 days later, when students are already overwhelmed" (P12).

The participants considered that making communication flexible around the students' needs and possibilities is the best option, considering the advisers' availability as well. For instance, while some advisers are willing to communicate synchronously by phone and video calls—in fact, they already do—others see it as unsustainable, as they work as advisers "in the wee hours of the morning" (P1) or simply they consider it would reduce flexibility and "the university would lose its spirit" (P12). Regardless of the chosen way of communication, most participants agreed that closer contact is needed to accompany students in a fully online learning environment.

Discussion

This case study focused on exploring the experiences of academic advisers while attending students with dis/abilities in a fully online university. We aimed to analyze the main advising practices employed by the participants to support these students as well as their reflections on how to make online advising more inclusive. We defined three main themes based on the participants' testimonies to answer our research questions: advisers' experiences attending different types of dis/abilities; strategies to advise these learners; and reflection on improving online advising for these students.

The advisers' profile determines how they address the demands and needs disclosed by learners. But rather than focusing on finding a suitable profile for professionals attending to students with dis/abilities, what is really important here is that all online advisers feel prepared to support all learners irrespective of their circumstances. To do so, supporting these advisers in enhancing their awareness of the diversity of needs among students would be an early consideration, so that they can adopt effective strategies to advise all learners. Even though improving the awareness of diversity in online higher education involves the entire online university community, it would be useful starting with advisers as they have the closest contact with students. Thus, online advisers could adopt an inclusive approach to support all learners proactively and effectively.

The advisers' experience supporting learners with dis/abilities is closely linked with the type and severity of their condition. They feel more overwhelmed while supporting students with nontraditional disabilities, such as mental health and chronic conditions, due to the lack of knowledge and guidelines on how to address these students' needs. In such cases, online advisers wished that they could receive support on how to advise these students by adopting an inclusive approach. According to literature, the lack of knowledge and support for advisers on disability issues has been a notable concern in higher education (Dunn, 2005; LaPadula, 2003; Tongsookdee, 2020).

Our results suggest that promoting advisers' knowledge about focusing their advising practices on UD principles in online higher education is a real necessity. Advising approaches typically based on students' demands exclude those learners who decide to keep their condition undisclosed. Therefore, it is urgent that online advisers shift their support practices into a proactive approach that promotes the inclusion of all learners. This means that online advising strategies should be designed in a way that helps students to gain autonomy and self-efficacy while progressing in their academic trajectory. In this sense, UD is a useful approach that suggests some guidelines to make information, processes, services, and resources accessible to all learners. By using this approach, institutions can promote learners' autonomy while accessing resources or processes independently and therefore to keep their condition undisclosed (Burgstahler, 2016; Scott et al., 2003). In any case, adopting this approach does not replace advisers' role of offering online learners the human touch they may need but gives them more chances and resources to support all learners.

Our results are consistent with the literature (Drake et al., 2013) in that advising strategies in higher education are framed in three blocks: emotional and instrumental support, administrative procedures, and advising and counseling practices. The advisers' psychoemotional and instrumental support to learners is a salient role in online higher education (Warren & Schwitzer, 2018). Therefore, it is convenient to define institutional strategies that guide advisers to improve their practices in these areas and provide them with the necessary resources that enable them to advise all learners effectively.

Collaboration and coordination between all the stakeholders involved in supporting students are also key to promoting inclusion in a fully online university. The advisers involved in coordinating strategies within their department were likely to support students effectively. Likewise, those who at least discussed the troubles they found and shared their experiences while attending to learners' needs with their colleagues to support each other also considered this informal collaboration very useful. Therefore, advising learners with diverse needs in a fully online university requires a well-structured institutional strategy and informal spaces in which the advisers can discuss, collaborate, and coordinate their strategies.

The advisers' testimonies are consistent with the literature regarding the effectiveness of combining different formats of communication particularly used in online learning (Argüello & Méndez, 2019; Pardy, 2016; Rimbau-Gilabert et al., 2011). There are no doubts regarding the suitability of asynchronous communication for these learners and online advisers. Nonetheless, all communication strategies should be based on UD to make interaction fluently and dynamic. For instance, advisers usually use synchronous interaction or asynchronous messages based on audiovisual formats to advise students with mental health conditions and learning dis/abilities. Incorporating diverse methods of interaction by combining audiovisual and text content and synchronous and asynchronous formats greatly enhances the communication between advisers and learners. Considering students with dis/abilities' diversity of needs, the communication processes should leverage the opportunities that diverse media offer in terms of flexibility, interactivity, and therefore accessibility, to facilitate their full involvement.

Conclusions

Advisers' practices in supporting students with different types of dis/abilities are key to promoting inclusion in online higher education. Therefore, even though this study shows that advisers attempt to address students' difficulties proactively, supporting the advisers' work is essential. Enhancing their knowledge of inclusive practices is fundamental to providing them with effective resources directed at meeting all learners' needs. Focusing the institutional support on collaborative and coordinated strategies among support services, advisers, and instructors to address the needs of the wide range of students jointly is also crucial.

Online advisers provide learners with emotional support, which is essential for all students and particularly for those with dis/abilities to succeed in online higher education. In this regard, strengthening the relationship between advisers and students, as well as with the rest of the university stakeholders, would greatly enhance their possibilities to support all learners. To do so, a communication strategy based on flexible and diverse forms of interaction would increase these actors' chances to collaborate, as well as receive and provide academic support aiming at promoting students' success equitably.

Acknowledgments

We thank Sílvia Mata for helping us to access the participants, the participants for sharing their experiences for the study, and Efrem Melián for helping us to proofread the manuscript.

Disclosure statement

No potential conflict of interest was declared by the authors.

Funding

This research was funded by the Universitat Oberta de Catalunya.

Geolocation information

This study was conducted at the Open University of Catalonia's 22@ building, Barcelona, Spain: 41.406719323451824°N, 2.1945476797315604°W.

ORCID

José Israel Reyes http://orcid.org/0000-0001-8420-4438
Julio Meneses http://orcid.org/0000-0003-4959-456X

References

Argüello, G., & Méndez, M. G. (2019). Virtual advising: A tool for retention, engagement, and success for the graduate distance learner. *Distance Learning*, *16*(2), 51–57.
Bornschlegl, M., & Caltabiano, N. J. (2022). Increasing accessibility to academic support in higher education for diverse student cohorts. *Teaching and Learning Inquiry*, *10*. https://doi.org/10.20343/teachlearninqu.10.13
Braun, V., & Clarke, V. (2006). Using thematic analysis in psychology. *Qualitative Research in Psychology*, *3*(2), 77–101. https://doi.org/10.1191/1478088706qp063oa
Braun, V., Clarke, V., & Rance, N. (2015). How to use thematic analysis with interview data. In A. Vossler & N. Moller (Eds.), *The counselling and psychotherapy research handbook* (pp. 183–197). SAGE Publications. https://doi.org/10.4135/9781473909847.n13

Burgstahler, S. (2016). The development of accessibility indicators for distance learning programs. *Research in Learning Technology*, *14*(1), 79–102. https://doi.org/10.1080/09687760500479753

Catalano, A. (2014). Improving distance education for students with special needs: A qualitative study of students' experiences with an online library research course. *Journal of Library & Information Services in Distance Learning*, *8*(1-2), 17–31. https://doi.org/10.1080/1533290X.2014.902416

Debenham, M., Whitelock, D. M., Fung, P., & Emms, J. M. (1999). Online educational counselling for students with special needs: Building rapport. *Research in Learning Technology*, *7*(1), 19–25. https://doi.org/10.1080/0968776990070104

Drake, J. K. (2011). The role of academic advising in student retention and persistence. *About Campus: Enriching the Student Learning Experience*, *16*(3), 8–12. https://doi.org/10.1002/abc.20062

Drake, J. K., Jordan, P., & Miller, M. A. (2013). *Academic advising approaches strategies that teach students to make the most of college*. John Wiley & Sons.

Dunn, S. (2005). A place of transition: Directors' experiences of providing counseling and advising to distance students. *Journal of Distance Education*, *20*(2), 40–57.

Kember, D., Trimble, A., & Fan, S. (2022). An investigation of the forms of support needed to promote the retention and success of online students. *American Journal of Distance Education*, *0*(0), 1–16. https://doi.org/10.1080/08923647.2022.2061235

Kilpatrick, S., Johns, S., Barnes, R., McLennan, D., & Magnussen, K. (2017). Exploring the retention and success of students with disability in Australian higher education. *International Journal of Inclusive Education*, *21*(7), 747–762. https://doi.org/10.1080/13603116.2016.1251980

Kocdar, S., & Bozkurt, A. (2022). Supporting learners with special needs in open, distance, and digital education. In O. Zawacky-Richter & I. Jung (Eds.), *Handbook of open, distance and digital education* (pp. 1–16). Springer. https://doi.org/10.1007/978-981-19-0351-9_49-1

LaPadula, M. (2003). A comprehensive look at online student support services for distance learners. *American Journal of Distance Education*, *17*(2), 119–128. https://doi.org/10.1207/S15389286AJDE1702_4

Lowenthal, P. R., Humphrey, M., Conley, Q., Dunlap, J. C., Greear, K., Lowenthal, A., & Giacumo, L. A. (2020). Creating accessible and inclusive online learning: Moving beyond compliance and broadening the discussion. *Quarterly Review of Distance Education*, *21*(2), 1–21.

Melián, E., & Meneses, J. (2022). Getting ahead in the online university: Disclosure experiences of students with apparent and hidden disabilities. *International Journal of Educational Research*, *114*, 101991. https://doi.org/10.1016/j.ijer.2022.101991

Miles, M. B., Huberman, A. M., & Saldaña, J. (2014). *Qualitative data analysis: A methods sourcebook* (3rd ed.). SAGE Publications.

Pardy, L. (2016). *Academic advising in British Columbia*. British Columbia Council on Admissions and Transfer. https://www.bccat.ca/pubs/Reports/AcademicAdvising2016.pdf

Rao, K., Torres, C., & Smith, S. J. (2021). Digital tools and UDL-based instructional strategies to support students with disabilities online. *Journal of Special Education Technology*. https://doi.org/10.1177/0162643421998327

Reyes, J. I., Meneses, J., & Melián, E. (2022). A systematic review of academic interventions for students with disabilities in online higher education. *European Journal of Special Needs Education*, *37*(4), 569–586. https://doi.org/10.1080/08856257.2021.1911525

Rimbau-Gilabert, E., Martinez-Arguelles, M., & Ruiz-Dotras, E. (2011). Developing models for online academic advising: Functions, tools and organisation of the advising system in a virtual university. *International Journal of Technology Enhanced Learning*, *3*(2), 124–136. https://www.inderscienceonline.com/doi/abs/ https://doi.org/10.1504/IJTEL.2011.039397

Scott, S., Mcguire, J., & Shaw, S. (2003). Universal Design for Instruction: A new paradigm for adult instruction in postsecondary education. *Remedial and Special Education*, *24*(6), 369–379. https://doi.org/10.1177/07419325030240060801

Simpson, O. (2013). *Supporting students for success in online and distance education* (3rd ed.). Routledge. https://doi.org/10.4324/9780203095737

Snow, W. H., & Coker, J. K. (2020). Distance counselor education: Past, present, future. *Professional Counselor*, *10*(1), 40–56. https://tpcjournal.nbcc.org/distance-counselor-education-past-present-future/ https://doi.org/10.15241/whs.10.1.40

Tait, A. (2014). From place to virtual space: Reconfiguring student support for distance and e-Learning in the digital age. *Open Praxis*, *6*(1), 5–16. https://doi.org/10.3316/informit.935850797583299

Thorpe, M. (2002). Rethinking learner support: The challenge of collaborative online learning. *Open Learning: The Journal of Open, Distance and e-Learning*, *17*(2), 105–119. https://doi.org/10.1080/02680510220146887a

Tippetts, M. M., Brandley, A. T., Metro, J., King, M., Ogren, C., & Zick, C. D. (2020). Promoting persistence: The role of academic advisors. *Journal of College Student Retention: Research, Theory & Practice*, Article 1521025120924804. https://doi.org/10.1177/1521025120924804

Tongsookdee, R. (2020). Academic advisors' experiences and needs working with students with disabilities: A case of Chiang Mai University. *International Journal of Child Development and Mental Health*, *7*(2), 21–32. https://he01.tci-thaijo.org/index.php/cdmh/article/view/196292

Warren, G., & Schwitzer, A. M. (2018). Two-year college distance-learning students with psychological disorders: Counseling needs and responses. *Journal of College Student Psychotherapy*, *32*(4), 270–281. https://doi.org/10.1080/87568225.2017.1396518

Xie, J., & Rice, M. F. (2021). Professional and social investment in universal design for learning in higher education: Insights from a faculty development programme. *Journal of Further and Higher Education*, *45*(7), 886–900. https://doi.org/10.1080/0309877X.2020.1827372

Yin, R. K. (2009). *Case study research: Design and methods* (4th ed). Sage Publications.

Yin, R. K. (2012). *Applications of case study research* (3rd ed.). SAGE.

Young-Jones, A. D., Burt, T. D., Dixon, S., & Hawthorne, M. J. (2013). Academic advising: Does it really impact student success? *Quality Assurance in Education*, *21*(1), 7–19. https://doi.org/10.1108/09684881311293034

◊ OPEN ACCESS

Promoting potential through purposeful inclusive assessment for distance learners

Poppy Gibson ⓘ, Rebecca Clarkson ⓘ, and Mike Scott ⓘ

ABSTRACT
The number of students with disabilities, which covers a range of conditions including physical and cognitive impairments, is on the rise. Further and higher education institutions are obliged to ensure that teaching and assessment is inclusive. This is particularly pertinent since the pandemic as many students have missed social opportunities that may have offered academic capital. We conducted a systematic review of relevant United Kingdom literature on how assessment for distance education in further education and higher education can be made inclusive in practical and purposeful ways. Assessment is the fundamental way that we measure students' understanding and progress; it is only through demonstrating knowledge against the set criteria and learning outcomes that students can pass assessments and earn credits toward completion of their degree. We found three key themes in promoting student potential: (a) purposeful and accessible feedback, (b) online group work opportunities, (c) student agency over assessment format.

Introduction

The term *disabilities* can cover a wide range of conditions, including physical, psychological, sensory, or cognitive impairments, that affect an individual's daily behaviors and functioning (Meleo-Erwin et al., 2021). It must also be noted that people with disabilities may have two or more conditions comorbidly, and thus may have a highly diverse range of accessibility needs, both physically and in terms of how they can access academic material (Meleo-Erwin et al., 2021).

An agenda of widening participation in higher education (HE) has led to an expansion in the number of students attending universities and, therefore, an increase in the diversity of these students (Connell-Smith & Hubble, 2018). This is supported by statistics showing that the number of students with disabilities enrolled in HE is on the rise (Pino & Mortari, 2014). The SARS-CoV-2 pandemic has shown an increase in

---

This is an Open Access article distributed under the terms of the Creative Commons Attribution-NonCommercial-NoDerivatives License (http://creativecommons.org/licenses/by-nc-nd/4.0/), which permits non-commercial re-use, distribution, and reproduction in any medium, provided the original work is properly cited, and is not altered, transformed, or built upon in any way.

the number of students with social phobias and anxiety (de Figueiredo, et al., 2021; Loades et al., 2020; Meherali et al., 2021) and that students who endured their further education (FE) studies during the pandemic missed out on social opportunities that may have offered academic capital (Aristovnik et al., 2020). These factors demonstrate the importance, now more than ever, that we ensure our teaching and assessment are as inclusive as possible.

Stentiford and Koutsouris (2021) conducted a scoping review of inclusive pedagogies in HE yet deemed the term itself problematic, and question whether inclusive pedagogies should just mean good teaching for all. An inclusive educational experience aims to make FE and HE accessible, relevant, and engaging for all (Thomas & May, 2010) and it is essential that institutions fulfill their obligation to all students to promote progress. Underpinning this is a recognition that assessment is a major aspect of learning (Race, 2014) where an understanding of students' differences must be valued (Hockings, 2010). Students must, therefore, be given the chance to demonstrate their achievement using assessments that are fair and appropriate to them (Thomas & May, 2010).

Assessment in FE and HE is underpinned by the *Equality Act* (Government of the United Kingdom, 2010), which for a practitioner means having a legal duty of care to both anticipate and make reasonable adjustments in teaching for any student with protected characteristics, which includes for example age, disability, race, sex, and religion or belief. In FE, direct observation of assessment is included within the Office for Standards in Education, Children's Services and Skills (2019) inspection framework. Within the context of HE policy, inclusive assessment sits as part of the Quality Assurance Agency for Higher Education (2018) assessment framework. In the framework is a requirement that assessment should be "inclusive and equitable" (p. 5), which outlines that students' needs should be considered in the design of an assessment and that no individual or group should be at a disadvantage (Office of the Independent Adjudicator, 2017). Specific groups mentioned that may require reasonable adjustments include students from different cultural or educational backgrounds, those with additional learning needs, or those with protected characteristics (Quality Assurance Agency for Higher Education, 2018).

Assessment is the fundamental way that we measure students' understanding and progress; it is only through demonstrating knowledge against the set criteria and learning outcomes that students can pass assessments and earn credits toward completion of their degree. In distance education, where face-to-face contact is limited or non-existent, and for students with disabilities for whom access may be increasingly challenged, it is fundamental that tutors make the most of feedback (Kasch et al., 2021), offering formative opportunities, ensuring students are assessed on the task, and given clear grading criteria.

It is essential that educators include and empower students through the inclusive nature of the assessments they set. Self-assessment, peer assessment, and then tutor feedback on formative assessment are all useful tools in a student's journey toward the summative submission (Alqassab et al., 2018). There are several steps that can be taken to ensure that assessment is inclusive and equitable. Plymouth University (2014), for example, created a seven-step approach to assessment design, which places choice and diverse methods at its center, along with underlying principles of good assessment design, use of technology, student participation, and reflection. These steps demonstrate that there can be flexible methods of assessment that meet the needs of students (Quality Assurance Agency for Higher Education, 2018) and benefit more than just the intended students (Hockings, 2010).

Educators must ensure that inclusive practice helps feed into assessment. Accessibility on online platforms is key (Baguma & Wolters, 2021). It is important that students can access their virtual learning environment (VLE) to read content as well as work on, and submit, assessments. VLE spaces must be accessible and should help encourage a feeling of community which can be done through guiding students through the spaces, ensuring uniform layout, and using the announcements tool to boost important documents. For students who may not voluntarily engage much in online communication, it is important that when they do engage, the VLE is clear and easy to navigate (Michel et al., 2021).

Research questions and methodology

Following a brief scoping review of the literature forming the introduction for this article, the following research questions were posed:

- What does an inclusive online assessment look like in terms of supporting distance learners with disabilities?
- How does the role of peer learners and the peer relationship fit into inclusive distance education?
- How can assessment feedback be inclusive and relevant for distance learners?

Utilizing systematic review

Once these questions had been formed, it was necessary to design a systematic review to ensure as much recent and relevant literature as possible was identified, appraised, and synthesized. Systematic reviews must adhere to a clear design based on certain criteria to be able to carry out this process.

Step 1: Preliminary scoping of research and question validation

The preliminary scope of literature, as outlined above, helped to ensure validity of the proposed idea and the feasibility of the research questions. A simple search on EBSCOhost and Google Scholar confirmed that there was adequate material for review.

Step 2: Inclusion and exclusion criteria

To be eligible for inclusion in this review, papers needed to be student-focused, include considerations of students with distance learning or disabilities, and be of recent date and appropriate geographical location (ideally based in the United Kingdom). Exclusion criteria were unavailable full texts; abstract only papers; dated publications >10 years. While most of the literature is from <5 years, some older sources were also included if relevant to help answer the research questions.

Step 3: Search strategy and article identification

Search terms were defined in light of the earlier scoping review: assessment, students with disabilities, inclusion, inclusive distance education.

Step 4: Database search, library created, and results imported onto an Excel spreadsheet for thematic analysis

This literature review was conducted in ERIC, Scopus, and EBSCOhost, with a focus on collecting relevant peer-reviewed journal articles. Any articles deemed suitable for further analysis were added to an online library and then imported into an Excel spreadsheet for review.

Thematic analysis

This literature review used a thematic approach. The thematic approach seeks to draw upon recurrent themes to explore alternative perspectives within a field of study, giving the researcher agency in project design (Braun & Clarke, 2006). As the literature was gathered, themes were explored through thematic analysis (TA). TA is perhaps a tool rather than a methodology in itself (Braun & Clarke, 2022). Due to the autonomous nature of TA, which gives the researcher agency in project design, it is therefore essential that the research is conducted in a way to provide rigor and trustworthiness, achieved through collaboration between authors as the co-researchers for the literature review (Braun & Clarke, 2022).

Findings

Work by Moriña and Biagiotti (2021) highlighted that for students with disabilities who complete their courses and make progress, qualities of self-advocacy, self-awareness, and self-esteem were key. In response to the three posed research questions (presented earlier), three key themes emerged around promoting outcomes for distance learners with disabilities. These three themes were drawn from the literature and illustrate how educators can promote student potential in distance education through the inclusive assessments that are provided at tertiary level:

- purposeful and accessible feedback
- online group work opportunities
- student agency over assessment format.

Purposeful and accessible feedback

Feedback and indeed *feedforward* are both terms that are commonly used in FE and HE. These can be defined as being types of information given to the learner about their achievement in relation to agreed learning expectations and should be aimed specifically at fostering improvement (Black et al., 2003; Broadfoot et al., 2002). For feedback to be effective and move the learning forward, it must direct the student's attention to what is next rather than focusing on how the student performed (Wiliam, 2011), be accurate, and focus on the learning outcomes and success criteria that have been shared with the students (Hattie, 2012). Feedback should be given promptly (or as soon after the learning as possible), but learners will also need to be given the opportunity to reflect and act on any feedback they receive to improve. When it comes to positive feedback, there is value in praise as part of the feedback comments; offering a student two or more points of praise helps foster a positive relationship with their education (Wulandari, 2022).

Feedback can only function formatively if the information given to the student is used by them to improve performance. However, there is evidence that written feedback and feedforward are not much used to improve future work (Sambell, 2011). Personalized assessment support in the form of student and staff tutorials can be seen as a positive approach to feedback and feedforward that helps to ensure that this information is used to favorable effect. Staff-student dialogues where there is a conversation about assessment are seen by learners to be fundamental to increasing student assessment literacy. A dialogue "shifts the balance of responsibility" (Bloxham & Campbell, 2010, p. 292) onto the student by ensuring the conversation is about aspects of the assignment that are important to them. This is supported by Alexander (2017), who suggested that the benefits of this type of talk support deeper learning. This contrasts with the focus on providing written feedback and feedforward, which can be monologic and potentially casts the student in a passive role.

Johnson and Cooke (2016) highlighted that for distance learners, employing a range of feedback formats may best meet the needs of all students, with opportunity for engagement with a variety of technologies. While written feedback sheets may be helpful, the use of audio and video feedback for students has gained impetus in recent years (McCarthy, 2015). Audio feedback offers expression, pronunciation, and emphasis for students (Middleton et al., 2009). Students may find audio feedback as being easier to engage with and understand, may have more depth, and may also be more personal than written feedback (Merry & Orsmond, 2008); building the personal bond can be key in keeping students engaged with their studies when on a distance program. In support of this, Ribchester et al. (2007) found that students engaged better with their tutors following the receipt of audio feedback, as the feedback felt more personal and it often allows tutors to embroider the discussion with feedforward steps due to the conversational narrative style of the feedback being given. Video feedback has also been shown to be useful for students in tertiary levels of education. One important point from the literature is that, due to the connection that may be made through the active engagement for the viewer, video feedback may be easier for students to act upon (McCarthy, 2015). For some students, being able to see or hear their tutor may help make the feedback more accessible as not only does it mean they can digest the comments without reading them but the tone and expression are present to aid understanding and support delivery. An overview of these three assessment feedback format types is summarized in Table 1.

Table 1. An overview of three assessment format types (adapted from McCarthy, 2015, p. 153).

Feedback format	Time implications	Affordances	Limitations
Audio	Fast to record feedback. May be slow to distribute.	Can be conceived as more personal than written feedback. Vocal tone and emphasis can improve understanding of feedback. Strong comprehension of feedback.	Comparatively large file size. Slower to distribute. Requires digital access to listen to feedback. No visual element involved.
Video	Slow to record and render feedback. Slow to distribute to students.	Feedback is engaging. Feedback is dynamic. Can be conceived as more personal than written feedback. Vocal tone and emphasis can improve understanding of feedback. Greater insight into student performance. Strong comprehension of feedback.	Comparatively large file size. Greater staff workload to produce feedback files. Slower to distribute. Requires digital access to view to feedback.
Written	Fast to write feedback and distribute to students.	A rubric can allow for faster interpretation of specific assessment criteria. Small file size. Fast to produce and distribute. Can be conceived as more formal. Can be printed out and read at any time.	Feedback is limited to text: no visual or aural element involved. Feedback is static. Can be conceived as less substantial or detailed.

The communicative act of dialogic feedback (Ajjawi & Boud, 2018) can also be fostered in a context of peer assessment. When the context of the learning and assessment, interaction between peers, and relationships is built into the feedback (Ajjawi & Boud, 2017; Esterhazy & Damşa, 2019; Telio et al., 2016), feedback becomes more than just giving information and more about creating a dialogue. When coupled with access to learning and assessment criteria, rubrics (grading schemes), and other assignment resources, this can foster students' understanding of quality, allowing them to make judgments based on their knowledge of the criteria (Ajjawi & Boud, 2018; Boud & Molloy, 2013; Esterhazy & Damşa, 2019).

In support of this, the planned and integrated use of the online learning platform for distance education for learners with disabilities is essential. In place of face-to-face contact time, carefully designed structure, and additional content, are needed to engage and educate the users. Examples of essays and assignments, and the associated assessment criteria and mark scheme, can be made available to students on the platform and provided in online sessions for them to analyze in small groups (Sadler, 1989, 2010). Clear written instructions and checklists for the assignments can also be presented on the module pages, as well as being delivered verbally in online sessions (Anglia Ruskin University, 2022; Teeside University, 2022). These measures will enable students to voice any concerns about the assignments, understand the standard to aim for, and see where they might need to improve (Sambell et al., 2013). Another benefit of online learning platforms is that formative feedback and marking opportunities are integrated. Written feedback and feedforward can be differentiated for students by using different colors (e.g., for content, grammar). This is something that is recommended for students with dyslexia (Anglia Ruskin University, 2022; Teeside University, 2022) but may be beneficial for all.

Online group work opportunities

Wang (2022) stated that value and meaningful learning is found through the social presences that can be fostered online in distance education. Difficulties in FE and HE have arisen in recent years because of the ongoing pace of technological development, owing in part to social media demands, putting pressure on education systems (Castro, 2019). As a consequence of the COVID-19 pandemic, additional barriers to group work and engagement, as well as overcoming obstacles to accessing the materials online, were experienced (Goodrich, 2021). The causal effects of the pandemic on education systems have meant governmental, institutional, and policy initiatives in supporting learners and maintaining quality teaching and assessment have been a high-priority focus with universities (Watermeyer et al., 2021). It is essential that institutions support students and staff with digital illiteracy, particularly within teaching and support in HE to further improve student agency with the usage of digital technologies.

An example of the impact on educational systems during the pandemic is a study by Paterson and Prideaux (2020) on how positive interdependence, individual accountability, teaching presence, authenticity, and group skills development were used to reduce group work issues and encourage collaborative group work within a HE online environment. Paterson and Prideaux found that group work issues identified by students included having a lack of group work skills and negative perceptions of group work. By using distributed online group-based assessment tasks across six subjects, students were enabled to work in real-world scenarios and work was peer assessed, which allowed workloads and the contribution requirement to be balanced. This led to the promotion of real-world relevancy, industry-like experiences, and the contextualization of employability skills, which resulted in personal and professional development in the students.

The online learning experience should be tailored to the needs of the students, including their disabilities. However, colleges and universities fail to address equitable access, particularly for disabled students. Compare this to open educational resources (OER), which enable educators to create materials for a diverse set of individuals, including disabled students, which can be freely shared with communities online (Zhang et al., 2020). Although researchers have focused on developing authoring tools for accessible OER, many of the resources are still not fully accessible. Instead, focus should be put on developing tools that can help educators create and publish OER for disabled students as well as providing specific competencies and training for the educators to improve the impact of functional and accessibility diversity on the education system (Zhang et al., 2020).

Student agency over assessment format

According to the Organisation for Economic Co-operation and Development (2022, p. 1), student agency is defined as the "capacity to set a goal, reflect and act responsibly to effect change"; this implies that students not only have the ability to positively influence their own individual life but also those around them. Student agency can be obtained through building upon foundational skills, which allow the student to exercise their agency. This can include employability skills, collaborative skills, digital competences, and a capacity for lifelong learning. Agency has evolved as an increasingly integral idea in education, both as a goal and as a process to lead learners and to assist them in navigating the unknown. A social-cognitive perspective is one factor which focuses on agency as the mediating element connecting intentionality, self-reflection, and self-efficacy (Stenalt & Lassesen, 2022).

Co-agency is another factor to consider when it comes to creating student agency, as it allows tutors to realize the potential for student idea, interests, and questions. Tutors can build upon student ideas and experiences to enact their agency. Vaughn (2020, p. 109) highlighted how "Ms. Reyes seized this moment and reshaped her instruction to support her students' interests and incorporate students' background experiences into the lesson. Her flexible and adaptive approach was essential to cultivating this opportunity for student agency."

Distance education offers an interesting phenomenon where connections must be made in virtual spaces; students whose habitus is at odds with that of their online peers or the values of the FE and HE institutions may feel they do not belong or fit in, and this can affect their engagement and connection to their learning (Thomas, 2012). Having a personal tutor can help to bridge this gap and promote engagement, providing a gateway for students' learning, yet there is the downside that a tutor can be too personal, and this may have negative connotations for professional boundaries. Limits or restrictions of content during interaction, set by the institution, can help prevent this, especially if parameters are set to only discuss general issues, current events, and cultures for instance, rather than anything too personalized (Barron, 2021). Personal distance must be maintained, yet there is a fine balance finding this distance in distance education where the tutor may need to often make the first move to engage students in conversation (Barron, 2021).

Student agency plays an important role for learning particularly in the assessment literature within HE (Chong, 2021; Gravett, 2022; Nieminen & Hilppö, 2020). Student agency therefore needs to be factored into assessment and feedback for the student to actively engage with feedback rather than educators using feedback to deliver information to the student. The notion that students should have agency in the feedback processes to then be able to read, interpret, and use feedback reaches beyond FE and HE and becomes "a core capability for the workplace and lifelong learning" (Carless & Boud, 2018, p. 1315). Tai et al. (2021) shared three strategies for making assessment more inclusive:

- offering choice for students in how to present their work
- programmatic approaches to the assessment
- co-design of policies and assessment tasks that promote inclusion.

This agency over assessment is particularly valuable when students may have disabilities that make certain activities more challenging. Offering choice (Tai et al., 2021) allows students to choose a format in which they are most comfortable; for some, this may be an independent solo presentation, for example, while for others with social anxiety, a written essay or PowerPoint presentation may be preferable.

Suggestions for practice

The three key suggestions for practice drawn from our findings are as follows.

Advocate for student agency in assessment format

Ensure that appropriate nonacademic time is built into the program, perhaps at the start of the academic year, either through online group sessions, 1:1 personal tutorials or a task whereby students create a poster about themselves and their interests which is uploaded to the VLE. By getting to know students and their interests, a better relationship may be formed, which will encourage students with disabilities to share their academic experiences, so that they can be best supported. Ask students about past assessments they have undertaken during previous study: Which did they most enjoy and why? Which were least accessible and why?

Factor formative assessments into each assessment cycle that draws upon ungraded group work

Incorporating group work activities into formative assessments allows for both peer learning and peer assessment; distance learners can benefit from engaging in online, or virtual, communities of practice, learning from others, and self-checking their understanding of the module content (McLaughlan, 2021).

Use a range of feedback delivery and do not forget the value in positive feedback

As mentioned, try to use a variety of written, audio, and video feedback from the tutor as appropriate. Remember to always include at least one praise point, although two or more are preferred (Wulandari, 2022).

Areas for future research

There must be further studies into accessible assessments for neurodiverse students in both FE and HE, as well as consideration of the practices of neurodiverse staff. We encourage further research into the benefits of video and audio feedback for students with disabilities at both FE and HE levels.

Conclusion

This paper has reviewed the literature to consider how purposeful assessment can promote potential through engaging and support students with their learning at tertiary level. Three themes have been considered through how feedback can be made accessible, such as through the use of audio or video recordings as opposed to written documents, through the support of online group work opportunities, and through the promotion of student agency and offering choice in assessment to promote this agency. Spaces that are created on distance learning programs, such as on the institution's VLE, offer online communities of practice for students to aid their learning and understanding

(McLaughlan, 2021). Educators must remember that it is essential now more than ever to ensure teaching is as inclusive as possible; putting student agency at the core of assessment and feedback may be one of the key steps to achieving this goal.

ORCID

Poppy Gibson http://orcid.org/0000-0002-5971-8565
Rebecca Clarkson http://orcid.org/0000-0002-1380-1611
Mike Scott http://orcid.org/0000-0001-7688-2423

References

Ajjawi, R., & Boud, D. (2017). Researching feedback dialogue: An interactional analysis approach. *Assessment & Evaluation in Higher Education*, *42*(2), 252–265. https://doi.org/10.1080/02602938.2015.1102863

Ajjawi, R., & Boud, D. (2018). Examining the nature and effects of feedback dialogue. *Assessment & Evaluation in Higher Education*, *43*(7), 1106–1119. https://doi.org/10.1080/02602938.2018.1434128

Alexander, R. J. (2017). *Towards dialogic teaching: Rethinking classroom talk* (5th ed.). Dialogos.

Alqassab, M., Strijbos, J.-W., & Ufer, S. (2018). Training peer-feedback skills on geometric construction tasks: Role of domain knowledge and peer-feedback levels. *European Journal of Psychology of Education*, *33*(1), 11–30. https://doi.org/10.1007/s10212-017-0342-0

Anglia Ruskin University. (2022). *Inclusive learning and teaching*. https://aru.ac.uk/anglia-learning-and-teaching/good-teaching-practice-and-innovation/approaches-to-learning-and-teaching/inclusive-learning-and-teaching

Aristovnik, A., Keržič, D., Ravšelj, D., Tomaževič, N., & Umek, L. (2020). Impacts of the COVID-19 pandemic on life of higher education students: A global perspective. *Sustainability*, *12*(20), Article 8438. https://doi.org/10.3390/su12208438

Baguma, R., & Wolters, M. K. (2021). Making virtual learning environments accessible to people with disabilities in universities in Uganda. *Frontiers in Computer Science*, *3*, Article 638275. https://doi.org/10.3389/fcomp.2021.638275

Barron, J. (2021, November 18). *Boundaries, limitations and the ethical and professional codes and standards in a personal tutoring role*. Start Teaching. https://start-teaching.com/boundaries-limitations-and-the-ethical-and-professional-codes-and-standards-in-a-personal-tutoring-role/

Black, P., Harrison, C., Lee, C., Marshall, B., & Wiliam, D. (2003). *Assessment for learning: Putting it into practice*. Open University Press.

Bloxham, S., & Campbell, L. (2010). Generating dialogue in assessment feedback: Exploring the use of interactive cover sheets. *Assessment & Evaluation in Higher Education*, *35*(3), 291–300. https://doi.org/10.1080/02602931003650045

Boud, D., & Molloy, E. (2013). Rethinking models of feedback for learning: The challenge of design. *Assessment & Evaluation in Higher Education, 38*(6), 698–712. https://doi.org/10.1080/02602938.2012.691462

Braun, V., & Clarke, V. (2006). Using thematic analysis. *Qualitative Research in Psychology, 3*(2), 77–101. https://doi.org/10.1191/1478088706qp063oa

Braun, V., & Clarke, V. (2022). Conceptual and design thinking for thematic analysis. *Qualitative Psychology, 9*(1), 3–26. https://doi.org/10.1037/qup0000196

Broadfoot, P., Daugherty, R., Gardner, J., Harlen, W., James, M., & Stobart, G. (2002). *Assessment for learning: 10 Principles*. Nuffield Foundation and University of Cambridge.

Carless, D., & Boud, D. (2018). The development of student feedback literacy: Enabling uptake of feedback. *Assessment & Evaluation in Higher Education, 43*(8), 1315–1325. https://doi.org/10.1080/02602938.2018.1463354

Castro, R. (2019). Blended learning in higher education: Trends and capabilities. *Education and Information Technologies, 24*(4), 2523–2546. https://doi.org/10.1007/s10639-019-09886-3

Chong, S. W. (2021). Reconsidering student feedback literacy from an ecological perspective. *Assessment & Evaluation in Higher Education, 46*(1), 92–104. https://doi.org/10.1080/02602938.2020.1730765

Connell-Smith, A., & Hubble, S. (2018). *Widening participation strategy in higher education in England* [Briefing paper]. UK Parliament, House of Commons Library. https://commonslibrary.parliament.uk/research-briefings/cbp-8204/

de Figueiredo, C. S., Sandre, P. C., Portugal, L. C. L., Mázala-de-Oliveira, T., da Silva Chagas, L., Raony, Í., Ferreira, E. S., Giestal-de-Araujo, E., dos Santos, A. A., & Bomfim, P. O.-S. (2021). COVID-19 pandemic impact on children and adolescents' mental health: Biological, environmental, and social factors. *Progress in Neuro-Psychopharmacology and Biological Psychiatry, 106*, Article 110171. https://doi.org/10.1016/j.pnpbp.2020.110171

Esterhazy, R., & Damşa, C. (2019). Unpacking the feedback process: An analysis of undergraduate students' interactional meaning-making of feedback comments. *Studies in Higher Education, 44*(2), 260–274. https://doi.org/10.1080/03075079.2017.1359249

Goodrich, A. (2021). Online peer mentoring and remote learning. *Music Education Research, 23*(2), 256–269. https://doi.org/10.1080/14613808.2021.1898575

Government of the United Kingdom. (2010). *Equality Act 2010*. https://www.legislation.gov.uk/ukpga/2010/15/contents

Gravett, K. (2022). Feedback literacies as sociomaterial practice. *Critical Studies in Education, 63*(2), 261–274. https://doi.org/10.1080/17508487.2020.1747099

Hattie, J. (2012). *Visible learning for teachers: Maximizing impact on learning*. Routledge.

Hockings, C. (2010). *Inclusive learning and teaching in higher education: A synthesis of research*. Higher Education Academy. https://documents.advance-he.ac.uk/download/file/document/2682?_ga=2.171678372.505918052.1666991824-1605041052.1666991824

Johnson, G. M., & Cooke, A. (2016). Self-regulation of learning and preference for written versus audio-recorded feedback by distance education students. *Distance Education, 37*(1), 107–120. https://doi.org/10.1080/01587919.2015.1081737

Kasch, J., van Rosmalen, P., Löhr, A., Klemke, R., Antonaci, A., & Kalz, M. (2021). Students' perceptions of the peer-feedback experience in MOOCs. *Distance Education, 42*(1), 145–163. https://doi.org/10.1080/01587919.2020.1869522

Loades, M. E., Chatburn, E., Higson-Sweeney, N., Reynolds, S., Shafran, R., Brigden, A., Linney, C., McManus, M. N., Borwick, C., & Crawley, E. (2020). Rapid systematic review: The impact of social isolation and loneliness on the mental health of children and adolescents in the context of COVID-19. *Journal of the American Academy of Child & Adolescent Psychiatry, 59*(11), 1218–1239. https://doi.org/10.1016/j.jaac.2020.05.009

McCarthy, J. (2015). Evaluating written, audio and video feedback in higher education summative assessment tasks. *Issues in Educational Research, 25*(2), 153–169. http://iier.org.au/iier25/mccarthy.html

McLaughlan, T. (2021). Facilitating factors in cultivating diverse online communities of practice: A case of international teaching assistants during the COVID-19 crisis. *The International*

Journal of Information and Learning Technology, 38(2), 177–195. https://doi.org/10.1108/IJILT-05-2020-0074

Meherali, S., Punjani, N., Louie-Poon, S., Abdul Rahim, K., Das, J. K., Salam, R. A., & Lassi, Z. S. (2021). Mental health of children and adolescents amidst COVID-19 and past pandemics: A rapid systematic review. *International Journal of Environmental Research and Public Health, 18*(7), Article 8073432. https://doi.org/10.3390/ijerph18073432

Meleo-Erwin, Z., Kollia, B., Fera, J., Jahren, A., & Basch, C. (2021). Online support information for students with disabilities in colleges and universities during the COVID-19 pandemic. *Disability and Health Journal, 14*(1), Article 101013. https://doi.org/10.1016/j.dhjo.2020.101013

Merry, S., & Orsmond, P. (2008). Students' attitudes to and usage of academic feedback provided via audio files. *Bioscience Education, 11*(1), 1–11. https://doi.org/10.3108/beej.11.3

Michel, C., Pierrot, L., & Solari-Landa, M. (2021). VLE limits and perspectives for digital integration in teaching practices. In T. De Laet, R. Klemke, C. Alario-Hoyos, I. Hilliger, & A. Ortega-Arranz (Eds.), *Technology-enhanced learning for a free, safe, and sustainable world* (pp. 96–109). Springer International Publishing. https://doi.org/10.1007/978-3-030-86436-1_8

Middleton, A., Nortcliffe, A., & Owen, R. (2009). *Igather: Learners as responsible audio collector of tutor, peer and self-reflection.* Sheffield Hallam University. http://research.shu.ac.uk/lti/awordinyourear2009/docs/Middleton-Nortcliffe-Owens-iGather_final.pdf

Moriña, A., & Biagiotti, G. (2021). Academic success factors in university students with disabilities: A systematic review. *European Journal of Special Needs Education*, 1–18. https://doi.org/10.1080/08856257.2021.1940007

Nieminen, J. H., & Hilppö, J. A. (2020). Methodological and conceptual suggestions for researching the interplay of assessment and student agency. In P. J. White, R. Tytler, J. Ferguson, & J. Cripps Clark (Eds.), *Methodological approaches to STEM education research* (vol. 1, pp. 87–107). Cambridge Scholars Publishing

Office of the Independent Adjudicator. (2017). *The good practice framework: Supporting disabled students.* https://www.oiahe.org.uk/media/1039/oia-good-practice-framework-supporting-disabled-students.pdf

Office for Standards in Education, Children's Services and Skills. (2019). *Further education and skills inspection handbook.* https://www.gov.uk/government/publications/further-education-and-skills-inspection-handbook-eif

Organisation for Economic Co-operation and Development. (2022). *Student agency for 2030.* https://www.oecd.org/education/2030-project/teaching-and-learning/learning/student-agency/Student_Agency_for_2030_concept_note.pdf

Paterson, T., & Prideaux, M. (2020). Exploring collaboration in online group-based assessment contexts: Undergraduate business program. *Journal of University Teaching & Learning Practice, 17*(3). https://ro.uow.edu.au/cgi/viewcontent.cgi?article=2038&context=jutlp

Pino, M., & Mortari, L. (2014). The inclusion of students with dyslexia in higher education: A systematic review using narrative synthesis: The inclusion of students with dyslexia in HE. *Dyslexia, 20*(4), 346–369. https://doi.org/10.1002/dys.1484

Plymouth University. (2014). *7 steps to inclusive assessment.* https://www.plymouth.ac.uk/uploads/production/document/path/2/2401/7_Steps_to_Inclusive_Assessment.pdf

Quality Assurance Agency for Higher Education. (2018). *UK Quality Code – Advice and guidance*: Assessment. https://www.qaa.ac.uk/docs/qaa/quality-code/advice-and-guidance-assessment.pdf?sfvrsn=ca29c181_4

Race, P. (2014). *Making learning happen: A guide for post-compulsory education* (3rd ed.). SAGE.

Ribchester, C., France, D., & Wheeler, A. (2007, September 12–14). *Podcasting: A tool for enhancing assessment feedback?* [Conference presentation]. 4th Education in a Changing Environment Conference at the University of Salford, England. http://www.ece.salford.ac.uk/proceedings/papers/15_07.pdf

Sadler, D. R. (1989). Formative assessment and the design of instructional systems. *Instructional Science, 18*(2), 119–144. https://doi.org/10.1007/BF00117714

Sadler, D. R. (2010). Beyond feedback: Developing student capability in complex appraisal. *Assessment & Evaluation in Higher Education*, *35*(5), 535–550. https://doi.org/10.1080/02602930903541015

Sambell, K. (2011, August 3). Rethinking feedback in higher education: An assessment for learning perspective. ESCalate. http://escalate.ac.uk/8410

Sambell, K., McDowell, L., & Montgomery, C. (2013). *Assessment for learning in higher education*. Routledge.

Stenalt, M. H., & Lassesen, B. (2022). Does student agency benefit student learning? A systematic review of higher education research. *Assessment & Evaluation in Higher Education*, *47*(5), 653–669. https://doi.org/10.1080/02602938.2021.1967874

Stentiford, L., & Koutsouris, G. (2021). What are inclusive pedagogies in higher education? A systematic scoping review. *Studies in Higher Education*, *46*(11), 2245–2261. https://doi.org/10.1080/03075079.2020.1716322

Tai, J., Ajjawi, R., & Umarova, A. (2021). How do students experience inclusive assessment? A critical review of contemporary literature. *International Journal of Inclusive Education*, 1–18. https://doi.org/10.1080/13603116.2021.2011441

Teeside University. (2022). Principles of inclusivity. *LTE Online*. https://blogs.tees.ac.uk/lteonline/learning-and-teaching/guides/inclusivity-for-teaching-and-learning-support/principles-of-inclusivity/

Telio, S., Regehr, G., & Ajjawi, R. (2016). Feedback and the educational alliance: Examining credibility judgements and their consequences. *Medical Education*, *50*(9), 933–942. https://doi.org/10.1111/medu.13063

Thomas, L. (2012). *Building student engagement and belonging in higher education at a time of change: A summary of findings and recommendations from the What Works? Student Retention & Success programme*. Higher Education Academy. https://www.advance-he.ac.uk/knowledge-hub/building-student-engagement-and-belonging-higher-education-time-change-final-report

Thomas, L., & May, H. (2010). *Inclusive learning and teaching in higher education*. Higher Education Academy. https://www.advance-he.ac.uk/knowledge-hub/inclusive-learning-and-teaching-higher-education

Vaughn, M. (2020). What is student agency and why is it needed now more than ever? *Theory into Practice*, *59*(2), 109–118. https://doi.org/10.1080/00405841.2019.1702393

Wang, Y. (2022). Exploring the relationships among the dimensions of a community of inquiry in an online learning environment. *Distance Education*, *43*(3), 353–368. https://doi.org/10.1080/01587919.2022.2088481

Watermeyer, R., Crick, T., & Knight, C. (2021). Digital disruption in the time of COVID-19: Learning technologists' accounts of institutional barriers to online learning, teaching and assessment in UK universities. *International Journal for Academic Development*, 1–15. https://doi.org/10.1080/1360144X.2021.1990064

Wiliam, D. (2011). *Embedded formative assessment*. Solution Tree Press.

Wulandari, Y. (2022). Effective feedback to improve students' writing skills. *Educalitra: English Education, Linguistics, and Literature Journal*, *1*(1), 10–17. https://jurnal.unupurwokerto.ac.id/index.php/educalitra

Zhang, X., Tlili, A., Nascimbeni, F., Burgos, D., Huang, R., Chang, T.-W., Jemni, M., & Khribi, M. K. (2020). Accessibility within open educational resources and practices for disabled learners: A systematic literature review. *Smart Learning Environments*, *7*(1), Article 1. https://doi.org/10.1186/s40561-019-0113-2

Identifying accessibility factors affecting learner inclusion in online university programs

Rita Fennelly-Atkinson ⓘ, Kimberly N. LaPrairie ⓘ, and Donggil Song ⓘ

ABSTRACT
As postsecondary online programs increase, the accessibility of online course content becomes a serious issue in higher education. There is currently little information about how postsecondary institutions address online course accessibility. This exploratory mixed-methods study examined the degree to which university online course checklists represent accessibility criteria and which criteria were most and least represented in university checklists. Further, this study also examined the relationship between several university factors. This review of university online course checklists against the Web Content Accessibility Guidelines criteria revealed some areas that may warrant closer inspection for researchers and universities. Results indicated that online program enrollment was linked with how the university handled accessibility compliance and how they trained faculty regarding online course accessibility. These findings have implications for how learner inclusion in online programs can be impacted at the university level.

Introduction

Globally, disability is considered an essential component of addressing inequities perpetuated by inaccessible technology or technology-enabled environments. Around the world, accessibility is emerging as a critical issue in ensuring human rights, equality, and social participation for people with disabilities (Ferri & Favalli, 2018; Goggin et al., 2019; Yang & Chen, 2015). Because so much information is accessed online, the inaccessibility of web-based content and learning environments impedes disabled students from benefiting "fully and equally" (Laufer Nir & Rimmerman, 2018). Further, inaccessibility perpetuates a digital divide that excludes disabled people as technology evolves (Ferri & Favalli, 2018). Creating accessible online environments is a central tenet of the social disability model, which focuses on social responsibility to accommodate the environment so everyone can participate fully (Bogart & Dunn, 2019; Magnus & Tøssebro, 2014; Persson et al., 2015).

As postsecondary online programs increase, the accessibility of online course content presents a serious issue in higher education. Universities are responsible for providing accessible web platforms, such as learning management systems (Golden, 2008; Myers, 2004), and faculty are responsible for designing or using accessible content (Coleman & Berge, 2018; deMaine, 2014). While the accessibility of online educational programs is essential to providing inclusive access to all learners, one does not need to identify as disabled to benefit. Accessibility benefits all people but has been found especially helpful for learners with disabilities, second language learners, and those from communities with low resources (Crossland et al., 2016; Yesilada et al., 2015). According to Fennelly-Atkinson (in press), "accessibility represents a design challenge in transforming online education from ableist to inclusionary paradigms of practice."

As online education programs increase, institutions have the challenge of addressing accessibility for growing amounts of digital content that is also more complex. Research regarding university accessibility primarily focused on websites (Curl & Bowers, 2009; Hackett & Parmanto, 2005) using now-outdated guidelines. Currently, the term *accessibility* is intertwined with ideas, policies, and legislation that ensures people with disabilities can equitably access online services, including educational instruction. More importantly, accessibility legislation has changed how students are served regardless of whether they identify as having a disability. To honor the variable preferences of people who identify as having a disability (American Psychological Association, 2020), we use person- and identity-first language interchangeably throughout this article.

While legal compliance does not address all dimensions of inclusion, they are necessary for setting a baseline for accessible technology (Hamraie, 2018). In the United States of America, people with disabilities have been provided with specific rights regarding access to digital and physical environments, education, and technology, according to the U.S Department of Justice Civil Rights Division (2009). These types of laws represent efforts in anti-discrimination toward disabled people (Ferri & Favalli, 2018; Hamraie, 2018; Laufer Nir & Rimmerman, 2018) rather than efforts to be fully inclusive. While this study focused on setting a baseline understanding of how postsecondary online programs address compliance with accessibility standards, we hope the findings will support moving toward more inclusive design practices. This means that the "inclusive disability design" (Goggin et al., p. 298, 2019) of accessible technology should be collaboratively designed with disabled people with an intersectional approach (Hamraie, 2018).

Participation in online distance education programs

About 24 million students were enrolled in a course hosted on a learning management system in 2018 in the United States of America and Canada (Hill, 2018). These enrollment figures present students who may be encountering digital course content that should be accessible regardless of whether the course is offered face-to-face, blended, or entirely online. Institutions providing online distance education programs are more likely to encounter accessibility compliance issues.

Overall enrollment in U.S. higher education in 2016 was about 20 million and decreased for traditional face-to-face instructional settings (U.S. Department of

Education et al., 2017). Of these students, 19.5% (approximately 3.9 million) self-reported a disability that would likely qualify them for accommodations and accessible content (Campbell & Wescott, 2019).

As traditional enrollment is declining, there is an upward trend in the number of students enrolling in distance education courses, which comprised about 32% (approximately 6.4 million) of all enrolled students in 2016 (Seaman et al., 2018). While there are no specific reports on the subject, a 19.5% representation of students with disabilities can be assumed to calculate estimates in the higher education population. These calculations suggest that 1.25 million students with a disability were participating in distance education programs across the United States of America before the COVID-19 pandemic.

COVID-19 pandemic impact on enrollment

Enrollment in primarily online programs increased in 2020–2021 due to the COVID-19 pandemic, which caused most universities in the United States of America to shift all instruction online (Miller, 2021). Although concrete data is unavailable, the pandemic has facilitated unprecedented participation in online higher education. It is unknown how this will impact the long-term representation of disabled students in online enrollment. Regardless, the increasing number of disabled students participating in higher education programs represents a growing population that necessitates a university strategy to address accessibility compliance issues.

Legal aspects of serving disabled students

It is important to acknowledge the history of disability and law to understand the emerging trends and issues that may impact their policies, training, and instructional decisions for online instruction. Since the accessibility of university online content and courses fits within a broader context surrounding disability rights and access, it is essential to delineate the legal and sometimes nuanced aspects of recent legal requirements that specifically pertain to online course content.

The legal context accommodating disabled students

The United States of America passed multiple pieces of legislation that collectively require government agencies, federally funded organizations, public educational institutions, and businesses or organizations that provide services to the public to make their content or services accessible to varying degrees. The laws and guidelines that address the legal implications of making online content accessible include the *Americans with Disabilities Act* (ADA), *Individuals with Disabilities Education Act*, Sections 504 and 508 of the *Rehabilitation Act*, and the Web Content Accessibility Guidelines (WCAG) (Office for Civil Rights, 2018; Pan, 2017; U.S. Department of Justice Civil Rights Division, 2009).

These laws require postsecondary institutions to ensure that disabled people have physical and virtual access to spaces and services without being discriminated against.

Adopted as part of Section 508 by the U.S. Access Board in 2017, WCAG is the most relevant when looking at the accessibility of online instructional content (U.S. General Services Administration [U.S. GSA], 2017).

While many public educational institutions have systems for handling physical accommodations, the transition to websites and online distance education programs has revealed a lag in having an accessible online presence. Universities traditionally provided disabled students with instructional and physical accommodations to meet their needs. However, a slew of disability lawsuits has clarified and expanded what the terms disability and reasonable accommodations mean in the context of online environments (Madaus, 2011).

Since 2015, a growing number of lawsuits have targeted the accessibility of university websites and instructional digital content (Accessibility Works, 2017; Launey & Aristizabal, 2017; UsableNet, 2019). The advent of the Internet, coupled with the increased use of devices, expanded the opportunities to serve students with digitized content in physical and online classrooms. Madaus (2011) noted the rise of technology provided increased opportunities for universities to serve disabled students while simultaneously creating online learning opportunities in which students may be underserved.

This surge in legal action can be attributed to a combination of increased use of online resources for daily personal, educational, and employment activities; a 2017 federal update to web accessibility regulations; and several landmark cases in federal and state courts (Kuykendall, 2017; Vu et al., 2019). As further confirmation, disabled students experienced more issues accessing appropriate equipment, Internet, technical support, instructional materials, and accommodations during the COVID-19 pandemic (Scott & Aquino, 2020). Further, disability resource professionals reported that more students were requesting accommodations while disability office budgets were being cut during COVID-19 (Scott & Aquino, 2021). Essentially, universities are faced with complying with a changing legal landscape as the demand for online education programs increases.

Legal precedence for accessibility requirements in online education

The WCAG 2.0 criteria specify accessibility requirements for all types of digital content and address a wide range of topics such as images, audio, video, website functionality, and mobile access. However, these guidelines were designed for developers of web content, authoring tools, and evaluation tools and did not easily translate to lay users (World Wide Web Consortium [W3C], 2016). The practical reality is that universities must ensure accessibility of digital content posted on their instructional platforms or school-generated content hosted elsewhere to meet WCAG compliance (Cullipher, 2017).

The most recent WCAG requirements have not been used extensively to evaluate course content in the literature (Kuykendall, 2017). However, evidence suggests that course compliance may be low based on the current number of pending legal cases (Accessibility Works, 2017; Launey & Aristizabal, 2017; UsableNet, 2019).

The only certainty is that legal action against postsecondary institutions has risen across the country, and 75% of federal cases specifically reference WCAG (Bowersox, 2019; UsableNet, 2019, 2020). Although COVID-19 initially led to an overall decrease in accessibility lawsuits due to closed courts, students with disabilities have increasingly sued institutions due to online learning issues (Vu et al., 2020; Weissman, 2020). Most of these lawsuits targeted accessibility issues, which gave prominence to institutional improvements of accessibility in a digital learning environment (Weissman, 2020).

Of note are the cases involving Harvard University, the Massachusetts Institute of Technology, and the University of California, Berkeley, in which lawsuits targeted inaccessible video and audio content used for educational purposes (Bowersox, 2019). According to the Bowersox article (published by the legal firm McAfee & Taft), this signals a shift in how the law is applied. Universities have previously relied on a system in which students requested accommodations through a disability office. This is now shifting toward an expectation that online content meets minimum accessibility requirements without a specific accommodation request (Bowersox, 2019).

The state of university accessibility compliance

Universities tackle compliance with disability law through various methods. Based on a survey of 183 colleges and universities, institutions used one, some, or none of the following options: formal accessibility policies, mandatory or optional training for faculty, services offered by disability offices to students and staff, and systematization and management of online education (WICHE Cooperative for Educational Telecommunications & The Campus Computing Project, 2010).

Without a systematic method for ensuring accessibility compliance, institutions make themselves vulnerable to complaints and lawsuits (Parry, 2010). While having a systematic method for addressing the compliance of educational content is critical, it is also important that educators feel comfortable and knowledgable in creating or reviewing content for accessibility compliance. A 2014 Web Accessibility in Mind (WebAIM) Survey of Web Accessibility Practitioner Results included 35 educators who revealed that 29% felt very proficient, 60% felt somewhat proficient, and 11% felt not very proficient with accessibility standards (J. Smith, personal communication, March 26, 2018). A report from the Center on Technology and Disability recommended several ways institutions can work towards compliance with WCAG 2.0 standards, including performing accessibility audits, identifying non-compliant materials, and creating a plan to update non-compliant resources (Crossland et al., 2016).

Potential costs of noncompliance

It is unclear how much universities are paying to resolve litigation, complaints, or court decrees. However, data on specific cases provided a potential range of costs associated with non-compliance. The simple act of making a plan to address accessibility issues costs about $25,000 (Cullipher, 2017). Yet, that is a minuscule amount compared to litigation costs.

Several court decrees resulted in estimates of an institution paying up to $1 million for case costs and accessibility compliance implementation (Cullipher, 2017). In one case, a public university paid $800,000 to settle a lawsuit based on an unresolved federal complaint filed by a student who could not complete coursework because of inaccessible web content (Rowland et al., 2014). While many universities with extensive online course programs may face a costly reality, institutions considering offering online programming can proactively address accessibility without extensive development costs (Rowland et al., 2014).

To date, it is imprecise how legal action has impacted the accessibility of online education. In the case of the University of California, Berkeley, the lawsuit resulted in the removal of more than 20,000 publicly available videos and lectures due to the cost of adding captions (Rowland, 2017). Meanwhile, the Massachusetts Institute of Technology case led to an agreement to make content accessible (National Association of the Deaf, 2020). Since accessibility guidelines have only been encoded into law for several years, the full impact of legal action on online course accessibility is unknown. Although these findings present use-case summaries, they created a general expectation for the potential cost of being noncompliant with accessibility guidelines.

Understanding WCAG 2.0

Due to increased access and use of the internet and devices, Section 508 of the *Workforce Rehabilitation Act* was most recently updated in 2018 to align with WCAG 2.0 Level AA requirements developed by the W3C (U.S. GSA, 2018). Embedded within these principles are the specific WCAG 2.0 success criteria or accessibility requirements which can be measured with various evaluation tools (U.S. GSA, 2018).

Previous research regarding university accessibility compliance focused on websites (Cullipher, 2017; Curl & Bowers, 2009; Foley, 2011; Hackett & Parmanto, 2005; Roig-Vila et al., 2014; Shawar, 2015); however, most of this work was conducted years ago using now-outdated WCAG 1.0 guidelines. Currently, very little research focuses on the accessibility of online educational content using current guidelines. An evaluation of online course design checklists showed that researchers concentrated on holistic expectations more aligned with universal design for learning (UDL), navigation, and clear pedagogical expectations (S. Baldwin et al., 2018; S. J. Baldwin & Ching, 2019). Further, the discussion about accessible instruction focused on meeting basic learner needs (Carlsen et al., 2016). While this research is essential to developing quality and pedagogically sound online education, there is little information available about how universities address online course accessibility. A recent study on online quality assurance frameworks found deep variation in how accessibility was addressed (Lowenthal et al., 2021).

Purpose of this study and research questions

The purpose of this exploratory mixed-methods study was twofold and addressed the following research questions:

1. Which WCAG 2.0 accessibility criteria were most and least represented in university online course checklists?

2. Was there a correlation between enrollment in online bachelor's programs, faculty credentials and training score, type of ADA compliance, and a composite WCAG score?

Theoretical framework

This study also relied on the conceptual frameworks of accessibility principles, UDL, and the core principles of personalized learning, as shown in Figure 1. This framework relied on the premise that accessibility principles guide technical and legal requirements for online content. Meanwhile, the UDL principles influenced how content is designed for online environments. Lastly, the concepts of personalized learning provided a pedagogical foundation for online instruction.

Methods

This exploratory mixed-methods study determined if there is a relationship between enrollment, faculty training score, type of ADA compliance used by the institution, and accessibility score (based on WCAG criteria presence in university online course checklists). Using a convergent design, online course checklists were evaluated using qualitative methods concurrently with quantitative data collection and analysis (Creswell & Plano Clark, 2018). Online course checklists were evaluated and coded using the 16 identified WCAG success criteria. Codes were assigned based on the criteria being (1) not present, (2) partially present, and (3) fully present. The resulting criterion scores for each university were summed to create an overall WCAG score used in further analysis.

Once the coding was complete, the data were analyzed with IBM SPSS Statistics version 26. The enrollment ranking, faculty training score, type of ADA compliance, and WCAG score were analyzed using Spearman's correlation coefficient to determine any relationships between the variables.

Sample

This study used a purposive sample of 35 universities generated from the U.S. News & World Report's (2019) best online bachelor's programs rankings. It was generated by identifying universities that offered an online bachelor's degree program, were publicly funded, and had a publicly available online course checklist from the top 100 ranked institutions. The sample of the universities ($N = 35$) enrolled about 2,000 students in their online programs ($M = 2050.74$, $SD = 2858.67$).

Materials and data sources

A web search using the university name, "online course checklist," and "online accessibility course checklist" was used to identify subjects that had publicly posted course checklists. To be considered a checklist, the posted content had to include specific guidance on how to design a course. Universities that directed users to the WCAG 2.0

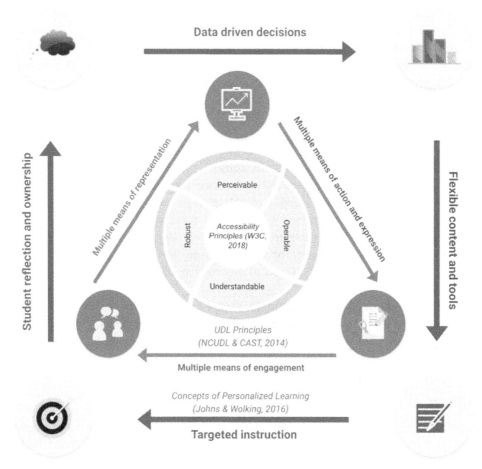

Figure 1. Principles of accessibility, UDL, and personalized learning.
Note. This theoretical framework centers on the principles of accessibility (W3C, 2018) within the context of UDL (National Center on Universal Design for Learning & Center for Applied Special Technology, 2014) and personalized learning (Johns & Wolking, 2016).

guidelines (World Wide Web Consortium, 2016), training, accessibility services, or policy without the presence of specific guidance in developing accessible courses were excluded from consideration. According to Cohen et al. (2011), a sample size of 30 is the minimum needed to conduct any type of statistical analysis, which indicates that the sample size was sufficient.

Data sources

All information used in this study was secondary data obtained from U.S. News & World Report rankings and publicly available information and documents posted on university websites (U.S. News & World Report, 2019). The U.S. News & World Report ranking data used for this study included enrollment, faculty credentials and training score, and ADA compliance. Enrollment consisted of university-reported data for online bachelor's degree programs (U.S. News & World Report, 2019). Faculty credentials and training scores were determined out of 100 as calculated by U.S. News & World Report on how well a university prepared instructors to teach remotely. The ADA compliance consisted of university-reported data on how it addressed course ADA compliance (U.S. News & World Report, 2019). The WCAG 2.0 criteria were obtained from the W3C Web Accessibility Initiative (W3C Web Accessibility Initiative, 2017) and Web Accessibility in Mind (2018).

WCAG criteria used to code online course checklists

The WCAG 2.0 Level A and AA standards consist of 38 success criteria (W3C, 2019). Since staff is often provided accessibility guidance via a checklist, the criteria were evaluated to determine the applicability to online course design or creation. Of the 38 success criteria, 16 were determined to have met the conditions based on whether the success criterion was applicable to course content that is created, selected, used, or designed by a course designer or instructor and whether a course designer or instructor could reasonably be expected to ensure that course content meets the success criteria.

Criteria that did not meet these conditions were considered the institution's responsibility and excluded from consideration in this study. The remaining measures were used to evaluate online course checklists to determine how well they were represented.

Constructs

University enrollment in the online bachelor's program, faculty credentials and training scores, and the type of ADA compliance, as reported by U.S. News & World Report (2019), were transformed into categorical variables.

Enrollment

Enrollment was transformed based on the Carnegie classification of institutions of higher education by the Indiana University Center for Postsecondary Research (2017) and categorized as very small, less than 999; small, 1,000 to 2,999; medium, 3,000 to 9,999; and large, more than 10,000.

Faculty score

The faculty score was transformed based on a traditional grading scale: A, 90 to 100; B, 80 to 89; C, 70 to 79; D, 60 to 69; and F, 0 to 59 (National Center for Education Statistics, 2011).

Type of ADA compliance

The type of ADA compliance was based on four categories determined by U.S. News & World Report (2019): central office reviews each course, central office reviews sample of courses, academic units held responsible, and individual faculty held responsible.

Composite scores of WCAG criteria representation

University course checklists were evaluated and scored using the 16 WCAG 2.0 success criteria. Scores were assigned based on the presence of the criterion (scored as 0), the criterion was partially represented to any degree (scored as 1), or the criterion was fully present even if simplified language was used (scored as 2).

For example, criterion 1.4.1 specifies that color cannot be the only method to convey information or the presence of hyperlinks. A score of 0 was assigned if the checklist did not address the criterion at all, a score of 1 was assigned if the checklist addressed the use of color for conveying information and did not mention links, and a score of 2 was assigned if the checklist thoroughly addressed the criterion. Moreover, a composite WCAG score was calculated as a mean of the 16 WCAG 2.0 criteria for each university. This composite score represented a measure that summarizes several equally-weighted indicators into a single score (Babbie, 2013; Ravallion, 2012).

Data analysis

All data were analyzed using descriptive statistics, frequency statistics, and Spearman's correlation coefficient using IBM SPSS Statistics version 26. Spearman's correlation coefficient was used to determine the strength of a relationship, if any was found (Stats Tutor, n.d.). The assumptions of this method were met.

Results

Descriptive statistics

The data was analyzed with IBM SPSS Statistics version 26 for all statistical tests. The study variables included enrollment in the online bachelor's program ($M = 2050.74$, $SD = 2858.67$), faculty credentials and training score ($M = 81.43$, $SD = 7.47$), and type of ADA compliance ($M = 2.54$, $SD = 1.31$).

Research question 1

The first research question addressed which accessibility criteria were most and least represented in university online course checklists. Of the 35 university online course checklists evaluated, none fully or partially addressed all 16 criteria, as shown in Table 1. Online course checklist evaluation data was analyzed using descriptive statistics and frequencies.

The least represented criteria ($M \leq .30$) were sensory characteristics, labels or instructions, page titles, and images of text. Sensory characteristics refer to instructions that include features such as sound, shape, or color (W3C, 2018). Labels and instructions are required when a person enters information (W3C, 2018). Page titles should describe the purpose, while images of text are not recommended (W3C, 2018).

In contrast, the most represented criteria ($M \geq 1.30$) were captions for prerecorded video, link purpose in context, alternative text for non-text content, and contrast. Captions can include open or closed captioning for prerecorded audio or video media (W3C, 2018). Web links should be displayed as meaningful text rather than the direct

Table 1. Composite WCAG scores.

WCAG 2.0 Success Criteria	M (N = 36)	SD	Not present (f)	Partially present (f)	Present (f)
Composite score of WCAG criteria representation	0.81	0.34	–	–	–
1.3.3 Sensory Characteristic	0.08	0.37	34	1	1
3.3.2 Labels or Instructions	0.11	0.40	33	2	1
2.4.2 Page Titled	0.19	0.58	32	1	3
1.4.5 Images of Text	0.25	0.65	31	1	4
1.2.5 Audio Description (Prerecorded)	0.42	0.77	27	3	6
1.3.2 Meaningful Sequence	0.50	0.74	23	8	5
1.2.3 Audio Description or Media Alternative (Prerecorded)	0.75	0.84	18	9	9
2.3.1 Three Flashes or Below Threshold	0.78	0.99	22	0	14
1.4.1 Use of Color	0.83	0.85	16	10	10
1.2.4 Captions (Live)	1.06	0.75	9	16	11
1.3.1 Info and Relationships	1.14	0.76	8	15	13
1.2.1 Prerecorded Audio-only and Video-only	1.19	0.89	11	7	18
1.4.3 Contrast (Minimum)	1.31	0.82	8	9	19
1.1.1 Non-text Content	1.36	0.59	2	19	15
2.4.4 Link Purpose (In Context)	1.42	0.91	10	1	25
1.2.2 Captions (Prerecorded)	1.61	0.77	6	2	28

Note. Composite WCAG scores for each criterion from least to greatest.

link URL (W3C, 2018). Alternative text should be included for non-text contexts such as emoticons, buttons, and images (W3C, 2018). For images and text, contrast ratios must meet a minimum level of difference (W3C, 2018).

Research question 2
Spearman's correlation coefficient was used to determine if there was a correlation between enrollment, faculty training score, type of ADA compliance, and the composite WCAG score. There was a significant positive correlation between online program enrollment and type of ADA compliance, $r_s = .656$ [.390, .832], $p < .001$; and online program enrollment and faculty credentials and training score, $r_s = .357$ [.021, .628], $p = .035$. There was no significant relationship between any other variables, as shown in Table 2.

Discussion

Overall, the results indicate that universities could improve their practices regarding online course accessibility. Universities can address more complex accessibility issues by implementing more robust accessibility practices.

Going beyond simple accessibility practices

The results indicate that universities are more likely to include accessibility criteria that are easier to check in their online course checklists while omitting or not fully addressing more complex guidelines. The most represented WCAG 2.0 criteria in the university's online course checklists were link purpose in context, alt text for non-text content, and captions for prerecorded video. These criteria are relatively intuitive and straightforward. These types of accessibility issues are usually identified using automated evaluation tools, many of which are integrated into learning management systems.

Table 2. Correlation between study variables using Spearman's correlation coefficient.

	Online program enrollment	Faculty training score	Type of ADA compliance	Composite WCAG score
Online program enrollment	–	.357**	.656*	.167
Faculty credentials and training score	.357**	–	.295	−.016
Type of ADA compliance	.656*	.295	–	.142
Composite WCAG score	.167	−.016	.142	–

*$p < .001$.
**$p = .035$.

On the other hand, the least represented WCAG 2.0 criteria encompass more complex guidelines. These consist of sensory characteristics, labels or instructions, images of text, page titles, and audio descriptions. These accessibility criteria usually necessitate manual evaluation by a person (W3C WAI, 2017). As a result, the Pacific ADA Center (n.d.) recommends that organizations use an accessibility evaluation methodology. The W3C WAI (2017) also proposes that each institution craft an accessibility evaluation plan which may include a combination of tools for use throughout the design process, the potential use of specialized tools, and the inclusion of some team members with a high level of accessibility knowledge.

However, the inclusion of technical accessibility guidelines in quality assurance frameworks, or online course checklists for the purposes of this study, is not the only way to address online content accessibility. Technical and legal requirements, while sometimes off-putting to designers and course instructors, provide helpful guidance and resources (Lowenthal et al., 2021). Lowenthal et al. (2021) found that high-quality frameworks directly addressed accessibility and included UDL, which provided design context. By combining accessibility with UDL and pedagogical strategies, the way online educational content is designed can be more comprehensively addressed to ensure inclusion and usability (Mancilla & Frey, 2021; Nieves et al., 2019; Pace & Schwartz, 2008). As a result, accessible online courses require a robust strategy that centers on learner access and usability needs while also addressing the technical and pedagogical aspects.

Enrollment points to a need for comprehensive accessibility strategies

Two significant positive relationships were found. The first was between online program enrollment and the type of ADA compliance. The second was between online program enrollment and faculty training scores. This suggests that the size of an online program impacts how the university handles accessibility compliance and faculty training.

Increased online program enrollment may be an indicator of accessibility practices because of the natural implications that occur. For example, higher enrollment may lead to expanded class offerings which could necessitate additional training and processes. Universities may also allocate additional funding or resources to ensure high-quality experiences as online programs grow. While the results of this study cannot explain how enrollment functionally impacted accessibility practices, they do allude to areas of further exploration.

Utility of a checklist as an indicator of accessibility

The lack of a relationship between the composite WCAG score and the other variables could be due to several reasons. The composite WCAG score represented an indirect measure of accessibility practices and may not describe the full extent of efforts a university takes to address accessibility. These results indicated a limit to the utility of a checklist as a gauge for accessibility practices. It is recommended that future studies use other measures to assess accessibility practices.

While checklists offer an opportunity to ensure online content is accessible, they can only be reliably used as one component of a larger accessibility strategy. On their own, checklists are insufficient to address the complexity and technical aspects of accessible online course content. As a result, a checklist could be useful in reminding designers and instructors of key practices, but they are not an adequate measure of how well an institution addresses accessibility in online courses.

Recommendations for practice

The literature offered several recommendations related to the findings of this study. First, institutions should develop a compliance strategy that does not rely solely on individuals (Burke et al., 2016). Second, accessibility can only be comprehensively addressed through a collaborative effort between the institution and instructors or designers. This includes the allocation of staffing and monetary resources to determine and fix accessibility issues in online courses. As the results suggested, training and compliance strategies are examples of comprehensive institutional measures that are more likely to impact accessibility practices.

Limitations

The findings of this study are limited by the use of secondary and self-reported data. Further, the small sample size of this study limits the generalizability of the results. In addition, the use of online course accessibility checklists is simply an indicator to examine university practices. The presence of a university course checklist was not and cannot be used as an indicator of compliance nor of the quality of online content used for instruction.

Future research

Accessible online instruction is an issue of concern for all universities. The results of this study indicate that a deeper examination of how enrollment impacts faculty training and accessibility compliance may reveal additional insight. Future research should consider how specific interventions, policies, or strategies affect course compliance. Additionally, future studies should move toward assessing accessibility through a more intersectional approach in collaboration with people with disabilities.

Disclosure statement

No potential conflict of interest was declared by the authors.

ORCID

Rita Fennelly-Atkinson http://orcid.org/0000-0003-4726-0662
Kimberly N. LaPrairie http://orcid.org/0000-0002-7149-5544
Donggil Song http://orcid.org/0000-0002-0306-6721

References

Accessibility Works. (2017, November 15). *2017 web accessibility ADA lawsuit statistics show the surge accelerating*. https://www.accessibility.works/blog/2017-web-accessibility-ada-lawsuit-statistics-2017/

American Psychological Association. (2020). *Publication manual of the American Psychological Association* (7th ed.). https://doi.org/10.1037/0000165-000

Babbie, E. R. (2013). *The practice of social research* (13th ed.). Wadsworth Cengage Learning.

Baldwin, S., Ching, Y. H., & Hsu, Y. C. (2018). Online course design in higher education: A review of national and statewide evaluation instruments. *TechTrends, 62*, 46–57. https://doi.org/10.1007/s11528-017-0215-z

Baldwin, S. J., & Ching, Y.-H. (2019). An online course design checklist: Development and users' perceptions. *Journal of Computing in Higher Education, 31*, 156–172. https://doi.org/10.1007/s12528-018-9199-8

Bogart, K. R., & Dunn, D. S. (2019). Ableism special issue introduction. *Journal of Social Issues, 75*(3), 650–664. https://doi.org/10.1111/josi.12354

Bowersox, E. (2019, March 1). Municipalities and universities new targets in ADA website accessibility lawsuits. *McAfee & Taft EmployerLINC*. https://www.mcafeetaft.com/municipalities-and-universities-new-targets-in-ada-website-accessibility-lawsuits/

Burke, D. D., Clapper, D., & McRae, D. (2016). Accessible online instruction for students with disabilities: Federal imperatives and the challenge of compliance. *Journal of Law & Education, 44*(2), 135–181.

Campbell, T., & Wescott, J. (2019). *Web tables: Profile of undergraduate students: Attendance, distance and remedial education, degree program and field of study, demographics, financial aid, financial literacy, employment, and military status: 2015–16*. U.S. Department of Education National Center for Education Statistics. https://nces.ed.gov/pubs2019/2019467.pdf

Carlsen, A., Holmberg, C., Neghina, C., & Owusu-Boampong, A. (2016). *Closing the gap: Opportunities for distance education to benefit adult learners in higher education*. UNESCO Institute for Lifelong Learning. k https://unesdoc.unesco.org/ark:/48223/pf0000243264

Cohen, L., Manion, L., & Morrison, K. (2011). *Research methods in education* (7th ed.). Routledge.

Coleman, M., & Berge, Z. L. (2018). A review of accessibility in online higher education. *Online Journal of Distance Learning Administration*, *21*(1), 1–8. http://www.westga.edu/~distance/ojdla/spring211/coleman_berge211.html

Creswell, J. W., & Plano Clark, V. L. (2018). *Designing and conducting mixed methods research* (3rd ed). SAGE Publications.

Crossland, A., Gray, T., Reynolds, J., Wellington, D., & Zhou, A. ((2016, October). *Digital accessibility toolkit: What education leaders need to know*. American Institutes for Research, Center on Technology and Disability.

Culliphier, V. (2017). (2017, November 13). Schools and organizations that serve education: Beware OCR complaints addressing online accessibility. *Medley's Cyber Tech & E-Commerce*. https://www.lexislegalnews.com/articles/21999/commentary-schools-and-organizations-that-serve-education-beware-ocr-complaints-addressing-online-accessibility

Curl, A. L., & Bowers, D. D. (2009). A longitudinal study of website accessibility: Have social work education websites become more accessible? *Journal of Technology in Human Services*, *27*(2), 93–105. https://doi.org/10.1080/15228830902749229

deMaine, S. D. (2014). From disability to usability in online instruction. *Law Library Journal*, *106*(4), 531–560. https://www.repository.law.indiana.edu/facpub/2871

Fennelly-Atkinson, R. (in press). Ableism versus inclusion: A systems view of accessibility practices in online higher education. In B. Hokanson, M. Exter, M. Schmidt, & A. Tawfik (Eds.), *Toward inclusive learning design: Social justice, equity, and community*. Springer-Verlag.

Ferri, D., & Favalli, S. (2018). Web accessibility for people with disabilities in the European Union: Paving the road to social inclusion. *Societies*, *8*(2), 40–58. https://doi.org/10.3390/soc8020040

Foley, A. (2011). Exploring the design, development and use of websites through accessibility and usability studies. *Journal of Educational Multimedia and Hypermedia*, *20*(4), 361–385. http://www.editlib.org/p/37621/

Goggin, G., Ellis, K., & Hawkins, W. (2019). Disability at the centre of digital inclusion: Assessing a new moment in technology and rights. *Communication Research and Practice*, *5*(3), 290–303. https://doi.org/10.1080/22041451.2019.1641061

Golden, N. (2008). Access this: Why institutions of higher education must provide access to the internet to students with disabilities. *Vanderbilt Journal of Entertainment and Technology Law*, *10*(2), 363–411. https://scholarship.law.vanderbilt.edu/jetlaw/vol10/iss2/3

Hackett, S., & Parmanto, B. (2005). A longitudinal evaluation of accessibility: Higher education web sites. *Internet Research*, *15*(3), 281–294. https://doi.org/10.1108/10662240510602690

Hamraie, A. (2018). Mapping access: Digital humanities, disability justice, and sociospatial practice. *American Quarterly*, *70*(3), 455–482. https://doi.org/10.1353/aq.2018.0031

Hill, P. (2018, January 22). Preliminary data on K-12 LMS market. *eLiterate*. https://eliterate.us/preliminary-data-k-12-lms-market/

Indiana University Center for Postsecondary Research. (2017). *Size & setting classification description*. http://carnegieclassifications.iu.edu/classification_descriptions/size_setting.php

Johns, S., & Wolking, M. (2016). *The core four of personalized learning: The elements you need to succeed*. Education Elements. https://www.edelements.com/hubfs/Core_Four/Education_Elements_Core_Four_White_Paper.pdf

Kuykendall, H. (2017, February 22). Section 508 and WCAG: How updated federal accessibility standards map to WCAG 2.0. *Microassist Digital Accessibility Digest*. https://www.microassist.com/digital-accessibility/section-508-and-wcag/

Laufer Nir, H., & Rimmerman, A. (2018). Evaluation of web content accessibility in an Israeli institution of higher education. *Universal Access in the Information Society*, *17*(3), 663–673. https://doi.org/10.1007/S10209-018-0615-7/TABLES/5

Launey, K. M., & Aristizabal, M. (2017, August 22). Website accessibility lawsuit filings still going strong. *ADA Title III: News & Insights*. https://www.adatitleiii.com/2017/08/website-accessibility-lawsuit-filings-still-going-strong/

Lowenthal, P. R., Lomellini, A., Smith, C., & Greear, K. (2021). Accessible online learning: A critical analysis of online quality assurance frameworks. *The Quarterly Review of Distance Education*, *22*(2), 15–29.

Madaus, J. W. (2011). The history of disability services in higher education. *New Directions for Higher Education, 154*, 5–15. https://doi.org/10.1002/he.429

Magnus, E., & Tøssebro, J. (2014). Negotiating individual accommodation in higher education. *Scandinavian Journal of Disability Research, 16*(4), 316–332. https://doi.org/10.1080/15017419.2012.761156

Mancilla, R., & Frey, B. (2021, May 20). *Professional development for digital accessibility: A needs assessment*. Quality Matters. https://www.qualitymatters.org/sites/default/files/research-docs-pdfs/QM-Digital-Accessibility-Professional-Development-WP.pdf

Miller, M. D. (2021, March 17). A year of remote teaching: The good, the bad, and the next steps. *The Chronicle of Higher Education*. https://www.chronicle.com/article/a-year-of-remote-teaching-the-good-the-bad-and-the-next-steps

Myers, E. L. (2004). Disability and technology. *Montana Law Review, 65*(2), 1–20. https://scholarworks.umt.edu/mlr/vol65/iss2/3

National Association of the Deaf. (2020, February 18). *Landmark agreements establish new model for online accessibility in higher education and business* [Press release]. https://www.nad.org/2020/02/18/landmark-agreements-establish-new-model-for-online-accessibility-in-higher-education-and-business/

National Center for Education Statistics. (2011). *High school transcript study: How is grade point average calculated?* https://nces.ed.gov/nationsreportcard/hsts/howgpa.aspx

National Center on Universal Design for Learning & Center for Applied Special Technology. (2014). *The three principles of UDL*. http://www.udlcenter.org/aboutudl/whatisudl/3principles

Nieves, L. H., Moya, E. C., & Soldado, R. M. (2019). A MOOC on universal design for learning designed based on the UDL paradigm. *Australasian Journal of Educational Technology, 35*(6), 30–47. https://doi.org/10.14742/ajet.5532

Office for Civil Rights. (2018). *Protecting students with disabilities*. https://www2.ed.gov/about/offices/list/ocr/504faq.html#introduction

Pace, D., & Schwartz, D. (2008, December). Accessibility in post secondary education: Application of UDL to college curriculum. *US-China Education Review, 5*(12), 20–26. https://www.davidpublisher.com/Public/uploads/Contribute/55b719eb35778.pdf

Pacific ADA Center. (n.d.). *Accessibility testing*. AccessibleTech.Org. Retrieved August 28, 2022, from https://accessibletech.org/testing/

Pan, J. (2017, September 26). (2017, September 26). *508, ADA, WCAG: What's the difference?* Logic Solutions. https://www.logicsolutions.com/508-ada-wcag-accessibility-difference/

Parry, M. ((2010, November 11). ADA compliance is a 'major vulnerability' for online programs. *The Chronicle of Higher Education*. https://www.chronicle.com/blogs/wiredcampus/ada-compliance-a-major-vulnerability-for-online-programs/28136

Persson, H., Åhman, H., Yngling, A. A., & Gulliksen, J. (2015). Universal design, inclusive design, accessible design, design for all: Different concepts—one goal? On the concept of accessibility—historical, methodological and philosophical aspects. *Universal Access in the Information Society, 14*(4), 505–526. https://doi.org/10.1007/s10209-014-0358-z

Ravallion, M. (2012). Mashup indices of development. *The World Bank Research Observer, 27*(1), 1–32. https://doi.org/10.1093/wbro/lkr009

Roig-Vila, R., Ferrández, S., & Ferri-Miralles, I. (2014). Assessment of web content accessibility levels in Spanish official online education environments. *International Education Studies, 7*(6), 31–45. https://doi.org/10.5539/ies.v7n6p31

Rowland, C. (2017, March 10). UC Berkeley decision results in universal inaccessibility. *WebAIM*. https://webaim.org/blog/uc-berkeley-inaccessibility

Rowland, C., Goetze, L., & Whiting, J. (2014). *GOALS cost case study: Costs of web accessibility in higher education*. National Center on Disability and Access to Education. http://www.ncdae.org/documents/GOALS_Cost_Case_Study.pdf

Scott, S., & Aquino, K. (2020). *COVID-19 transitions: Higher education professionals' perspectives on access barriers, services, and solutions for students with disabilities.* Association on Higher Education and Disability. https://higherlogicdownload.s3.amazonaws.com/AHEAD/38b602f4-ec53-451c-9be0-5c0bf5d27c0a/UploadedImages/COVID-19_/AHEAD_COVID_Survey_Report_Barriers_and_Resource_Needs.pdf

Scott, S., & Aquino, K. (2021). *COVID-19 transitions: An update on access, barriers, and supports nine months into the pandemic.* Association on Higher Education and Disability. https://higherlogicdownload.s3.amazonaws.com/AHEAD/38b602f4-ec53-451c-9be0-5c0bf5d27c0a/UploadedImages/COVID-19_/AHEAD_COVID_Report_wave_2_final.pdf

Seaman, J. E., Allen, I. E., & Seaman, J. (2018). *Grade increase: Tracking distance education in the United States.* Babson Survey Research Group. http://onlinelearningsurvey.com/reports/gradeincrease.pdf

Shawar, B. A. (2015). Evaluating web accessibility of educational websites. *International Journal of Emerging Technologies in Learning, 10*(4), 4–10. https://doi.org/10.3991/ijet.v10i4.4518

Stats Tutor. (n.d.). *Spearman's correlation.* Retrieved July 17, 2022, from https://www.statstutor.ac.uk/topics/correlation/spearmans-correlation-coefficient/

U.S. Department of Education, Institute of Education Sciences, & National Center for Education Statistics. (2017). *Table 303.20. Total fall enrollment in all postsecondary institutions participating in Title IV programs and annual percentage change in enrollment, by degree-granting status and control of institution: 1995 through 2016* [Digest of Education Statistics 20]. https://nces.ed.gov/programs/digest/d17/tables/dt17_303.20.asp?current=yes

U.S. Department of Justice Civil Rights Division. (2009). *A guide to disability rights laws.* https://www.ada.gov/cguide.htm

U.S. General Services Administration. (2017, November 10). *Accessibility news: The Section 508 update.* https://www.section508.gov/blog/accessibility-news-the-section-508-Update

U.S. General Services Administration. (2018, May). *Design & develop: Applicability & conformance.* https://www.section508.gov/develop/applicability-conformance/

U.S. News & World Report. (2019). *Best online bachelor's programs.* https://www.usnews.com/education/online-education/bachelors/rankings

UsableNet. (2019). *2018 ADA web accessibility recap: Lawsuit report.* https://cdn2.hubspot.net/hubfs/3280432/2019_UsableNet_WebAccessibilityLawsuit_Infographic_FINAL.pdf

UsableNet. (2020). *2020 midyear ADA website and app accessibility report.* https://f.hubspotusercontent30.net/hubfs/3280432/2020_Mid-Year_Accessibility_Lawsuit_Report_final_July1.pdf

Vu, M. N., Launey, K. M., & Ryan, S. (2019, January 31). Number of federal website accessibility lawsuits nearly triple, exceeding 2250 in 2018. *ADA Title III: News & Insights.* https://www.adatitleiii.com/2019/01/number-of-federal-website-accessibility-lawsuits-nearly-triple-exceeding-2250-in-2018/

Vu, M. N., Launey, K., & Ryan, S. (2020, September 2). Federal ADA Title III lawsuit numbers drop 15% for the first half of 2020 but a strong rebound is likely. *ADA Title III.* https://www.adatitleiii.com/2020/09/federal-ada-title-iii-lawsuit-numbers-drop-15-for-the-first-half-of-2020-but-a-strong-rebound-is-likely/

Web Accessibility in Mind. (2018). *WCAG 2.0 checklist.* https://webaim.org/standards/wcag/WCAG2Checklist.pdf

Weissman, S. (2020, September 8). Universities face digital accessibility lawsuits as pandemic continues. *Diverse Issues in Higher Education.* https://diverseeducation.com/article/189682/

WICHE Cooperative for Educational Telecommunications, & The Campus Computing Project. (2010). *2010 managing online education survey.* https://www.campuscomputing.net/content/2010/11/13/2010-managing-online-education-survey

World Wide Web Consortium. (2016, January 5). *How to meet WCAG 2.0: A customizable quick reference to Web Content Accessibility Guidelines 2.0 requirements (success criteria) and techniques.* https://www.w3.org/WAI/WCAG20/quickref/20160105/

World Wide Web Consortium. (2018, June 5). *Web Content Accessibility Guidelines (WCAG) 2.1.* https://www.w3.org/TR/WCAG21

World Wide Web Consortium. (2019, October 4). *How to meet WCAG (Quickref reference): A customizable quick reference to Web Content Accessibility Guidelines (WCAG) 2 requirements (success criteria) and techniques.* https://www.w3.org/WAI/WCAG21/quickref

World Wide Web Consortium Web Accessibility Initiative. (2017, December 23). *Selecting web accessibility evaluation tools.* https://www.w3.org/WAI/test-evaluate/tools/selecting/#cannot

Yang, Y. T., & Chen, B. (2015). Web accessibility for older adults: A comparative analysis of disability laws. *The Gerontologist, 55*(5), 854–864. https://doi.org/10.1093/geront/gnv057

Yesilada, Y., Brajnik, G., Vigo, M., & Harper, S. (2015). Exploring perceptions of web accessibility: A survey approach. *Behaviour & Information Technology, 34*(2), 119–134. https://doi.org/10.1080/0144929X.2013.848238

Higher education leaders' perspectives of accessible and inclusive online learning

Amy Lomellini ⓘ, Patrick R. Lowenthal ⓘ, Chareen Snelson ⓘ, and Jesús H. Trespalacios ⓘ

ABSTRACT
Online learning can potentially meet increasingly diverse students' needs in higher education, including disabled students. However, institutions have historically struggled in providing accessible and inclusive online learning. Higher education online learning leaders, those who manage instructional designers, are in a unique position to help institutions strategize and create accessible and inclusive online courses. In this qualitative study, we interviewed nine higher education online learning leaders to understand leaders' perceptions about how institutions provide accessible and inclusive online learning. Results demonstrated that despite varying conceptualizations of accessibility and inclusivity, online learning leaders perceive an insufficient but growing emphasis in higher education. Overall, participants described instructional designers as the most knowledgeable and skilled in this area. Participants described a lack of agency for instructional design teams and a need to advocate for buy-in from senior leadership. They also described strategies (e.g., faculty development, quality standards, and accessibility checkers) to support faculty.

Enrollments in online higher education courses and programs have continued to grow over the last 2 decades. This has resulted in an increasingly diverse student body taking online courses. In particular, a growing number of disabled students are choosing to learn online these days (De Los Santos, 2019). The flexibility of learning online can help disabled students mitigate the effects of symptoms, medications, and physical barriers on campus (e.g., poor acoustics in lecture halls for students with hearing disabilities or long distances between buildings for students with mobility issues) (Bartz, 2020; Kent, 2016). However, online learning also has the potential to present barriers to student learning outcomes (Kent, 2016; Nieminen & Pesonen, 2020). For instance, inaccessible digital materials (e.g., documents that are not designed for compatibility with assistive technologies) and the unorganized presentation of content can halt academic progress for students who rely on assistive technology or who have learning, attention, or focus disabilities (Bartz, 2020; Fichten et al., 2009). The COVID-19 pandemic, and the rush to move courses online, further exposed barriers like these (Anderson, 2020; Burgstahler, 2022). On the other hand, courses intentionally designed for accessibility help disabled students meet their academic goals (Burgstahler, 2015).

Confronted with the reality that online learning might not be meeting the needs of disabled students, institutions of higher education and online learning leaders—that is, those in charge of managing online learning on campuses—in particular, have recently increased their attention on providing accessible and inclusive online courses (Fenneberg, 2022; Lewicki-Townley et al., 2021; Oyarzun et al., 2021). However, questions remain about what institutions of higher education and online learning leaders are actually doing to provide accessible and inclusive online learning and whether it is enough (Garrett et al., 2021; Linder et al., 2015). Given this and the importance of helping all students succeed in learning online, we set out to explore online learning leaders' perspectives on accessible and inclusive online learning in higher education. In the following paper, we present the results of our inquiry and its implications for research and practice.

Background

Traditionally, institutions of higher education have thought of disability in medical terms. A medical model of disability conceptualizes disability as a person's lack of ability to do something due to a health concern (World Health Organization, 2011). Thinking of disability in this way led institutions to adopt the practice of requiring students to disclose their disability before any accommodations of support could be identified (Dolmage, 2017). Accommodations often include extra time on tests, separate testing locations, alternative formats of instructional materials, and/or the use of assistive technology (Ketterlin-Geller & Johnstone, 2006). This approach, though, can be confusing and stigmatizing to disabled students who may face doubt, suspicion, and a lack of understanding from faculty and their peers (Cook et al., 2009; Harris et al., 2019; Sarrett, 2017), as well as time-consuming and costly (Harris et al., 2019). For reasons like these, many students prefer not to disclose their disability at all, leaving institutions of higher education struggling to understand and meet their needs (Izzo et al., 2008; McAndrew et al., 2012; Roberts et al., 2011; Schelly et al., 2011).

More recently, society and institutions of higher education specifically have begun to conceptualize disability and diversity differently. Among other ideas, institutions are now seeing value in approaching accessibility proactively rather than retroactively (Lomellini & Lowenthal, 2022; Seale, 2020). However, there is still considerable debate about the best ways to do this and whose job it is to ensure online courses in particular are designed with accessibility in mind (Linder et al., 2015; Singleton et al., 2019). Faced with this, online learning leaders have begun looking for scalable institutional investments, including faculty development initiatives and instructional design support, to support campus-wide cultural shifts toward proactive accessible and inclusive course design strategies (Burgstahler, 2022; Westine et al., 2019). Cultural shifts never happen easily. Research suggests that a collaborative approach among students, faculty, instructional designers, disability services providers, administrators, and leaders is needed to improve accessibility at institutional levels (Burgstahler, 2015; Gladhart, 2009; Oyarzun et al., 2021). Resources and training can help increase faculty and instructional designers' awareness and skills while policies and procedures can identify clear responsibilities and support structures (Gladhart, 2009; Izzo et al., 2008; Linder et al., 2015; Xie & Rice, 2021).

Online learning has the potential to improve access to higher education for all learners, including disabled students (Black et al., 2015; Burgstahler, 2022; Satterfield et al., 2015). However, reducing barriers for disabled students in online learning involves buy-in from leadership and an institutional paradigm shift to support proactive accessible and inclusive course design initiatives (Burgstahler, 2022; Seale, 2020). Previous studies about accessible and inclusive online learning have examined the perceptions of faculty (Westine et al., 2019), students (Bartz, 2020), and to a lesser degree, instructional designers (Singleton et al., 2019; Xie, Gulinna, Rice et al., 2021), but few studies have addressed online learning leaders' perceptions (Garrett et al., 2021). Leaders are uniquely situated between instructional designers doing the hands-on work with faculty and administrators setting institutional priorities and planning. Thus, this study sought to address the gap in the literature by exploring how online learning leaders perceive the challenges and opportunities related to accessible and inclusive online learning at their institutions.

Method

While many online learning leaders acknowledge that online accessibility needs to be a priority (Linder et al., 2015; Garrett et al., 2021), research has shown that a lack of clear policies, responsibilities, professional development, and stakeholder buy-in can hinder effective accessibility and inclusion efforts (Burgstahler, 2022; Linder et al., 2015; Singleton et al., 2019). What remains unclear is how online learning leaders are addressing these issues and how they perceive the barriers and strategies related to inclusive online course design at their institutions.

Given the aforementioned problems and the lack of literature on this topic, the purpose of this qualitative study was to understand online learning leaders' perceptions of providing an increasingly diverse student body accessible and inclusive online learning experiences. This study sought to answer the following research questions:

1. What are leaders' perceptions of the current state of institutions' ability to provide accessible and inclusive online learning?
2. How are institutions providing accessible and inclusive online learning experiences?

Research design

We used a qualitative research design with semi-structured interviews to answer the research questions (see the Appendix). Qualitative research is helpful to understand complex stories of individuals' lived experiences (Creswell & Poth, 2018). Additionally, qualitative research can help challenge traditional assumptions (Creswell & Poth, 2018). In this case, digital accessibility issues are often assumed to be the concern of disability services and faculty (Tobin & Behling, 2018). This study investigated this assumption by exploring the role of online learning departments in accessible and inclusive online learning.

Positionality

It is important to note that I (A. L.) identify as a disabled person, researcher, student, instructional designer, and more recently, associate director of online learning at an institution of higher education. This study was conducted using the theoretical lens of disability inquiry studies, which empowers disabled people rather than focusing on biological constraints (Creswell & Poth, 2018). In particular, the study was informed by the diversity model of disability, which celebrates disability pride and the social model of disability, in which accessibility is viewed as a shared social responsibility instead of an individual's problem. Through this lens, meeting the needs of disabled students can shift toward a proactive, collaborative venture to address barriers in online learning instead of attempting to "fix" students' bodies. To counteract potential bias in this study, I (A. L.) used strategies such as providing participants with the transcript to check that their intentions were accurately conveyed, remaining neutral during interviews, collaborating with other researchers, and reporting all views, including dissenting opinions.

We use disability-first language (i.e., "disabled students") to celebrate disability pride (Andrews et al., 2022), to align with the disability community's movement of reclaiming historically dehumanizing terms as a means of empowerment (Vivanti, 2019), and to reflect the cultural preferences certain groups (i.e., "Deaf students" and "autistic students") (Dunn & Andrews, 2015; Sarrett, 2017). We recognize that language is continuously evolving and that preferences vary in the diverse disability community.

Sample and context

Nearly every college or university offers some courses and programs online (Garrett et al., 2021). However, the resources and support available to create online courses and programs vary by institution in the United States of America (Garrett et al., 2021). On one end of the continuum are institutions like the University of Central Florida and Arizona State University that have dozens of staff dedicated to offering courses and programs online; on the other end of the continuum are small liberal arts colleges that might not employ any instructional designers. Given the lack of literature and the exploratory nature of this study, we employed a maximum variation sampling strategy to gather data and perspectives from a diverse sample (Creswell & Poth, 2018). We were interested in identifying common themes despite variation (Patton, 2002).

To maximize sample variation, I used LinkedIn and institutional websites to search for the titles "Director of Online Learning" and "Director of Instructional Design." She recorded institution size according to the Carnegie classification of institutions of higher education: small (full-time equivalent enrollment of 1,000–2,999), medium (full-time equivalent of 3,000–9,999), and large (full-time equivalent of at least 10,000) (American Council on Education, 2022). After obtaining Institutional Review Board approval, I sent recruitment emails to leaders. Ultimately, nine participants, representing three large institutions, four medium-sized institutions, and two small institutions of higher education responded and were interviewed. Participants had an average of 4 years of experience in their current role (range: 2–9.5 years) and an average of nearly 18 years of experience in additional roles in education including management, instructional design, and teaching (range: 10–30 years). Three participants held doctoral degrees (Doctor of Philosophy or Doctor of Education), five held master's degrees, and one participant's degree is unknown.

Data collection

The semi-structured interviews were conducted via Zoom. Research has shown that participants in virtual interviews report positive feedback because visual cues from researchers remain similar to face-to-face interviews (Mirick & Wladkowski, 2019). I followed a semi-structured protocol to ensure consistency throughout the different interviews. This protocol was originally tested and refined during a pilot study with an online learning leader. The interviews included questions such as "What barriers do institutions face with providing accessible and inclusive online learning experiences?" and "What strategies is your institution, or other institutions, using to provide accessible and inclusive online courses?" (see the Appendix for the full protocol). I also maintained a journal to take notes during and after the interviews to reflect on the themes that arose.

Data analysis

The interviews were transcribed, edited for accuracy, and imported into NVivo for coding and qualitative analysis. To analyze the interview data, I read the transcripts several times to become familiar with the data presented. Then, I used NVivo to organize the data and coding process. While it can be difficult to decide what constitutes a piece of data to analyze when coding, ultimately we allowed the data to tell the story (Chenail, 2012). We focused on the themes and natural chunks that emerged from the data as opposed to a line-by-line analysis (Elliot, 2018). I used Miles et al. (2020) iterative, cyclical qualitative data analysis model to analyze the data. During the first cycle of coding, chunks of data were summarized. Then, during the second cycle of coding, the summaries were grouped together to create themes or pattern codes to demonstrate relationships and meaning. I frequently consulted with the other researchers to discuss themes.

Reliability, validity, and trustworthiness

The interviews were semi-structured and followed a consistent protocol to increase reliability (Fowler & Cosenza, 2009). Transcripts were presented to participants to verify accuracy and help maintain credibility and increase trustworthiness (Creswell & Poth, 2018). This strategy helped to ensure that participants felt the transcript was an accurate representation of their thoughts on the topic. The use of leaders from various institutions helped provide alternative perspectives (Creswell & Poth, 2018). I also reflected on my role and positionality throughout the interviews and data analysis to further ensure transparency and trustworthiness. We collaborated to discuss the emergent themes and reflect on the research process to minimize potential bias and increase credibility. We have included the interview protocol in this report to increase transparency.

Table 1. Themes and descriptions of higher education leaders' perspectives of accessible and inclusive online learning.

Theme	Description
Varying conceptualizations of accessible and inclusive online learning	Participants understand accessible online learning as the technical requirements that meet standards and laws but see inclusive online learning as a newer idea of creating a learning environment that is accessible but also welcoming to all learners.
Insufficient but growing emphasis on accessibility and inclusivity	Participants felt that institutions do not currently place enough emphasis on providing accessible and inclusive online learning, but it is becoming more of a priority. They generally felt that the field is doing better in this area, but there is still room to grow.
Instructional designers possess the knowledge and skills, but lack the agency to enact change	While participants generally viewed instructional designers as being the most knowledgeable and skilled, they felt hindered by a lack of agency because faculty were ultimately responsible for online course content.
Online learning leaders are advocating for buy-in and support	Participants positioned themselves as advocates who need to obtain buy-in and prioritize accessibility and inclusivity. When speaking with senior administrators, participants emphasized retention, recruitment, and litigation. With faculty, participants focused on student experience and relied on top-down support.
Instructional designers use faculty development, quality standards, and accessibility checkers to support faculty	Given instructional designers' consultative role, participants focused efforts on faculty training, quality assurance standards, and accessibility checker tools to support faculty in designing accessible and inclusive online courses.

Results

It became clear from interviewing online learning leaders that from their perspective, institutions are making progress toward providing students with more accessible and inclusive online courses, however institutions still remain hindered by varying conceptualizations of terminology, lack of clear responsibilities, and a lack of support from senior leadership. At the same time, online learning leaders felt positioned as advocates to fight for the necessary buy-in, resources, and tools to support accessibility and inclusion initiatives. The central theme that emerged from the data was a sense of urgency to capitalize on growing awareness, but frustration with current barriers preventing a cultural shift to fully supporting accessible and inclusive online learning. We identified five themes (see Table 1), which we discuss in greater detail as they relate to the research questions in the rest of this section.

What are leaders' perceptions of the current state of institutions' ability to provide accessible and inclusive online learning?

Theme 1: Varying conceptualizations of accessible and inclusive online learning

We began the interviews by asking participants about their definition of "accessible and inclusive online." Generally speaking, participants viewed accessible and inclusive online learning as designing learning experiences and instructional materials for the widest possible audience to meet educational objectives regardless of disability, preference, need, or background.

When discussing accessible and inclusive online learning, participants frequently mentioned universal design for learning (UDL). In fact, they discussed the need for institutions to take a proactive approach to course design (e.g., using UDL) to meet the needs of students who do not disclose their disabilities or needs but also highlighted the importance of reducing barriers for all learners. For instance, one person stated:

> [If] everything is built with universal design in mind, then you're not going to have to do too much if someone like needs a special accommodation, or they may not even need a special accommodation.

Online learning leaders, though, differentiated between accessibility and inclusivity. They viewed accessibility as the "nuts and bolts" or technical requirements (e.g., captions, transcripts, alt text) related to course design. Meeting accessibility requirements was also viewed as "overwhelming," "daunting," and "very challenging." Accessibility was described as an older, more established, and defined topic, but less "sexy" and more challenging to get faculty engaged. Inclusivity, on the other hand, was described as "intriguing," "interesting," and a more broad but less clearly defined way of meeting the needs of all students. The differentiation between the terms is illustrated with the following quotes:

> [They are] two separate but kind of related things. So, I see an accessible course as one where students with learning disabilities would be able to fully participate in the course. And I see that as a subset of inclusive courses. So, an inclusive course is one that's fully accessible, but also welcoming to students from all different types of backgrounds.

We asked participants if they believed that accessibility and inclusivity were included in diversity, equity, and inclusion (DEI). Some felt that the underlying principles were aligned, but accessibility and inclusivity may not be receiving enough emphasis due to the broader focus of DEI.

> I believe it has been something that has really been a focus for a long time, and so I think as DEI has kind of become more prominent in higher ED institutions and education in general, I think it was an easy success for a lot of departments to say, "oh yeah we're being inclusive because we're providing captioning on videos" or whatever that like that's an easy kind of a thing. But um, but I see those initiatives pushing things to a lot more broader audience.

Overall, participants talked about how accessibility and inclusivity strategies are essentially ways to meet the needs of "all" learners. Participants described accessibility as being specifically for disabled students but helpful for all students. Inclusivity was perceived as a broader term, including ethnically and racially diverse students, nontraditional students, first-generation students, but often less focused on disabled students.

Theme 2: Insufficient but growing emphasis on accessibility and inclusivity

We were interested in better understanding what online learning leaders thought about institutions, both their own and others, ability to provide accessible and inclusive online learning. Three key themes emerged from the data. The overall sentiment from participants was that while interest and support are growing, whether that be due to recent lawsuits and/or the COVID pandemic, institutions are not currently placing enough emphasis on providing accessible and inclusive online courses. One participant expressed:

> I think that's getting better and I think the spotlight has been shone on this issue with this move to remote learning. Because I think it's become very clear that for many students, some of these accessibility features are critical for them to continue learning.

Participants expressed a desire to improve accessible and inclusive online learning strategies at their institutions but described how administrative barriers prevent widespread adoption. One participant noted, "I think we need to do more, but don't have administrative support or not the right tools to actually do it more broadly." They went on to say, "So I think there's an emphasis in the instructional design field. It's just getting it down to faculty and administration."

Participants felt that the accessible and inclusive online learning is more of a priority within the field of instructional design. They even talked about inclusivity being an increasingly listed desired knowledge and skill area in instructional design job postings, unlike 5 years ago:

> I've noticed that more and more job postings specify inclusivity as like knowledge and skill ability area that somebody should have when they applied for the job. That didn't exist years ago. That definitely was not on there. I don't even know if it was 5 years ago, but it's becoming more and more common to see that listed on job postings.

Despite perceptions of progress, participants expressed that there is more work to be done in the instructional design field as well. One participant noted that only six out of 20 recent people interviewing for online learning–related jobs "sounded like they knew something about [accessibility and inclusivity]." One leader pushed for more from the field by emphasizing the opportunity to support all students in their desire to learn by setting the expectation in the field that "every person might need to do this a little bit differently and that's okay because...there's no straight path to the answer."

Overall, participants felt that the growing emphasis presented an opportunity to capitalize on the momentum by investing in the instructional designers' knowledge and skills in this area, while advocating for increased buy-in and support from senior leadership.

Theme 3: Instructional designers possess the knowledge and skills, but they lack the agency to enact change

When we asked participants to describe the knowledge and skills of the faculty and instructional designers at their institution, participants noted the challenge that while faculty are responsible for the content, their knowledge and skills in providing accessible and inclusive online learning were relatively low. They described how there were some "rock stars" who understood the importance and could do the work, but that there were other faculty in which accessibility and inclusivity were not "on their radar" and would need a lot of "hand holding" to do the work. Participants described the challenge to help faculty see beyond their own experiences when they would say things like, "I don't have any students like that," "My students have never needed this before," and "No student has ever asked me for this." Participants described the difficulty in convincing faculty to learn about and implement effective accessible and inclusive practices in their online courses because faculty were often faced with competing priorities and a lack of time and resources.

Instructional designers were viewed as having the most knowledge and skills with creating accessible and inclusive online learning on campuses, but their lack of agency created a barrier to the implementation of accessible and inclusive design strategies. Participants were confident in their instructional designers' ability to design accessible and inclusive online courses. However, many talked about how their instructional designers could use more training on the "newer" concept of inclusive course design. Many participants described how they had at least one accessibility "guru" on their team. The following quotes illustrate this theme:

> My instructional designer is way above and beyond my skills and knowledge in accessibility, specifically. She's our guru and she can look at something and tell me what's wrong with it and what needs to be fixed and I have to dig a little bit.

> I think the team is very strong right now in terms of foundational [accessibility] principles, but then we're always looking for ways to improve and learn new ways of integrating some of these ideas into our work.

All participants expressed that instructional designers were critical in supporting the success and implementation of accessible and inclusive course design strategies regardless of official responsibility or titles. In fact, one participant described investing in one team member to become the institutional guru in this area despite accessibility not being an official part of their role:

> And so, we've actually kind of invested heavily in one of our staff to get a lot of training and be the main accessibility person, even though she does not have that in her title.

Participants described how the instructional designers were doing the day-to-day work because of their knowledge and skills in this area despite not having the official responsibility or authority over the course content. Ultimately, most participants perceived accessibility and inclusivity in online courses as the faculty's responsibility. Some participants described institutional policies and procedures (e.g., official digital accessibility policies and/or requirements in faculty's contracts) that designate faculty as responsible, while other participants described an unofficial perception that faculty should be responsible because they control the course content. Overall, most participants felt that the instructional designers at their institutions were simply there to support the faculty. One participant stated:

> We're not the content experts ... we can't go in and make their document how they want it, but we can help them make it accessible to their students. So, at the end of the day, it's the faculty's course, the faculty is responsible for that, but we want to make the job as easy as possible.

Another participant, though, expressed that accessibility and inclusivity should be everyone's responsibility, while yet another one felt that without a policy it was nobody's responsibility. Others felt the provost was ultimately responsible for providing accessible and inclusive online learning, but that an institution's instructional designers and Office of Disability Services were responsible for making it happen, as illustrated in the following quote:

> It probably ultimately falls on our VP of Academics. That's probably where the buck would stop when it came to an audit. It's probably between me and the Disability Services Director on like the day-to-day things.

Amid the confusion about who is actually responsible, instructional designers were generally perceived as the go-to experts for accessibility and inclusivity on campus; however, participants felt that instructional designers' lack of agency prevented them from enacting effective strategies. One participant noted:

> For the most part, learning designers and faculty developers are in a service role and have limited purview to do more than advise and consult.

Participants believed increasing the utilization of instructional design teams across the institution would better serve students. One participant described:

> Our group should be partnered with the Provost and they should be constantly turning to us and saying … "Hey, all these faculty need you." And "hey all you faculty, you need them. And we're not going to be okay if you don't use them."

Participants felt instructional design teams were doing the work because they possess the required knowledge and skill; however, instructional designers lack the official responsibility or agency to enact the desired institutional culture shift to more accessible and inclusive online courses.

Overall, online learning leaders described accessibility as challenging and felt that it may get lost in broader inclusivity initiatives. Participants perceived the current state of accessibility and inclusivity in online higher education as an area that is gaining attention but hindered by a lack of clear responsibilities.

How are institutions providing accessible and inclusive online learning experiences?

After we had a better understanding of participants' perceptions, we wanted to know more about how their institutions were actually providing accessible and inclusive online learning.

Theme 4: Online learning leaders are advocating for buy-in and support

Online learning leaders expressed that part of their role is to communicate the importance of creating accessible and inclusive online courses to their teams, faculty, and leadership at their institution. Participants described strategies to convince stakeholders to make accessibility and inclusivity a priority and to provide ongoing support to accomplish this work. One participant stated:

> I'm probably the only person at the university who is tuned in to it. So, I need to be knowledgeable enough to then communicate out what we need to do as an institution.

Participants expressed that the broad range of requirements, standards, and best practices related to accessibility and inclusivity combined with diverse student needs often paralyzed institutions and faculty and left them not knowing where to begin. To combat this, participants described strategies to convince administrators and faculty to prioritize this work.

Administrative buy-in. Participants described how administrators often would take an all-or-nothing approach. For instance, making all documents accessible was deemed impossible, so some administrators thought that they should not even attempt it. A participant described needing to be the "voice of reason" to get administrative buy-in and help them understand how to take smaller steps. Others noted that institutions generally want to do the right thing, but they are unclear how and instead wait until the problem presents itself.

Participants talked about how they leverage the mission, retention, recruitment, and litigation when talking with senior leadership in efforts to get administrative buy-in to prioritize accessible and inclusive online courses. The following quote illustrates this theme:

> The mission of my unit is to increase access to educational experiences and if you want to [recruit] more and different types of people, [accessibility and inclusivity have] to be a part of what you think about and what you do.

Participants leveraged senior leadership to motivate faculty to accomplish the work. They talked about how with high-level support, they are better able to plan, prioritize, and meet their goals related to accessible and inclusive online courses. For instance, one school's provost disseminated a statement about the importance and expectations of accessible online courses at the request of the online learning leader:

> We asked the interim Provost, could you just send a letter out laying down the law and like 'this is what's expected?' And you know, we gave him the language [to send out]. But he really added to it. So, I mean it came down like 'This is like what needs to happen.'

Another provost required faculty to caption their own videos and take mandatory accessibility training:

> We had an amazing provost ... she backed us up. She actually put it in their contracts ... they had to sign a piece of paper saying they would take the [accessibility training] class.

On the other hand, one participant cautioned the top-down approach and favored "creating a parade that people would like to join versus saying you have to do this."

Faculty buy-in. Participants believed that faculty generally want to support students, but often feel overwhelmed by the scope and technical abilities required to design accessible and inclusive online learning. To obtain faculty buy-in, participants described the "delicate balance to be a change agent... [and how] getting folks to change depends on the person you're working with." Conversations with faculty focused less on legal aspects of accessibility and more on the student experience. "It's not just the law, it's the right thing to do" was a common talking point for participants in this study.

Overall, online learning leaders felt compelled to advocate for buy-in at all levels and believed it was within their role to advance accessibility and inclusivity at the institution.

Theme 5: Instructional designers use faculty development, quality standards, and accessibility checkers to support faculty

Given that faculty were generally perceived by participants as responsible for online course content (either officially or unofficially), participants described how instructional design teams provide faculty development, leverage quality course design standards, and utilize accessibility checkers to facilitate the implementation of accessible and inclusive online course design strategies.

Faculty development offerings. Participants described offering drop-in hours, courses, webinars, workshops, "lunch and learns," tutorials, and even presenting at faculty meetings about accessibility and inclusivity; however, it was difficult to ascertain the effectiveness of these strategies. One participant stated:

> [The training offered] wasn't well attended, so I'm not sure how effective they were. I probably would be a little blurb on a compliance audit that says, 'this is what we tried to work towards compliance,' but beyond that, I don't think they were very effective.

Course design quality assurance frameworks. Participants also mentioned how they leverage quality course design standards (e.g., Quality Matters Rubric; Online Course Quality Review Rubric) to discuss and increase accessibility, consistency, and quality of online courses. However, they described that they often had mixed success with this approach because without support from deans, chairs, and the provost, some faculty simply resist quality assurance frameworks. One leader stated, "there's little to no appetite for [quality assurance programs]...unless a college or department chair or head says, 'I need all the courses in my program to be certified.'" Participants even cautioned the reliance on standards because they may not actually meet individual students' needs. One leader described standards as the minimum bar. In their view, "there's the right thing to do, what's required by law, and then there's going the extra mile to find out if those things are actually meeting [students'] needs."

Accessibility checker tools. Participants talked a lot about accessibility tools such as Blackboard Ally and the Universal Design Online Content Inspection Tool. Both tools scan content and files in a learning management system for accessibility issues, flag potential barriers, and provide feedback to help content creators improve the course's accessibility. Participants talked about how using these tools can initiate conversations with faculty by highlighting accessibility issues and helping them learn how to remediate the problems. The following is an example of a participant's perspectives on tools like these:

> Definitely Ally has been a good strategy ... To me what it does, it brings it to the forefront right? Instead of you just putting a document up and getting no indication whatsoever what's going on, that little gauge helps people see that something's going on in the background.

Some noted that Blackboard Ally was useful to intrigue faculty when it was first adopted but interest dwindled. On participant noted:

> I felt like Ally served a big purpose in the first few semesters that we had it and then it did its job in terms of like getting people to where they needed to be. So, for every faculty member who is going to be swayed by that red mark, was swayed by it and now it's kind of like it's helpful for new faculty.

Others questioned the validity of the accessibility scores provided by these tools. They described how they had found through their own testing that some low-scoring content was not as inaccessible as the tool made it seem. What started as a strategy to help faculty learn to remediate their content, shifted into a way for instructional designers to provide faculty with ongoing assistance. One participant stated:

> I think it's been helpful for our instructional design staff even more so than the faculty. Because our instructional design staff is very much focused on making sure those course sites initially are fully accessible, and this is just another tool to help them double-check what they're doing and how things are working.

Online learning leaders perceive their role as advocates to obtain buy-in from senior administrators and faculty alike. Given the consultative role of instructional designers and their lack of agency to enact change, participants developed initiatives such as providing diverse faculty development offerings, leveraging quality assurance standards, and using accessibility checkers to support an institutional shift toward further awareness and prioritization of accessible and inclusive online learning.

Discussion

This study investigated leaders' perceptions of the current state of institutions' ability to provide accessible and inclusive online learning and the strategies they used to do the work in this area. The results of this study align with previous studies that demonstrated that accessibility and inclusivity are becoming increasingly more of a priority for institutions of higher education (Garrett et al., 2021; Lomellini & Lowenthal, 2022; Rao, 2021). Yet, as evidenced by this study and others, there are still barriers to overcome.

Developing shared understandings of accessible and inclusive online learning

One key finding from our study is the need to develop a shared understanding of accessible and inclusive online learning. Leaders in this study described accessibility and inclusivity as interconnected but separate entities, which aligns with well-established definitions (Microsoft, 2016; W3C Web Accessibility Initiative, 2022). Accessibility is often defined as the technical application of standards and legal requirements aimed at supporting disabled users (W3C Web Accessibility Initiative, 2022). However, while intended to meet disabled people's needs, accessibility principles are often beneficial for all learners (Henry et al., 2014; Microsoft, 2016).

Inclusivity is a methodology to design ways for everyone to access, participate, and have a sense of belonging in the experience (Bonitto, 2021; Microsoft, 2016). Participants in this study often cited UDL as a guiding framework for opening conversations with faculty and providing related training. While UDL can be a helpful conversation starter for proactive design (Meyer et al., 2014), research has also shown that the broad scope and competing definitions of UDL can cause ambiguity of implementation and evaluation in research studies and in practice (Fornauf & Erickson, 2020). More research needs to be conducted to clarify concrete UDL strategies and understand the effectiveness in terms of recruitment, student experience, and retention (Fornauf & Erickson, 2020; Roberts et al., 2011).

There is also a growing interest in DEI due to the diversification of students with access to higher education, recent political events, and the inequities highlighted during the COVID pandemic (Burgstahler, 2022; Fenneberg, 2022). Institutions are increasingly developing programs and hiring administrators to help accomplish this important work. Participants in this study perceived inclusion in broader terms and felt that accessibility may get lost in DEI initiatives. It is important to consider accessible and inclusive design alongside other strategies that challenge inequity (Xie & Rice, 2021). Thus, questions remain on how accessibility and disability fit into DEI work (Fenneberg, 2022).

Barriers institutions currently face

As seen in this study and in other research, many of the barriers hindering institutions' ability to provide accessible and inclusive online learning stem from external demands on faculty (e.g., their available time to dedicate to course design), a lack of support from senior administration, and the challenge of shifting institutional cultures toward a social model of disability (De Los Santos et al., 2019; Singleton et al., 2019).

Faculty often have limited time, competing priorities, and narrow perspectives when it comes to accessibility and inclusivity (Oyarzun et al., 2021; Xie, Gulinna, & Rice, 2021). Some accessibility requirements, such as captioning videos, can be time-consuming and overwhelming (Morris et al., 2016). Participants in this study discussed struggles with requiring and/or supporting faculty to caption their multimedia content when faculty believe they do not have students who require captions or believe that since they never needed captions during their own education, that it was less important. These findings align with previous research demonstrating that some faculty may rely on teaching methods learned from their own educational experiences and struggle to think of diverse learners' needs (Singleton et al., 2019). Research suggests that when faculty embrace the social model of disability that puts a shared onus of accessibility on the curriculum and content creators instead of the individuals, they are more likely to engage with inclusive course design strategies (Ginsberg & Schulte, 2012; Meyer et al., 2014). Training to help faculty see past their own learning experiences can help institutions obtain the necessary faculty buy-in to do this work and seek out assistance from other departments.

The delegation of responsibility remains a persistent barrier to the implementation of accessibility strategies and policies (Linder et al., 2015). While faculty are often ultimately responsible for course content, the results of this study align with previous research in that faculty are content matter experts who may need additional support and training to design accessible and inclusive online learning

(Lowenthal & Lomellini, 2022; Singleton et al., 2019; West et al., 2016; Xie, Gulinna, & Rice, 2021). There is often no designated point person for online accessibility. Instead, responsibilities are split among faculty, instructional designers, and additional offices supporting faculty who operate on different timetables with different priorities (Linder et al., 2015; Mancilla & Frey, 2020). Participants in this study described institutional silos and the paralysis institutions face without a responsible party. Instructional design teams are in a unique position to lead the charge by leveraging their knowledge and skills in this area, their relationships with faculty, and faculty development initiatives (Xie, Gulinna, & Rice, 2021). Participants in this study reported that instructional design teams are doing the work, whether they are officially responsible or not. However, instructional designers also have varying levels of knowledge and commitment to inclusive design strategies (Lowenthal & Lomellini, 2022; Singleton et al., 2019; Xie, Gulinna, & Rice, 2021). Participants in this study emphasized the need to invest in their team's knowledge in this area to continue to be able to meet the needs of diverse online learners.

Additionally, resources including time, money, and staff to assist in this area are generally scarce (Oyarzun et al., 2021). This makes planning and prioritizing accessibility and inclusivity all the more important to create the most effective pathways to removing barriers to student success (Rao, 2021; Tobin & Behling, 2018). It can often be difficult to change longstanding processes and ways of thinking in higher education, including a reliance on a reactive model of accommodations that help individual disabled students but fail to address the underlying barrier (Burgstahler, 2022). Online learning leaders are challenged to help institutions and faculty see the value in proactive models of accessible and inclusive online course design (Seale, 2020).

Strategies to get buy-in and to provide ongoing support

Online learning leaders need to find strategic means to encourage buy-in and provide ongoing support to better serve diverse students in online environments. Based on our results and other studies, leaders and institutions need to advocate for a proactive approach and find ways to recruit buy-in from senior leadership and faculty to continue to advance accessible and inclusive course design initiatives (Seale et al., 2020). However, senior leaders often need to be convinced to make providing accessible and inclusive online course design a priority worth investing in. When speaking with administrators, research suggests appealing to recruitment, retention, and satisfaction (Linder et al., 2015; Tobin & Behling, 2018). Interestingly, participants in this study also leveraged legal requirements and recent litigation in conversations with administrators. The literature tends to suggest shifting the focus away from legal terms and toward more student-centered approaches (Izzo et al., 2008; Tobin & Behling, 2018; Xie & Rice, 2021).

Research suggests reframing accessibility by focusing conversations with faculty on how accessible and inclusive design can help improve learning experiences for all students (Singleton et al., 2019; Xie & Rice, 2021). Aligning with previous research (Izzo et al., 2008), participants in this study found appealing to faculty's desire to improve the student learning experience to be the most effective, especially when senior leadership supported accessible and inclusive course design initiatives (Oyarzun et al., 2021). Strategies from the literature include identifying specific areas for improvement and setting measurable goals in collaboration with instructional designers and other support staff to respect faculty's limited time and experience in this area (Seale et al., 2020; Singleton et al., 2019; Tobin & Behling, 2018). Mirroring previous research (Linder et al., 2015), participants in this study emphasized the importance of making the work doable by suggesting faculty take small, proactive steps towards more inclusive course design.

Research suggests that faculty want training in this area and training can result in increased implementation of accessible and inclusive design strategies in their courses (Dallas et al., 2014; Izzo et al., 2008; Lombardi et al., 2011; Schelly et al., 2011; Wynants & Dennis, 2017). Yet, prior to the COVID-19 pandemic in the spring of 2020, only 17% of institutions had faculty development related to making content accessible (Garrett et al., 2021). Instructional design units have the opportunity to fill this gap with focused, effective faculty development initiatives (Xie, Gulinna, Rice et al., 2021). However, the knowledge and skills of instructional designers can also vary (Lowenthal & Lomellini, 2022; Singleton et al., 2019). Participants in this study relied heavily on one "accessibility guru" in many cases to lead the team and faculty in furthering initiatives in this area. This aligns with previous research demonstrating that instructional designers may be informally taking on this responsibility regardless of their level of training (Linder et al., 2015).

Participants in this study and previous research also emphasized leveraging course design quality assurance programs that include accessibility and inclusivity standards (e.g., Quality Matters) for additional training in this area (Lowenthal et al., 2021). Participants in this study mentioned using accessibility checker tools such as Ally or the Universal Design Online Content Inspection Tool as a means of providing data and starting and guiding conversations with faculty. More research needs to be conducted to determine the effectiveness of such tools on the implementation of accessible course design strategies.

Opportunities for future growth

As institutions become more aware of the importance of accessibility and inclusivity, there is an opportunity to integrate best practices from the start and maintain them in the process of designing online courses (Xie, Gulinna, Rice et al., 2021). Educating administrators and training faculty in this area can help ensure that future content is developed to meet the needs of diverse learners, including those with disabilities (Tobin & Behling, 2018). Once administrators have a better understanding of the importance, there is an opportunity for them to clarify responsibility to streamline effective implementation of the strategies already mentioned (Linder et al., 2015).

Additionally, the lack of utilization of instructional design teams and their consultative role can also hinder institutions' ability to provide online learning that meets the needs of diverse learners (Garrett et al., 2021). Some participants in this study also struggled with whether centralizing instructional design units would provide more control or authority to implement best practices. Regardless, increasing utilization of instructional designers has led to increased engagement and accessibility (Garrett et al., 2021).

Conclusion

This study was limited by self-selection bias, small sample size, and a variety of institutional barriers that may impact strategies to support accessible and inclusive online course design. Another possible limitation could be participants' concerns about social norms and wanting to be seen as doing the "right" thing in terms of addressing the needs of diverse learners. To counter these concerns, the researcher attempted to minimize any perceived judgment by remaining impartial throughout the interviews. The researcher assured participants that their answers were confidential and that their identities would not be compromised.

A better understanding of online learning leaders' perspectives is an important step in national and global initiatives to ensure online courses are accessible to all students (Linder et al., 2015). The results of this study are intended to add to the understanding of challenges, successes, and opportunities for improvement in inclusive online education.

Online learning is full of potential to meet diverse learners' needs, yet it can also be full of barriers. This is especially true for disabled students when online courses are not designed proactively with accessibility and inclusivity in mind. For institutions to rise to the challenge of fully engaging disabled students in online learning, leaders will need to advocate for and implement clear visions accessibility and inclusivity (Burgstahler, 2022). Online learning leaders are in a unique position to advise stakeholders in the creation of policies, responsibilities, and support structures while leading instructional design teams in the implementation of accessible and inclusive online course design practices. However, research in this area is nascent and questions remain about how to effectively address the issues of full inclusion and engagement of disabled students in online higher education.

Disclosure statement

No potential conflict of interest was declared by the authors.

ORCID

Amy Lomellini http://orcid.org/0000-0002-2977-3010
Patrick R. Lowenthal http://orcid.org/0000-0002-9318-1909
Chareen Snelson http://orcid.org/0000-0002-5201-2957
Jesús H. Trespalacios http://orcid.org/0000-0002-3162-3601

References

American Council on Education. (2022). *The Carnegie classification of institutions of higher education: Size & setting classification description.* https://carnegieclassifications.acenet.edu/classification_descriptions/size_setting.php

Anderson, G. (2020, April 6). Accessibility suffers during pandemic. *Inside Higher Ed.* https://www.insidehighered.com/news/2020/04/06/remote-learning-shift-leaves-students-disabilities-behind

Andrews, E. E., & Forber-Pratt, A. J. (2022). Disability culture, identity, and language. In M. L. Wehmeyer, & D. S. Dunn (Eds.), *The positive psychology of personal factors: Implications for understanding disability* (pp. 27–40). Lexington Books. https://lccn.loc.gov/2021044033

Bartz, J. (2020). All inclusive?! Empirical insights into individual experiences of students with disabilities and mental disorders at German universities and implications for inclusive higher education. *Education Sciences, 10*(9), Article 10090223. https://doi.org/10.3390/educsci10090223

Black, R. D., Weinberg, L. A., & Brodwin, M. G. (2015). Universal Design for Learning and instruction: Perspectives of students with disabilities in higher education. *Exceptionality Education International, 25*(2), 1–26. https://doi.org/10.5206/eei.v25i2.7723

Burgstahler, S. (2015). Opening doors or slamming them shut? Online learning practices and students with disabilities. *Social Inclusion, 3*(6), 69–79. https://doi.org/10.17645/si.v3i6.420

Burgstahler, S. (2022). Leveling the playing field for students with disabilities in online opportunities. In M. Bonous-Hammarth (Ed.), *Bridging marginality through inclusive higher education. neighborhoods, communities, and urban marginality* (pp. 235–250). Palgrave Macmillan. https://doi.org/10.1007/978-981-16-8000-7_11

Chenail, R. J. (2012). Conducting qualitative data analysis: Reading line-by-line, but analyzing by meaningful qualitative units. *The Qualitative Report, 17*(1), 266–269. https://nsuworks.nova.edu/tqr/vol17/iss1/12/

Cook, L., Rumrill, P. D., & Tankersley, M. (2009). Priorities and understanding of faculty members regarding college students with disabilities. *International Journal of Teaching and Learning in Higher Education, 21*(1), 84–96. https://www.isetl.org/ijtlhe/pdf/ijtlhe567.pdf

Creswell, J. W., & Poth, C. N. (2018). *Qualitative inquiry and research design: Choosing among five approaches* (4th ed.). SAGE.

Dallas, B. K., Upton, T. D., & Sprong, M. E. (2014). Post-secondary faculty attitudes toward inclusive teaching strategies. *Journal of Rehabilitation, 80*(2), 12–20. https://doi.org/10.9743/JEO.2015.2.1

De Los Santos, S. B., Kupcznski, L., & Mundy, M.-A. (2019). Determining academic success in students with disabilities in higher education. *International Journal of Higher Education, 8*(2), 16–38. https://doi.org/10.5430/ijhe.v8n2p16

Dolmage, J. T. (2017). *Academic ableism: Disability and higher education*. University of Michigan Press. https://doi.org/10.3998/mpub.9708722

Dunn, D. S., & Andrews, E. E. (2015). Person-first and identity-first language: Developing psychologists' cultural competence using disability language. *American Psychologist, 70*(3), 255–264. https://doi.org/10.1037/a0038636

Elliott, V. (2018). Thinking about the coding process in qualitative data analysis. *The Qualitative Report, 23*(11), 2850–2861. https://nsuworks.nova.edu/tqr/vol23/iss11/14/

Fenneberg, L. (2022). Student affairs-academic affairs collaborations to support diverse communities. In M. Bonous-Hammarth (Ed.), *Bridging marginality through inclusive higher education* (pp. 19–41). Palgrave Macmillan. https://doi.org/10.1007/978-981-16-8000-7_2

Fichten, C. S., Ferraro, V., Asuncion, J. V., Chwojka, C., Barile, M., Nguyen, M. N., Klomp, R., & Wolforth, J. (2009). Disabilities and e-learning problems and solutions: An exploratory study. *Educational Technology & Society, 12*(4), 241–256. https://drive.google.com/file/d/1bpOvlrQLZ2D7TRQQqADi-EQ4QZNcfMdj/view

Fornauf, B. S., & Erickson, J. D. (2020). Toward an inclusive pedagogy through universal design for learning in higher education: A review of the literature. *Journal of Postsecondary Education and Disability, 33*(2), 188–199. https://higherlogicdownload.s3.amazonaws.com/AHEAD/38b602f4-ec53-451c-9be0-5c0bf5d27c0a/UploadedImages/JPED/JPED_Vol_33/33_issue_2/JPED_33_2_.pdf

Fowler, F. J., & Cosenza, C. (2009). Design and evaluation of survey questions. In L. Bickman, & D. J. Rog (Eds.), *The SAGE handbook of applied social research methods* (pp. 375–412). SAGE. https://doi.org/10.4135/9781483348858.n12

Garrett, R., Simunich, B., Legon, R., & Fredericksen, E. E.(2021). *CHLOE 6: Online learning leaders adapt for a post-pandemic world*. Quality Matters & Encoura. https://www.qualitymatters.org//sites/default/files/research-docs-pdfs/QM-Eduventures-CHLOE-6-Report-2021.pdf

Gladhart, M. A. (2009). Determining faculty needs for delivering accessible electronically delivered instruction in higher education. *Journal of Postsecondary Education and Disability, 22*(3), 185–196. https://higherlogicdownload.s3.amazonaws.com/AHEAD/38b602f4-ec53-451c-9be0-5c0bf5d27c0a/UploadedImages/JPED_ARCHIVE/22/jped_22_3_export__1_.doc

Ginsberg, S. M., & Schulte, K. (2012). Instructional accommodations: Impact of conventional vs. social constructivist view of disability. *Journal of the Scholarship of Teaching and Learning, 8*(2), 84–91. https://scholarworks.iu.edu/journals/index.php/josotl/article/view/1702

Harris, P. S., Gould, R., & Mullin, C. (2019). *ADA research brief: Higher education and the ADA*. ADA National Network Knowledge Translation Center. https://adata.org/sites/adata.org/files/files/ADA%20Research%20Brief_Higher%20Education%20and%20the%20ADA_FINAL.pdf

Henry, S. L., Abou-Zahra, S., & Brewer, J. (2014). The role of accessibility in a universal web. In *Proceedings of the 11th Web for All Conference* (pp. 1–4). Association for Computer Machinery. https://doi.org/10.1145/2596695.2596719

Izzo, M. V., Murray, A., & Novak, J. (2008). The faculty perspective on universal design for learning. *Journal of Postsecondary Education and Disability, 21*(2), 60–72. https://higherlogicdownload.s3.amazonaws.com/AHEAD/38b602f4-ec53-451c-9be0-5c0bf5d27c0a/UploadedImages/JPED_ARCHIVE/21/JPED_21_2_Text__2_.doc

Kent, M. (2016). *Access and barriers to online education for people with disabilities*. National Center for Student Equity in Higher Education. https://www.ncsehe.edu.au/publications/access-and-barriers-to-online-education-for-people-with-disabilities/

Ketterlin-Geller, L. R., & Johnstone, C. (2006). Accommodations and universal design: Supporting access to assessments in higher education. *Journal of Postsecondary Education and Disability, 19*(2), 163–172. https://higherlogicdownload.s3.amazonaws.com/AHEAD/38b602f4-ec53-451c-9be0-5c0bf5d27c0a/UploadedImages/JPED_ARCHIVE/19-2/JPEDVol19No2.doc

Levicky-Townley, C., Garabedian Stork, M., Zhang, J., & Weatherford, E. (2021). Exploring the impact of Universal Design for Learning supports in an online higher education course. *Journal of Applied Instructional Design, 10*(1). https://doi.org/10.51869/101/clt

Linder, K. E., Fontaine-Rainen, D. L., & Behling, K. (2015). Whose job is it? Key challenges and future directions for online accessibility in US institutions of higher education. *Open Learning, 30*(1), 21–34. https://doi.org/10.1080/02680513.2015.1007859

Lombardi, A., Murray, C., & Gerdes, H. (2011). College faculty and inclusive instruction: Self-reported attitudes and actions pertaining to universal design. *Journal of Diversity in Higher Education, 4*(4), 250–261. https://doi.org/10.1037/a0024961

Lomellini, A., & Lowenthal, P. R. (2022). Inclusive online courses: Universal design for learning strategies for faculty buy-in. In J. E. Stefaniak & R. Reese (Eds.), *The instructional designer's training guide: Authentic practices and considerations for mentoring ID and ed tech professionals* (pp. 101–111). Routledge.

Lowenthal, P. R., & Lomellini, A. (2022). Creating accessible online learning: A preliminary investigation of educational technologists' and faculty's knowledge and skills. *Tech Trends*. https://doi.org/10.1007/s11528-022-00790-1

Lowenthal, P. R., Lomellini, A., Smith, C., & Greer, K. (2021). Accessible online learning: A critical analysis of online quality assurance frameworks. *Quarterly Review of Distance Education, 22*(2), 15–29.

Mancilla, R., & Frey, B. (2020). A model for developing instructional design professionals for higher education through apprenticeship. *The Journal of Applied Instructional Design, 9*(2). https://doi.org/10.51869/92rmbf

McAndrew, P., Farrow, R., & Cooper, M. (2012). Adapting online learning resources for all: Planning for professionalism in accessibility. *Research in Learning Technology, 20*(4), 345–361. https://doi.org/10.3402/rlt.v20i0.18699

Meyer, A., Rose, D. H., & Gordon, D. (2014). *Universal design for learning: Theory and practice.* CAST.

Microsoft. (2016). *Inclusive 101.* https://www.microsoft.com/design/inclusive/

Miles, M. B., Huberman, A. M., & Saldana, J. (2020). *Qualitative data analysis: A methods sourcebook* (4th ed.). SAGE.

Mirick, R. G., & Wladkowski, S. P. (2019). Skype in qualitative interviews: Participant and researcher perspectives. *Qualitative Report, 24*(12), 3061–3072. https://doi.org/10.46743/2160-3715/2019.3632

Morris, K. K., Frechette, C., Dukes, L. III, Stowell, N., Topping, N. E., & Brodosi, D. (2016). Closed captioning matters: Examining the value of closed captions for "all" students. *Journal of Postsecondary Education and Disability, 29*(3), 231–238. http://www.ahead-archive.org/uploads/publications/JPED/jped_29_3/JPED%2029_3_Final%20Doc.pdf

Nieminen, J. H., & Pesonen, H. V. (2020). Taking universal design back to its roots: Perspectives on accessibility and identity in undergraduate mathematics. *Education Sciences, 10*(12). https://doi.org/10.3390/educsci10010012

Oyarzun, B., Bottoms, B. L., & Westine, C. (2021). Adopting and applying the Universal Design for Learning principles in online courses. *Journal of Applied Instructional Design, 10*(1). https://doi.org/10.51869/jaid2021105

Patton, M. Q. (2002). *Qualitative research and evaluation methods* (3rd ed.). Sage.

Rao, K. (2021). Inclusive instructional design: Applying UDL to online learning. *The Journal of Applied Instructional Design, 10*(1). https://doi.org/10.51869/jaid2021104

Roberts, K. D., Park, H. J., Brown, S., & Cook, B. (2011). Universal Design for Instruction in postsecondary education: A systematic review of empirically based articles. *Journal of Postsecondary Education and Disability, 24*(1), 5–15. http://www.ahead-archive.org/uploads/publications/JPED/jped_24_1/JPED%2024_1%20FINAL%20DOCUMENT.pdf

Sarrett, J. C. (2017). Autism and accommodations in higher education: Insights from the Autism community. *Journal of Autism and Developmental Disorders, 48*, 679–693. https://doi.org/10.1007/s10803-017-3353-4

Satterfield, D., Lepage, C., & Ladjahasan, N. (2015). Preferences for online course delivery methods in higher education for students with autism spectrum disorders. *Procedia Manufacturing, 3*, 3651–3656. https://doi.org/10.1016/j.promfg.2015.07.758

Schelly, C. L., Davies, P. L., Spooner, C. L. (2011). Student perceptions of faculty implementation of Universal Design for Learning. *Journal of Postsecondary Education and Disability, 24*(1), 17–30. http://www.ahead-archive.org/uploads/publications/JPED/jped_24_1/JPED%2024_1%20FINAL%20DOCUMENT.pdf

Seale, J. (Ed.). (2020). *Improving accessible digital practices in higher education: Challenges and new practices for inclusion.* Springer Nature. https://doi.org/10.1007/978-3-030-37125-8

Seale, J., Burgstahler, S., & Havel, A. (2020). One model to rule them all, one model to bind them? A critique of the use of accessibility-related models in post-secondary education. *Open Learning, 37*(1), 6–29. doi:https://doi.org/10.1080/02680513.2020.1727320

Singleton, K., Evmenova, A., Jerome, M. K., & Clark, K. (2019). Integrating UDL strategies into the online course development process. *Online Learning, 23*(1), 206–235. https://doi.org/10.24059/olj.v23i1.1407

Tobin, T. J. & Behling, K.T. (2018). *Reach everyone, teach everyone: Universal design for learning in higher education.* West Virginia University Press.

Vivanti, G. (2019). Most appropriate way to talk about individuals with a diagnosis of autism? *Journal of Autism and Developmental Disorders, 50,* 691–693. https://doi.org/10.1007/s10803-019-04280-x

W3C Web Accessibility Initiative. (2022). *Accessibility, usability, and inclusion.* https://www.w3.org/WAI/fundamentals/accessibility-usability-inclusion/

West, E. A., Novak, D., & Mueller, C. (2016). Inclusive instructional practices used and their perceived importance by instructors. *Journal of Postsecondary Education and Disability, 29*(4), 363–374. http://www.ahead-archive.org/uploads/publications/JPED/jped_29_4/JPED29_4_FullDocument.pdf

Westine, C. D., Oyarzun, B., Ahlgrim-Delzell, L., Casto, A., Okraski, C., Park, G., Person, J., & Steele, L. (2019). Familiarity, current use, and interest in Universal Design for Learning among online university instructors. *The International Review of Research in Open and Distributed Learning, 20*(5), 20–41. https://doi.org/10.19173/irrodl.v20i5.4258

World Health Organization. (2011). *World report on disability.* https://www.who.int/publications/i/item/9789241564182

Wynants, S. A, & Dennis, J. M. (2017). Embracing diversity and accessibility: A mixed methods study of the impact of an online disability. *Journal of Postsecondary Education and Disability, 30*(1), 33–48. https://higherlogicdownload.s3.amazonaws.com/AHEAD/38b602f4-ec53-451c-9be0-5c0bf5d27c0a/UploadedImages/JPED/JPED_30_1__Full_Doc.pdf

Xie, J., & Rice, M. F. (2021). Professional and social investment in universal design for learning in higher education: Insights from a faculty development programme. *Journal of Further and Higher Education, 45*(7), 886–900. https://doi.org/10.1080/0309877X.2020.1827372

Xie, J., Gulinna, A., & Rice, M. F. (2021). Instructional designers' roles in emergency remote teaching during COVID-19. *Distance Education, 42*(1), 70–87. https://doi.org/10.1080/01587919.2020.1869526

Xie, J., Gulinna, A., Rice, M. F., & Griswold, D. E. (2021). Instructional designers' shifting thinking about supporting teaching during and post-COVID-19. *Distance Education, 42*(3), 331–351. https://doi.org/10.1080/01587919.2021.1956305

Appendix
Interview questions

The following interview protocol was used during the semi-structured interviews:

1. How long have you been working in the field of instructional design and technology?
2. What is your role at your university?
3. How did you gain the knowledge and skills needed to do your job? (e.g., Do you have a degree or coursework in instructional design and technology?)
4. What does accessible and inclusive online learning mean to you?
5. How would you describe your knowledge and skills on designing accessible and inclusive online? And your team? What about the faculty at your institution?
6. What challenges or barriers do institutions face with providing accessible and inclusive online learning experiences?

7. What strategies is your institution, or other institutions, using to provide accessible and inclusive online courses?
8. Do you think institutions are placing enough emphasis on providing accessible and inclusive online courses? Please explain.
9. Do you think the field, in general, is focused enough on accessible and inclusive online learning?
10. How can leadership improve an institution's ability to deliver accessible and inclusive online learning experiences?
11. Are there any factors that influenced your team's ability to provide accessible and inclusive online learning experiences?
12. Do you have any additional comments?

Serving students with disabilities in K-12 online learning: daily practices of special educators during the COVID-19 pandemic

Allison Starks

ABSTRACT
Online and distance education strategies offer a path for closing opportunity gaps for students with disabilities because of digital technologies' flexibility and capacity for differentiation, but fully online schooling does always guarantee an inclusive education. The COVID-19-induced shift to remote learning highlighted the need for more insight into inclusive practices for students with disabilities in online contexts, especially at the K-12 levels. The present study describes special education teachers' online teaching practices with students with disabilities and the necessary conditions for special educator use of technology in K-12 remote learning. Using in-depth interview ($N = 2\,0$) and survey data with special educators teaching during the COVID-19 pandemic, findings highlight specific strategies special educators use to differentiate instruction as well as innovations in hybrid content experiences and home-school partnerships across K-12 schooling. The practices of special educators teaching in online environments provide insights into how all educators can support learners with or without disabilities in K-12 distance education settings.

Introduction

Online and distance education strategies offer the potential for expanded learning opportunities for students with disabilities (Basham et al., 2020; U.S. Department of Education, 2017) and an increasing number of students with disabilities were enrolling in distance learning (National Center for Education Statistics, 2019) prior to the COVID-19 pandemic. With the shift to emergency remote learning during 2020, students in the United States of America receiving special education (SPED) services were effectively enrolled in online learning overnight. This transition raised significant questions about how students with disabilities would access a free and appropriate education (FAPE) guaranteed under SPED law (*Individuals with Disabilities Education Act*; IDEA, 2004) and special educators' role in facilitating fully online school.

IDEA (2004) was designed to ensure students had access to "a free appropriate public education that emphasizes special education and related services designed to meet their unique needs and prepare them for further education, employment, and independent living" (§ 1400). Given the dominance of digital spaces for the way people live, work, and learn, educators must consider how online learning experiences can provide an inclusive education for diverse students. Given the increasing role of technology in the general curriculum of K-12 schools (Vega & Robb, 2019) and the importance of technology fluency for future employment (World Economic Forum, 2020), opportunities to learn with technology are an important consideration for the legal rights of students with disabilities. However, the rapid shift to remote learning underscored how unprepared many schools in the United States of America were to provide FAPE in fully online settings, when some school districts opted not to provide instruction to all students because they doubted their ability to meet the needs of SPED students in online environments (Jones, 2020; Preston, 2020).

Emerging research from the pandemic-induced phases of remote learning suggest that SPED teachers attempted to provide accessible learning opportunities, access to peers, and consistent communication with families of students with disabilities but they also experienced significant challenges (Hirsch et al., 2021; M. F. Rice, 2022). Teachers reported declines in accommodations for students in online settings (Myers et al., 2021), and students received fewer service minutes during emergency remote learning compared to previous years, on average (U.S. Government Accountability, 2020). Although schools in the United States of America are no longer fully remote, many schools have continued to offer blended learning opportunities, and a number of students with disabilities are turning to online schools because traditional schooling does not sufficiently meet their needs (Ortiz et al., 2021). Thus, it is crucial to understand how practitioners can provide FAPE in online settings and ensure students' rights under IDEA (2004) are met. Scholars have called for all individualized education plans to consider digital contexts and make plans for how students with disabilities will access FAPE across digital modalities in the event of school closures or a student need to engage in remote learning for a period of time (M. F. Rice & Pazey, 2022). In order to plan for and provide FAPE in a digital age, it is helpful to understand the promising practices of special educators providing services in fully remote settings during the COVID-19 pandemic. Thus, rich descriptions of how special educators worked to provide accessible learning opportunities during fully online learning offer ideas for future accommodations, practices, and provisions in SPED.

The COVID-19 pandemic and shift to remote learning required many educators to adapt their teaching practices for online environments, and SPED teachers in particular experienced a sharp increase in workload in order to continue providing FAPE in online learning environments (M. F. Rice, 2022). Special educators needed to adapt their practices overnight, which was a significant task. However, there is also reason to think that SPED teachers in particular had a unique capacity for innovating in online environments due to their experience differentiating instruction based on diverse student needs and with adaptive technologies (Courduff et al., 2016).

This study documents how special educators adapted their teaching practices for online education in an attempt to fulfill the promise of FAPE for their students and created new digitally-mediated practices to meet the various needs of students with disabilities in K-12 schools during emergency remote learning. The practices and innovations of these special educators provide insights into how educators can support all learners in K-12 distance education settings. Facilitating conditions for meeting diverse needs of students in online learning are identified and underscored as important foundations for inclusive education.

Problems with distance education and online learning for students with disabilities

Distance education can be defined multiple ways, but it is largely understood to be learning and instruction that is planned, that may occur asynchronously or synchronously, and where the teacher and student are not geographically together (K. Rice, 2006). The terms *distance education*, *online learning*, and *virtual learning* appear in the review of prior research though I acknowledge the field's work to differentiate among these terms and the uniqueness of pandemic induced online teaching (Hodges et al., 2020). Because of the debate over whether distance education requires the use of technology, the terms *online learning* or *remote learning* will be used throughout this text.

Online learning and distance education were growing in popularity especially among students with diverse learning needs before the COVID-19-induced shift to online learning (Vasquez & Serianni, 2012). Parents of students with disabilities report enrolling in fully online learning in order to provide better learning opportunities for their students than traditional school, but research suggests that online schools do not always meet the standards of a FAPE as guaranteed by SPED law (Ortiz et al., 2021). Prior research outlines the potential and promise of technology to meet the diverse needs of learners, but little research exists describing the specifics of day to day instruction in online learning (Basham et al., 2015). One exception is a recent in-depth study of four teachers serving students with special needs which described how teachers used technologies during fully online learning to provide expanded access to the curriculum and to build relationships with students and families, but these teachers also reported needing more time, decision-making power, and training to continue using digital technologies (M. F. Rice, 2022). As more research is published from the pandemic era of online schooling, researchers are calling for more studies that explore how teachers find and use technologies to serve students with diverse learning needs (M. F. Rice, 2022). Scholars also call for more research into how to support students with disabilities' academic skills development such as reading (e.g., decoding texts, reading comprehension) in distance education (Vasquez & Serianni, 2012).

Although these gaps about best practice in online learning are still being explored, research points to which environmental elements create barriers to inclusive distance education including lack of specific online teaching strategies, insufficient teacher training, inaccessible digital content, and lack of home-school partnerships.

Lack of specific online teaching strategies

Educational technologies often provide options for differentiating the content, process, or product of learning (Hall et al., 2003). However, educators in online settings have repeatedly called for more guidance on how to use technology to meet the needs of students with disabilities (Basham et al., 2015). Prior research in distance education points to best practices in online course design for students with disabilities including text differentiation for different levels of readers and user-friendly supports for changing elements of online courses (M. F. Rice & Deshler, 2018), while experts recommend providing multiple ways to engage the learners and designing with universal design for learning (UDL) in mind (Lewis, 2021). However, it is unclear what specific online teaching strategies or tools special educators use in the daily practice of online teaching and how these strategies function to meet the needs of students with disabilities.

Lack of teacher training

Teacher training is a persistent problem for inclusive distance education (Kocdar & Bozkurt, 2022). A survey of online teachers found that 64% wanted more training in teaching students with disabilities in online formats, and 1 in 4 new online teachers did not receive any training at all for teaching online (Dawley et al., 2010). Most educators serving in online learning formats do not know what best practice looks like for students with disabilities (Cavanaugh et al., 2013) and have asked for more information on specific teaching strategies such as how to incorporate UDL frameworks into their instruction (Burgstahler, 2015). Research to date has not documented whether SPED teachers experience teacher training as a barrier to facilitating online learning in the same ways as general educators.

Inaccessible digital content

Digital environments are largely not designed with the needs of diverse users in mind (Alper & Goggin, 2017) to the point that the design of the technology itself can be a barrier to learning (Kocdar & Bozkurt, 2022). Prior research into online learning in higher education shows that educators usually try to retrofit content and instruction to a students' needs rather than planning with accessibility in mind from the beginning (Barnard-Brak & Sulak, 2010; Seale, 2014). A recent analysis of SPED guidance during the COVID-19 pandemic highlighted the need for more accessible digital content in K-12 schools and more informed decision making about purchasing (M. F. Rice & Pazey, 2022). Because students with disabilities are not considered in the design of online learning experiences, diverse students can find aspects of digital learning to be inaccessible (Burgstahler, 2015).

Weak home-school partnerships

Families of students with disabilities often report poor home-school communication and that school-driven efforts to use technology for communication do not always consider nondominant perspectives (Noguerón-Liu, 2017; Spann et al., 2003). These home-school partnerships are important for online learning because prior research suggests parental involvement in a student's virtual learning is predictive of student achievement (Black, 2009) and good parental support helps students stay organized and consistent with their virtual learning (K. Rice, 2006). It is unclear how teachers in online learning go about involving families with student learning, and how these home-school partnerships may be unique for students with disabilities.

UDL and the promise of online learning for students with disabilities

UDL is a conceptual framework for teaching and learning that emphasizes reducing barriers for learning. The UDL framework has three main principles: (1) multiple means of engagement in the learning process, (2) multiple ways of accessing and understanding information, and (3) multiple ways for students to show what they know and interact with learning partners (CAST, 2018). Because UDL emphasizes designing learning experiences with built in flexibility and adaptations, it has been endorsed as a helpful framework for integrating technology and creating online learning opportunities for students that are "born accessible" (Basham et al., 2020; U.S. Department of Education, 2017).

Digital technologies can help tailor instruction to diverse student needs. Learning opportunities expand for traditionally marginalized students when technology is integrated with curriculum in purposeful ways (e.g., UDL framework) (Ciampa, 2017; Margalit & Raskind, 2009) because students have access to more personalized learning opportunities. Technology integration offers potential for increased accessibility, differentiation, and collaboration (Edyburn, 2013; Smith & Okolo, 2010), and recent survey data suggests that special educators are eager to leverage this potential (Gallup, 2019). However, not much is known about how teachers use technology or principles of UDL in their day-to-day virtual instruction to meet the needs of students with dis- abilities (Burgstahler, 2015).

The present study documents special educators' innovations and practices during emergency remote learning, at a time when the majority of educators across the United States of America were forced into using digital technologies to facilitate student learning. Because K-12 special educators are trained in differentiating instruction, they were well positioned to leverage the potential of technology in new ways. These insights into on-the-ground experiences in K-12 distance education provide much needed detail on teachers' inclusive practices and facilitating conditions necessary for inclusion distance education.

Materials and methods

This study explores how special educators used technology to meet the needs of students with disabilities during periods of remote learning. In light of established research gaps, the present inquiry seeks to describe online teaching practices, how practices align (or not) with UDL and the necessary conditions for special educator use of technology in remote learning. These findings highlight potential strategies and facilitating conditions for accessible online learning for all students, especially students with diverse learning needs. Thus, the present study asks:

1. How did SPED teachers meet the needs of students with disabilities during remote learning?

2. What practices did SPED teachers use to meet diverse learning needs?
3. How did SPED teacher practices align with the UDL framework?
4. What conditions facilitated SPED teacher use of technology for inclusive remote learning?

A multiple case-study research design was used with semi-structured individual video-chat interviews ($N = 20$) lasting between 45 to 60 minutes, followed with teacher surveys ($N = 18$). Thematic coding and cross-case analysis was used to understand the practices of SPED teachers as well as the various conditions that facilitated SPED teacher use of technology. Prior research on special educators' practices with technology is limited and largely survey based (see Gallup, 2019). Rich descriptions of special educators' practices and innovations during remote learning, along with cross-case analysis, can expand understanding of how SPED teachers used technology to facilitate student learning opportunities.

Role of the researcher

The focus of this study was informed by my 10-year experience as both a SPED and general education classroom teacher and district technology coach. My prior experience integrating technology in K-12 contexts informed the shape of the protocols and the explicit focus on SPED.

Participant recruitment and selection

Twenty SPED teachers were recruited through professional networks and professional development sessions I taught through a state university during summer 2020, which skewed the sample toward participants teaching in California. Only full-time, lead (e.g., not paraprofessionals or student teachers) SPED teachers working in K-12 public schools in the United States of America that were normally held in person were eligible. Participants' primary role included case management and instruction (e.g., not coordinators or instructional coaches), with caseloads of students who qualified for SPED services. Eligible participants were emailed the study information sheet with details on confidentiality, data security, and study risks and benefits. SPED teachers were interviewed between May and September 2020 and given a $20 gift card.

Study participants

Participants included special educators working full time at K-12 public schools across five states (California, New Jersey, Virginia, Massachusetts, Texas). Almost all special educators had advanced degrees in SPED or were pursuing an advanced degree. Most teachers ($n = 14$) worked as inclusion or collaborating teachers, with the remaining teachers ($n = 6$) working in self-contained settings. The sample was evenly split between teachers serving elementary and secondary students (see Table 1), and the sample skewed toward schools with higher concentrations of free and reduced lunch (FARL) populations, with 11 teachers reporting between 50% and 100% FARL.

Table 1. Participant demographics.

Participant	Grade level	SPED role	FARL school %	State	Education	Years teaching
Olivia	K–5	Resource teacher & collaborating/inclusion teacher	0–25	NJ	(missing)	(missing)
Isabelle	K–5	Resource teacher & collaborating/inclusion teacher	75–100	MA	MA	5
Tina	K–5	Resource teacher & collaborating/inclusion teacher	0–25	CA	MA	20
Evelyn	K–5	Resource teacher & collaborating/inclusion teacher	75–100	CA	MA	25
Viola	K–5	Resource teacher & collaborating/inclusion teacher	75–100	CA	MA	17
Teresa	K–5	Self-contained/ special day class teacher	50–75	CA	BA (enrolled in MA)	(missing)
Noelle	K–5	Resource teacher & collaborating/inclusion teacher	25–50	MA	MA	5
Sofia	K–5	Self-contained/special day class teacher	75–100	CA	BA (enrolled in MA)	2
Diane	K–5	Resource teacher & collaborating/inclusion teacher	50–75	TX	MA	19
Emma	6–8	Collaborating/inclusion teacher	50–75	VA	MA	10
Louise	6–8	Collaborating/inclusion teacher	75–100	MA	MA	6
Laura	6–8	Collaborating/inclusion teacher	50–75	VA	MA	17
Clare	6–8	Self-contained/directed teacher	0–25	VA	MA	3
Amelia	6–8	Self-contained/directed teacher	0–25	CA	MA	2
Elizabeth	6–8	Collaborating/inclusion teacher	75–100	CA	MA	19
Ellen	9–12	Collaborating/inclusion teacher	25–50	CA	MA	10
Bryan	9–12	Self-contained/directed teacher	75–100	CA	BA	8
Sarah	9–12	Resource teacher & collaborating/inclusion teacher	25–50	CA	MA	28
Jonathan	9–12	Self-contained/directed teacher	25–50	CA	MA	8
Harper	9–12	Collaborating/inclusion teacher	75–100	CA	MA	14

Note. All names listed are pseudonyms. FARL = free and reduced lunch; NJ = New Jersey; MA = Massachusetts; CA = California; TX = Texas; VA = Virginia, BA = bachelor's degree, MA = master's degree.

Data collection and analysis

I conducted semi-structured interviews through Zoom which were automatically transcribed using the Otter.ai plug-in. Then I verified transcripts for accuracy. Interviews had three main sections and began with informed consent, information about confidentiality, and participant rights (see Appendix A). The first section of the interview centered on general demographic and belief information (e.g., special educator role, population served, general beliefs about technology), with remaining sections focused on technology resources and teaching practices both before and during the COVID-19 pandemic.

Interviews were analyzed using first-cycle and second-cycle coding methods (Saldaña, 2016) During first-cycle coding, descriptive, in-vivo, and process codes were used to analyze interview transcripts inductively with MAXQDA software. Deductive coding was also used, drawing upon a list of possible codes from an initial literature review on teacher technology integration, barriers to technology integration, and SPED technology use. Codebook development occurred alongside continued data collection, creating an iterative process (see Appendix B for code list).

I sought to improve trustworthiness through triangulation of interview findings with survey data, member checks, multiple cases to allow for comparisons, thick description to provide context, reflective and thematic memoing, and an interrater check using a second coder. Follow-up survey data provided important information for special educators' teaching context, beliefs about technology and SPED, and perceived barriers and enablers for online instruction. I conducted all coding but used two different peer review processes to establish reliability. I used a doctoral-level qualitative course working group to provide feedback on codebook development and shared pieces of anonymous transcripts with colleagues for open-ended coding to speak to validity of interpretations. To ensure dependability of findings, I used a second coder to code a random selection of 15% of interviews to yield interrater reliabilities of 92% across codes. I completed reflective memos following interviews in order to make observations, record insights and to reflect on the content of participants' interviews. These memos were used to inform coding and assess trustworthiness of later findings.

Second-cycle coding began when I coded the rest of the interviews and developed categories, themes, and concepts related to SPED teacher practices and the barriers and enablers for SPED teachers' use of technology with students. After the last interview, a subset of coded interviews was used to further revise and refine the codebook. Data from the follow-up teacher survey about teachers' perceived barriers for technology use and technology practices during the COVID-19 pandemic helped contextualize interview data.

The follow-up survey was emailed to participants immediately after the interview and asked about demographics, attitudes and beliefs about technology, technology use during the pandemic for teaching, confidence using technology, and teaching philosophy. Measures were based on previous literature related to technology integration, including the Perceived Affordances & Barriers of Technology (Blackwell et al., 2014), Technology Barrier Scale (Brush et al., 2008), Confidence Using Technology

(Hogarty et al., 2003), and the Teaching Philosophy subscale from Teaching, Learning, and Computing Survey (Becker, 2001).

Results

Special educators used a variety of strategies to provide accessible learning experiences for students with disabilities and to promote progress in the curriculum. Many of these strategies aligned with UDL in digital environments (see Table 2). At the same time, teachers also used digital technologies in ways that do not fit neatly into the UDL framework. One of the most widely reported and successful strategies for supporting student distance learning was strengthening home-school partnerships. Teachers used a variety of methods to communicate in more equitable and accessible ways with families, harnessing the power of digital technologies to include families in student learning experiences across the virtual school and physical home context. However, it is unclear how family partnerships factor into the design of learning environments using a UDL approach. Additionally, some SPED teachers recognized the limitations of 2D screen media alone to meet learner needs and used creative methods for creating hybrid physical and virtual learning experiences. This kind of innovation points to the problems with assuming technology can be used to facilitate learning for the widest variety of learners in all circumstances.

1. Differentiating engagement, access, and expression

Using digital technologies, special educators provided multiple pathways for students to engage with learning, access content, and show what they know. A list of these strategies for differentiation are included in Table 2.

Screencasting

SPED teachers used screencasting as a result of the shift to distance learning. Screencasting is a digital video recording of a computer screen that typically includes audio narration. SPED teachers recorded screencasts to show how to do something, to scaffold literacy experiences (e.g., digital read-aloud), and to support student organization. As a response to students' struggle with material Elizabeth reported, "doing a Screencastify and then sending that to them, then asking if they have any questions about that".

Special educators recorded screencasts for both students and family members to use. As Amelia described:

> I did a lot of like how-to videos for like when I made one specifically for one parent, because she's like, I don't know what I'm doing. And she didn't speak English as her first language... She was like, I need help. And so I made a video for her like this is how you check so and so's grade. And this is where you go, like if you need help with x y and z. These are the steps to get there.

Teachers also used screencasts as a way to provide audio information alongside the visual text of reading activities (see Table 2). Noelle created digital read alouds using screencasting and her videos were shared with each student in fifth grade rather than

Table 2. SPED teacher practices during remote learning and associated affordances.

Strategy	Description of teacher practices	Exemplar quote	What it does for students and/or families
Screencasting	Teachers record themselves to support learning. Uses varied including as how-to guides, read aloud, weekly update/overview of the course for students and parents, showing how to navigate to resources, think aloud/ talk aloud for academic activity, training parent digital training (how to support student academically in distance learning environment)	"So I recorded myself a lot on Screencastify … some of my students had trouble reading and decoding words, so I would record myself reading that ahead of time so that students could click on it and see the words as they're going." (Noelle)	Multiple representations for content (audio, video, sometimes text) Fosters digital literacy Encourages family support for student distance learning Makes thinking visible Expanded access: Asynchronous access to how-to, teacher information—can replay as much as needed
Online games for fluency and skills practice	Teachers used online games to provide multiple opportunities for skills practice (fluency) and to monitor student understanding/ personalize learning	"You could get instant feedback when you check for understanding using a Kahoot program where you're gauging how well they understand something." (Ellen)	Multiple ways to engage Checks for understanding, feedback to student, feedback to teacher (Kahoot) Excites learners Fluency practice
Customizing reading experiences	Teachers use technology to customize reading experiences Exchanging reading levels of texts, providing audio for texts, providing wide array of digital book choices, using built in reading comprehension quizzes to shape instruction	"And like a reading site like Newsela, I can have like five students reading the same article at different Lexile levels, and then like just with you learn like it's really great to be, I think technology, especially with like modifications, with being able to like modify and like differentiate is really amazing." (Harper)	Multiple ways to express Graduated levels of support Multiple ways to represent Supports decoding text and translation, customized display of information
Expanding expression in digital writing	Teachers used digital technologies to facilitate written expression in distance education by teaching students how to use various accessibility features (voice typing, speech to text), encouraging multiple drafting strategies, and to scaffold student writing skills through immediate teacher feedback.	"Some of my really reluctant writers, I'm thinking of one kiddo, in particular, who really his fine motor skills are so weak but he is such a smarty pants and his brain is really moving faster than his hands can do it and I often let him do the talking into the computer and that's been a good piece for him." (Olivia)	Multiple ways to express Access to assistive technology Various methods for communication Multiple ways to engage Feedback loops
Explicit teaching accessibility tools	Teachers (because of pandemic) prompted to teach explicitly how to use accessibility features like text to speech, speech to text, translation services	"Teaching them how to use like the text to speech extensions on on Chrome and then the translation because we have a lot of ELs." (Harper)	Multiple ways to express Access to assistive technology

just her caseload students, underscoring the ways that UDL can serve broader populations. Some teachers used screencasts to help students mentally organize, as Amelia explained: "I give them videos like, Hi everybody it's Friday and this is what we're going to be doing."

Online games for fluency and skills practice

Several special educators used online games during distance learning in order to gather feedback about student learning progress and to provide multiple opportunities for skills practice. Ellen used gaming platforms to inform her next instructional steps as described in Table 2. Feedback went to both teachers and students, where teachers gauged student progress through student performance and students received instant feedback through their progress in the game. Isabelle described her favorite math skills game to use with students saying:

> It had a very interactive feel. A lot of my students really struggle with fluency. And so one of my favorite things to do was they have a lot of fluency games like multiplication games that are racing games. My kids loved that, they had a great time … And they have all kinds of skills on this platform I actually never knew existed until the pandemic. And I actually think if we went back to face to face teaching next year, instead of doing worksheets and multiplication facts, I think it'd be way more fun and engaging for the students to play a racing game with me again.

Isabelle used an educational game purposefully to provide the fluency practice her students needed. Across the special educators who used educational gaming platforms, participants consistently pointed to the need for interactivity, immediate feedback, automatically leveled experiences, and appeal to students as features of a high-quality game for learning.

Customizing access to reading experiences

SPED teachers used the multiple modalities of digital technologies (e.g., visual, audio) and the built in features of various reading applications to meet the needs of students with diverse learning needs. Multiple SPED teachers started using reading applications with large digital libraries of high interest student texts during remote learning. These digital texts provided accessibility features such as built-in ways to change the reading level, picture dictionaries, text to speech, audiobooks, and translation services. Special educators felt that differentiated reading technologies opened up access to literacy in new ways. Olivia described her use of a reading application called EPIC! by saying:

> I also signed everybody up for EPIC! … And some of my students are like reading machines now. I mean because they can listen, they can read it and they have access to so many different books. It's incredible. I'm like, so thankful for it because I feel like you can't go to the public library.

Some special educators reported that their schools paid for subscriptions to various reading applications (e.g. EPIC! Books, RazKids, Lexia Core5) as a result of the shift to distance learning while others lamented the lack of sufficient software applications. As Olivia pointed out, these programs can provide personalized access to books that are available at a child's reading level, regardless of their ability to physically go to the library.

Expanded expression in digital writing

Special educators used technology to facilitate written expression by explicitly teaching students about accessibility features (e.g., voice-typing, speech-to-text) and modeling how to use them, encouraging multiple drafting strategies, and scaffolding student writing skills through immediate teacher feedback. Harper started teaching both SPED and general education students how to use speech-to-text tools and voice-typing in Google Docs with positive results, saying, "And I find that that's helped our students increase their amount or quantity of what they write because it's easier for them to say it. And it doesn't get stuck, you know in their fingers and stuff. So that's been really helpful." According to Olivia, younger students experience these benefits as well (see Table 2).

Multiple teachers talked about the affordances of collaborative word processing applications that allows for real time editing with multiple users to provide more timely and frequent writing feedback. Louise said, "We use Google Docs a lot ... which I really like because then I can then go in and watch them type and be providing feedback, like in the moment." Collaborative writing tools allowed Tina to give feedback asynchronously and monitor a student's writing progress across contexts:

> If it's something simple I can just highlight and type a little comment to them while they're with me. But for the most part it works because when they go back to their classrooms, I still have access to what they're working on. I can check in later and see what they did. And if they followed the direction, how much more they got, and I can make comments that they can then check, and then they can resolve whatever it is that I've suggested or comment back to me or whatever it is that you know needs to be done. And they don't have to be with me for us to have that interaction.

SPED teachers valued these kinds of opportunities to give writing feedback as a way to build students' writing fluency and skills.

Explicit teaching accessibility tools

The shift to distance learning prompted many SPED teachers in the sample to embrace digital accessibility tools and explicitly teach students how to use various accessibility tools including speech-to-text, text-to-speech, and translation services. Some special educators had introduced accessibility tools prior to distance learning, however many of them had not. As Diane noted, "Before this year, though, I really didn't use speech to text much."

Of the teachers that introduced accessibility tools to students before the pandemic, some reported student reluctance to use them during in-person instruction. Teachers believed students with disabilities felt singled out when using assistive technologies in front of their peers. However, the digital environment offered a different opportunity to use these technologies, especially when tools were introduced to the entire class. SPED teachers talked about how educators often assume students know how to use these tools or are motivated to do so, but a better practice is to explicitly teach how to use accessibility tools without assuming a prior digital literacy. It is also helpful for teachers to model use of these tools so students can understand their utility.

2. Physical manipulatives and virtual instruction

Although SPED teachers employed digital technologies to meet the needs of students with disabilities, some reported technology to be insufficient and explained how students needed a physical component alongside digital instruction. One in four teachers talked about how they made physical artifacts available to students in order to facilitate distance learning, while three additional teachers talked about their students' unfulfilled need for physical manipulatives or learning artifacts. Part of SPED teachers' innovation in distance education is in recognizing the limits of digital technology to meet all the needs of diverse learners.

Diane explained the limits of relying on virtual resources alone for the students she worked with:

> I think with the kids that I have, they definitely need the visual, they need the chart, they need to hold it in their hand, and they need to be able to manipulate it so they can see it ... And so, what I've had to do is I made bags for them, so they could take base 10 blocks home, so they could have it in charts and so forth ... so they are not fully 100% online without anything in their hands.

Multiple teachers created bags or kits that included physical manipulatives (e.g., magnetic letters, whiteboards, base 10 blocks, dice). SPED teachers felt these resources were crucial for students' learning because the physical items provided a chance to manipulate 3D objects to learn new things, to show what they know, to practice a skill, or to get feedback. Viola shared how she immediately recognized the needs of her students and distributed bags to each of her students' homes:

> So when we officially moved over to distance learning. I was just like there's no way I could do everything on screen. My kids need to physically have things. So I went around mask on, gloves on. I dropped off bags of stuff at each of their doorsteps. So, when we were reading a book they all had the book ... I use magnetic boards and letters and tiles and I also do Words Their Way, the cutting and sorting. I threw glue sticks, scissors and the stuff into a bag ... so that all my students have their resources in a bag and I could reference it, like 'okay guys, take out your magnetic board and follow what's on screen'.

Some teachers reported that simply providing a physical packet or workbook helped students engage with virtual instruction and reduce distraction. Students who had the physical workbook or paper packet did not need to use multiple tabs to work with a teacher and look at materials on the same screen. Emma explained how this works in real time:

> So if I'm zooming with a student, it's really hard for me to tell them how to pull up their Google Doc on one side, keep me on the other side or share. I'm going to share my screen now you don't see me or you or whatever, or you share your screen and now I can see yours. The amount of steps that it takes now to use the technology to get to that content [is] really difficult. So I have a lot of students that are wanting me to send paper pencil because they can then have their paper pencil in front of them. And we can zoom chat like we're together.

3. Leveraging smartphones for inclusive home-school partnerships

The affordances of a smartphone allows for teachers to partner with families to promote student learning in three main ways. First, smartphones allowed expanded parental involvement in a student's learning. Jonathan shared what this looked like in his virtual class:

> I make the parents do videos of their kids cooking breakfast, making lunch, going shopping. So the parents will text it to me, and then I can show it to the class. And that's been fun, because kids love to see themselves. And then the parents are getting kind of into it now. So now they're getting a little cool with their editing and lighting. And it's kind of fun.

Second, smartphones facilitated parent digital literacy development. SPED teachers reported using mobile technology to walk parents through accessing the correct platforms and digital spaces, which parents could then turn around and teach their child.

Third, the majority of participants talked about the unique power of texting to build partnerships between educators and students' family members throughout distance education. Many SPED teachers started using text messaging because it was a faster and more accessible method to communicate with families. Text messaging allowed families more time in crafting a response and did not require access to email or high speed internet. Viola described how texting was a "lifesaver" because phones were "the one piece of technology every household had, every parent had some kind of cell phone, smartphone, old iPhone or the newest iPhone". Clare explained further "there are just certain families that I couldn't get in touch with over the phone or email, but they would respond to my text in 30 seconds."

Prior to remote learning, many teachers relied on email to communicate with families. However, corresponding through email often required access to a desktop computer or laptop and high speed internet which were not available to all families. Laura explained:

> There were some families that didn't have an email address listed but they had a phone number. And so I would try texting first because I assumed it was a cell phone number … And yeah so it just came out of the fact that I didn't hear from them any other way.

In this way, text messaging offered more equitable opportunities for home-school partnerships across family resource levels.

The shift to remote learning prompted many special educators to reconsider their communication methods in light of their own assumptions about families. Clare described this process:

> Well, I, I think that just understanding that not everybody has access to email or internet or feels comfortable speaking over the phone was … a cultural thing that I did not, or an assumption, that I did not realize that I had been making about the families that I was working with.

Texting was preferable to voice phone calls as well. As Emma explained, "most of the time parents would much prefer to construct a response on their own time than be inundated with a phone call that they answer and then they don't know how to sort of process or what to say."

Text messaging was more inclusive for linguistically diverse families. Viola explained, "the parents who didn't speak a lot of English, when I texted in English, … they were able at least to show that to their own child or an older somebody in that household, and be like yeah the teacher wrote this." Texting allowed monolingual teachers to reach out to linguistically diverse families as Louise explained: "so texting is great because you can use Google Translate. And so I could translate what I want to say into Spanish, then translate their response back into English."

Facilitating conditions
Teachers talked about how certain conditions facilitated the use of technology to support students with diverse learning needs. These conditions consited of (1) student access to resources including devices, high-speed internet, digital literacy training, and accessible software, (2) technology infrastructure, (3) the ability to communicate with students and families, and (4) teacher technology training.

Though participants discussed the innovations and workarounds they used to support student learning in depth, they also reported various barriers to using technology for online learning.

Access to student resources
The majority of special educators reported that students did not have enough access to devices (61%) and home high-speed internet (89%). All special educators (100%) reported that student digital literacy skills were a barrier to remote learning. Almost half of all special educators (44%) reported insufficient or inaccessible software for students with disabilities.

Technology infrastructure
Half of all teachers (50%) reported issues with the reliability of technology for teaching and a lack of technology support. Teachers' responses point to the need for more technical and infrastructure support during remote learning.

Ability to communicate with families
Almost all teachers (89%) reported that their inability to communicate with students and their families presented a barrier to working with students during remote learning. Some special educators had success with contacting families and many found more inclusive ways to reach families during the shift to remote learning. However, the majority of SPED teachers in the sample expressed the need for more consistent and inclusive ways for schools to maintain partnerships with students and families around student learning.

Teacher training
Teachers expressed the need for more teacher education and time to learn about technology. The majority of teachers (67%) said lack of time to learn technology was a barrier to using technology with students, while 56% felt that they did not have enough training with technology. Often, teachers felt unprepared to integrate technology in ways that met the needs of diverse learners. SPED teachers talked about the need for explicit training in using technology to support students with diverse learning needs. When schools were able to provide this training or the conditions to facilitate collaborative learning among teachers themselves, teachers were able to innovate in new ways.

Discussion

With the increased uptake of online learning across K-12 environments, it is important to understand how educators can provide a free and appropriate education for students with disabilities. Research does not adequately address the actual practices special educators use with digital technologies in order to meet the needs of students with disabilities and how these practices might vary based on teachers' identities and teaching contexts (Carnahan & Fulton, 2013; M. F. Rice, 2022). The present study speaks to this important gap by describing the ways special educators (1) differentiated engagement, access and expression (2) offered hybrid physical and virtual learning experiences, and (3) created more inclusive home–school partnerships during remote learning. The rich description of special educator practices in online learning offers examples of learning opportunities that provide access to the general education curriculum and supports for academic progress. Facilitating conditions for inclusive education described here underscore the importance of inclusive decision making at the institutional level, rather than depending on the technology alone to meet the standards for FAPE in online settings. Special educators' reports of barriers to online instruction help to identify areas of improvement for K-12 settings.

Pandemic-induced shifts to inclusive online practices

SPED teachers used the built in flexibility of digital technologies to change the content, process or product of learning for students with disabilities. Teachers reported increased student access to learning when using screencasting, online gaming for fluency and feedback, customized reading experiences, scaffolded digital writing, and by explicitly teaching accessibility tools. These strategies removed barriers to student online learning by providing multiple forms of content presentation (e.g. audio, visual, tactile), scaffolded learning experiences (e.g., changing reading level, leveled skills practice), and various ways to express understanding (e.g., speech-to-text). Many of these methods promoted feedback loops between teacher and student, such as the use of collaborative writing software, online games, and built in reading checks within literacy applications. Notably, the majority of special educators reported shifts in their practice due to the reliance on remote learning. Many teachers began using digital technologies in ways that reflect updated notions of FAPE in the digital age such as explicitly teaching speech-to-text and text-to-speech tools, using technologies to provide faster and more specific feedback, and providing personalized content such as leveled reading. These are potential practices for ensuring students with disabilities have access to online learning opportunities similar to their general education peers.

Teachers recognized the limitations of online learning and provided physical manipulatives to students in order to create expanded learning opportunities. Multiple educators created physical material sets and distributed them to students with learning differences. Teachers felt these physical artifacts were necessary to meet the needs of their students.

Creating and maintaining partnerships with families was one of the most important inclusive practices for online learning according to SPED teachers. SPED teachers used technology to meet the various linguistic, cultural and economic needs of families, which helped them meet their legal obligations for communicating with students' families. Teachers recognized the limitations of relying on email to reach all families and instead employed texting to communicate, which allowed families to communicate with educators regardless of home technology access (desktop, high-speed internet), gave families time to craft responses, and allowed for families who speak multiple languages to communicate more easily. Similar to other accounts of parents' strengths when it comes to online learning and students with disabilities (M. F. Rice & Ortiz, 2021), special educators in this study considered home-school partnerships as crucial for serving students with disabilities in remote learning and that schools could be doing more to ensure consistent and inclusive communication with families. Strong home-school relationships allowed family members to supervise learning at home, expand learning experiences across home and school contexts and to connect learning to day to day family life. These methods represent a move toward strengths-based parental involvement strategies and away from deficit narratives about students with disabilities and their families.

Findings both affirm and challenge the utility of UDL as a framework for designing online learning experiences. Educators used technology in ways that aligned with UDL, but they also employed practices that did not fit neatly into the established UDL framework. Although UDL is often endorsed in educational technology, the present findings suggest that technology has limitations and at times is insufficient for meeting the needs of diverse learners. UDL focuses on removing barriers for learning at the student level, but it is unclear where families fit into the UDL framework. Because students most likely engage in virtual learning within the home context, it is important to articulate where families fit into UDL and what it looks like to remove barriers to learning at the family level, wherein a student experience is nested.

Barriers to inclusive online learning

Teachers talked about what conditions helped meet the needs of students with disabilities in online learning and what got in the way. Interview and survey data pointed to four main barriers to inclusive online learning including lack of (1) student access to resources including devices, high-speed internet, digital literacy training, and appropriate software, (2) technology infrastructure, (3) the ability to communicate with students and families, and (4) teacher technology training. These barriers manifest largely at the institutional level, where schools or districts make decisions about resource allocation, investments in technology infrastructure, teacher training, and home-school communication practices. Teachers who did not have institutional supports found short-term work arounds such as teaching themselves how to use technology or diverging from established home-school communication practices (e.g., email), but these practices would be more effective if adopted and supported at the institutional level.

Findings are consistent with previous research related to online learning as well as emerging research from the COVID-19 era of emergency remote learning. Survey data collected with teachers during the pandemic showed that barriers to online instruction included poor or no internet connection, lack of resources, and lack of teacher training. However, teacher participants also appreciated the differentiation and flexibility technology provided (Cardullo et al., 2021). Reviews of research related to online learning and SPED have found that digital materials used by K-12 schools are often inaccessible and that teacher preparation programs are unsure how to help SPED teachers ensure IDEA (2004) and inclusion online (M. F. Rice & Dykman, 2018). Institution-level support for special educators is key in making sure teachers have the resources, training, and access they need to support online learning for students with disabilities. School leaders are often in charge of choosing which online technologies to use with students and they need more guidance and information to make decisions that meet the needs of students with disabilities (M. F. Rice & Pazey, 2022). The strategies and tools described by participating special educators in this study highlight potential features to consider when choosing tools or planning teaching training experiences. Results also underscore the importance of facilitating conditions such as devices, high speed internet, equitable school wide strategies for home-school partnerships, and teacher training opportunities.

Moving forward with FAPE in the digital age

There are no federal guidelines that detail what SPED looks like in online settings (M. F. Rice & Dykman, 2018), but the provisions of IDEA (2004) necessitate inclusive online education practices. The shift to emergency remote learning showed us that schools have a long way to go to support inclusive education in fully online settings (M. F. Rice & Pazey, 2022), but these struggles have also pointed to areas for improvement. To ensure special educators are able to provide FAPE in online settings, teacher training programs can begin incorporating coursework that specifically addresses FAPE in digital contexts and how to use technology for instruction in online settings. School and district leaders can provide professional development to all educators that considers diverse needs of students when it comes to technology and legal requirements for accessibility. Teachers will also need the necessary devices, connectivity, and technology infrastructure to facilitate inclusive learning in online settings, which requires consistent funding and thoughtfulness about how funds will be distributed.

Limitations

The present study describes the various practices teachers used to create accessible online learning and is an important first step in building the evidence base of best practice in online learning for students with disabilities. The study is limited to teacher reports and did not include student level outcomes or student perceptions of accessibility. Data collection occurred within 6 months of the pivot to distance learning, making it difficult to collect student-level data. Future research that examines the relationship between inclusive teacher practices and student outcomes would add much needed insight into best practice in online teaching methods.

Conclusion

SPED teacher innovations and practices described here have implications for online teaching with students with disabilities. Because students with disabilities are entitled to a "free and appropriate education" (IDEA, 2004), which increasingly involves digital learning environments, it is crucial for all educators to understand how to support diverse learners online. By closely examining the successful practices of SPED teachers and facilitating conditions of those practices, this study makes an important contribution to the field's understanding of how teachers can create inclusive learning environments for students with disabilities.

Acknowledgments

I would like to thank Dr. Stephanie Reich for her supervision of this research.

Disclosure statement

No potential conflict of interest was declared by the author.

Funding

This work was supported by the U.S. Department of Education, Integrated Research Training: Language and Literacy Disabilities (IRT-LDD) Personnel Preparation Leadership Grant, #H325D190031.

ORCID

Allison Starks http://orcid.org/0000-0001-7074-5460

References

Alper, M., & Goggin, G. (2017). Digital technology and rights in the lives of children with disabilities. *New Media and Society*, *19*(5), 726–740. https://doi.org/10.1080/08923641003604251

Barnard-Brak, L., & Sulak, T. (2010). Online versus face- to-face accommodations among college students with disabilities. *The American Journal of Distance Education*, *24*, 81–91. https://doi.org/10.1080/08923641003604251

Basham, J. D., Blackorby, J., & Marino, M. T. (2020). Opportunity in crisis: The role of universal design for learning in educational redesign. *Learning Disabilities: A Contemporary Journal*, *18*(1), 71–91.

Basham, J. D., Stahl, S., Ortiz, K., Rice, M. F., & Smith, S. (2015). *Equity matters: Digital & online learning for students with disabilities*. Center on Online Learning and Students with Disabilities. https://centerononlinelearning.ku.edu/wp-content/uploads/2017/04/2015_COLSD_Annual-Publication_FULL-2.pdf

Becker, H. J. (2001, April 10). *How are teachers using computers in instruction?* [Paper presentation]. American Educational Research Association Annual Meeting, Seattle, WA, United States.

Black, E. W. (2009). *An evaluation of familial involvements' influence on student achievement in K–12 virtual schooling* [Master's thesis, University of Florida]. University of Florida Digital Collections. https://ufdc.ufl.edu/UFE0024208/00001

Blackwell, C. K., Lauricella, A. R., & Wartella, E. (2014). Factors influencing digital technology use in early childhood education. *Computers and Education, 77*, 82–90. https://doi.org/10.1016/j.compedu.2014.04.013

Brush, T., Glazewski, K. D., & Hew, K. F. (2008). Development of an instrument to measure preservice teachers' technology skills, technology beliefs, and technology barriers. *Computers in the Schools, 25*(1–2), 112–125. https://doi.org/10.1080/07380560802157972

Burgstahler, S. (2015). Opening doors or slamming them shut? Online learning practices and students with disabilities. *Social Inclusion, 3*(6), 69–79.

Cardullo, V., Wang, C. H., Burton, M., & Dong, J. (2021). K–12 teachers' remote teaching self-efficacy during the pandemic. *Journal of Research in Innovative Teaching & Learning, 14*(1), 32–45. https://doi.org/10.1108/JRIT-10-2020-0055

Carnahan, C., & Fulton, L. (2013). Virtually forgotten: Special education students in cyber school. *TechTrends, 57* (4), 46–52. https://doi.org/10.1007/s11528-013-0677-6

CAST. (2018). *Universal Design for Learning Guidelines version 2.2.* http://udlguidelines.cast.org

Cavanaugh, C., Repetto, J., Wayer, N., & Spitler, C. (2013). Online learning for students with disabilities: A framework for success. *Journal of Special Education Technology, 28*(1), 1–8. https://doi.org/10.1177/016264341302800101

Ciampa, K. (2017). Building bridges between technology and content literacy in special education: Lessons learned from special educators' use of integrated technology and perceived benefits for students. *Literacy Research and Instruction, 56*(2), 85–113. https://doi.org/10.1080/19388071.2017.1280863

Courduff, J., Szapkiw, A., & Wendt, J. L. (2016). Grounded in what works: Exemplary practice in special education teachers' technology integration. *Journal of Special Education Technology, 31*(1), 26–38. https://doi.org/10.1177/0162643416633333

Dawley, L., Rice, K., & Hinck, G. (2010). *Going virtual! 2010: The status of professional development and unique needs of K–12 online teachers.* Boise State University, Department of Educational Technology. https://aurora-institute.org/wp-content/uploads/goingvirtual3.pdf

Edyburn, D. (2013). Critical issues in advancing the special education technology evidence base. *Exceptional Children, 80*(1), 7–24. https://doi.org/10.1177/001440291308000107

Gallup. (2019). *Education technology use in schools.* New Schools Venture Fund. http://www.newschools.org/wp-content/uploads/2019/09/Gallup-Ed-Tech-Use-in-Schools-2.pdf

Hall, T., Vue, G., Strangman, N., & Meyer, A. (2003). *Differentiated instruction and implications for UDL implementation.* National Center on Accessing the General Curriculum. https://www.cast.org/products-services/resources/2014/ncac-differentiated-instruction-udl

Hirsch, S. E., Bruhn, A. L., McDaniel, S., & Mathews, H. M. (2022). A survey of educators serving students with emotional and behavioral disorders during the COVID-19 pandemic. *Behavioral Disorders, 47*(2), 95–107. https://doi.org/10.1177/01987429211016780

Hodges, C., Moore, S., Lockee, B., Trust, T., & Bond, A. (2020, March 27). The difference between emergency remote teaching and online learning. *EDUCAUSE Review, 3.* https://er.educause.edu/articles/2020/3/the-difference-between-emergency-remote-teaching-and-online-learning

Hogarty, K. Y., Lang, T. R., & Kromrey, J. D. (2003). Another look at technology use in classrooms: The development and validation of an instrument to measure teachers' perceptions. *Educational and Psychological Measurement, 63*(1), 139–162. https://doi.org/10.1177/0013164402239322

Individuals with Disabilities Education Act, 20 U.S.C. § 1400 [2004]. https://sites.ed.gov/idea/statute-chapter-33/subchapter-i/1400

Jones, C. (2020, March 24). Despite assurances of flexibility, educators fear liability in online instruction of special ed students. *EdSource.* https://edsource.org/2020/despite-assurances-of-flexibility-educators-fear-liability-in-online-instruction-of-special-ed-students/626898

Kocdar S., & Bozkurt A. (2022). Supporting learners with special needs in open, distance, and digital education. In O. Zawacki-Richter & I. Jung (Eds.), *Handbook of open, distance and digital education* (pp. 1–16). Springer. https://doi.org/10.1007/978-981-19-0351-9_49-1

Lewis, E. (2021). Best practices for improving the quality of the online course design and learners experience. *The Journal of Continuing Higher Education, 69*(1), 61–70. https://doi.org/10.1080/07377363.2020.1776558

Margalit, M., & Raskind, M. H. (2009). Mothers of children with LD and ADHD: Empowerment through online communication. *Journal of Special Education Technology, 24*(1), 39–49. https://doi.org/10.1177/016264340902400104

Myers, J., Witzel, B., Bouck, E., & Mathis, J. (2021). Middle school math teachers' perceptions of their classroom practices among students with disabilities before and during the pandemic: A pilot study. *Journal of Online Learning Research, 7*, 209–231. https://www.learntechlib.org/primary/p/219619/

National Center for Education Statistics. (2019). *Characteristics of public and private elementary and secondary schools in the United States: Results from the 2017–18 National Teacher and Principal Survey First Look* (Table 3, pp. 11–12). https://nces.ed.gov/pubs2019/2019140.pdf

Noguerón-Liu, S. (2017). Expanding notions of digital access: Parents' negotiation of school-based technology initiatives in new immigrant communities. *Equity and Excellence in Education, 50*(4), 387–399. https://doi.org/10.1080/10665684.2017.1395301

Ortiz, K. R., Rice, M. F., Curry, T., Mellard, D., & Kennedy, K. (2021). Parent perceptions of online school support for children with disabilities. *American Journal of Distance Education, 35*(4), 276–292. https://doi.org/10.1080/08923647.2021.1979343

Preston, C. (2020, March 31). "I hate COVID-19": Kids with disabilities struggle to adjust as schools close. *NBC News*. https://www.nbcnews.com/news/education/i-hate-covid-19-kids-disabilities-struggle-adjust-schools-close-n1172906

Rice, K. (2006). A comprehensive look at distance education in the K-12 context. *Journal of Research on Technology in Education, 38*(4), 425–448. https://doi.org/10.1080/15391523.2006.10782468

Rice, M. F. (2022). Special education teachers' use of technologies during the COVID-19 era (Spring 2020—Fall 2021). *TechTrends, 66*(2), 310–326. https://doi.org/10.1007/s11528-022-00700-5

Rice, M. F., & Deshler, D. D. (2018). Too many words, too little support: Vocabulary instruction in online earth science courses. *International Journal of Web-Based Learning and Teaching Technologies, 13*(2), 46–61. https://doi.org/10.4018/IJWLTT.2018040104

Rice, M. F., & Dykman, B. (2018). The emerging research base on online learning and students with disabilities. In K. Kennedy & R. Ferdig (Eds.), *Handbook of research on K-12 online and blending learning* (2nd ed., pp. 189–206). ETC Press.

Rice, M. F., & Ortiz, K. R. (2021). Parents' use of digital literacies to support their children with disabilities in online learning environments. *Online Learning Journal, 25*(3), 208–229. https://doi.org/10.24059/olj.v25i3.2407

Rice, M. F., & Pazey, B. L. (2022). Ensuring IDEA implementation for students with disabilities across instructional modalities. *Management in Education*. https://doi.org/10.1177/08920206221107102

Saldaña, J. (2016). *Coding manual for qualitative researchers* (3rd ed.). SAGE.

Seale, J. K. (2014). *E-learning and disability in higher education: Accessibility research and practice*. Routledge. https://doi.org/10.4324/9780203095942

Smith, S. J., & Okolo, C. (2010). Response to intervention and evidence-based practices: Where does technology fit? *Learning Disability Quarterly, 33*, 257–272. https://doi.org/10.1177/073194871003300404

Spann, S. J., Kohler, F. W., & Soenksen, D. (2003). Examining parents' involvement in and perceptions of special education services: An interview with families in a parent support group. *Focus on Autism and Other Developmental Disabilities, 18*(4), 228–237. https://doi.org/10.1177/10883576030180040401

U.S. Department of Education. (2017). *Reimagining the role of technology in education: 2017 National Education Technology Plan update*. https://tech.ed.gov/files/2017/01/NETP17.pdf

U.S. Government Accountability Office. (2020, November). *Distance learning: Challenges providing services to K-12 English learners and students with disabilities during COVID 19*. https://www.gao.gov/products/GAO-21-43#summary

Vasquez, E., III, & Serianni, B. A. (2012). Research and practice in distance education for K-12 students with disabilities. *Rural Special Education Quarterly, 31*(4), 33–42. https://doi.org/10.1177/875687051203100406

Vega, V., & Robb, M. B. (2019). *The Common Sense Census: Inside the 21st-century classroom*. Common Sense Media. https://www.commonsensemedia.org/sites/default/files/research/report/2019-educator-census-inside-the-21st-century-classroom_1.pdf

World Economic Forum. (2020). *The future of jobs report 2020*. http://www3.weforum.org/docs/WEF_Future_of_Jobs_2020.pdf

Appendix A
Interview Protocol

Let me tell you a little bit about the study you are participating in today. Prior to the COVID-19 pandemic, I was interested in the strengths and limitations of technology to meet the needs of students, and especially students with diverse learning needs. Now these issues have taken on more urgency as schools have shifted to remote learning models, and special educators are being asked to meet student needs completely online. My hope is to describe the special educator experience during the COVID-19 response to learn how teacher training and schools can better support students and teachers when it comes to technology.

The interview will take between 45 to 60 minutes and will be recorded. I will use the information you share for research purposes online. I will keep identities confidential and will not link any comments to specific individuals or schools. After the interview, I will send you a link to an online survey and an ID code you will use to keep your answers anonymous. After you complete the survey, I will reach out to finalize the details for your gift card.

Your participation in this study is voluntary. You may request at any time that we stop the interview or turn off the recording. You may also request at any time that I not include this interview in the study. Right now, I am going to give you a chance to review the study information sheet I sent previously to your email account. Do you have any questions?

Before we get into some of the technology specific questions, I'd like to ask a couple general questions about your role at school, the kinds of special education you provide, and general attitudes about technology.

GENERAL

- What is your title at school? What are the general responsibilities of your role?
- In general, what kind of special education teaching model (support, collab, parallel teaching, station teaching) do you use during a typical in-person school day? (planning lessons, reviewing for adaptation, co-teaching, small group instruction)
    - Has this changed during remote learning?
    - How so?
- What are the general needs of the students you serve?
- How do you view the relationship between special education and technology?
    - Do you think the relationship between teaching and technology differs for content area teaching? Why or why not?

[This next set of questions focuses on school technology use before COVID-19. After these, we will move into a few questions about what teaching looks like during emergency remote learning.]

BEFORE COVID

- Prior to COVID-19, what resources existed at your school that help teachers teach with technology?
    - equipment, knowledgeable people, time to experiment/learn, community
- Prior to the COVID-19 pandemic, how did you use technology for teaching?
    - For meeting specific needs of students (with/without special need)
    - For teaching tasks
- What kinds of things have helped you use technology as a teacher?
    - Teacher education courses / preservice teaching?
    - inservice/ teacher PD?
    - Learning from other teachers?
- Is there anyone you can turn to for help using technology for teaching?
    - Who are they?
    - How do they help?
- Prior to COVID-19, what got in the way of teaching with technology?
    - Specifically, is there anything that got in the way of using technology to meet the needs of special education students?

[Now we are going to move into some questions about teaching specifically during the COVID-19 pandemic.]

COVID-19 Specific

- Please describe your school's current remote learning plan for students—if there is one.
    - Are there any specific plans for students with special needs?
        - ■ Service delivery, IEP meetings, etc.
    - How were these plans communicated?
- What kinds of accommodations for students were easier to adapt for online learning? What kinds of accommodations were more difficult?
- What are some of the biggest challenges for teaching (in a remote learning environment) right now?
    - Has your school found any solutions for these issues?
- Please describe what collaboration with general education teachers look like right now.
- What resources do you use to teach remotely/meet the needs of students?
    - Technology
    - People
    - Communities
- How are cell phones being used to connect with students or families (if at all)?
- What gets in the way of meeting student needs remotely?
- What kinds of things would be helpful for your teaching right now?
- In what ways was your school prepared or unprepared for the shift to remote learning?
- How does collaboration with teachers, students, and families changed with the shift to remote learning?
    - What strategies have been especially helpful in partnering with families?

[For this last part of the interview, I am going to ask your thoughts about changes that could be made as a result of the COVID-19 pandemic.]

Looking forward

- What kinds of professional development would help teachers who are teaching in remote learning environments or for teaching with technology in general?
- What changes, if any, do you think your school should make after this experience?
- What has surprised you about teaching in a remote learning model?
- What are some of your biggest concerns, if any, about the students you serve during remote learning?
- Is there anything else you would like to say about technology integration, special education, or remote learning?

Appendix B
List of codes
Demographics

- caseload
- school context
- SPED role
- grade taught

Teacher practices with tech

- using tech for comprehension monitoring/intervention
- accessibility training
- differentiating presentation of material
- scaffolding attention
- gamifying
- building social skills
- home communication
- personalizing
- platforms used with students

Innovations and workarounds

- language translation workarounds
- bureaucracy workarounds
- providing hands on materials
- incentive systems
- coaching home on tech use
- tech for SEL needs
- screencasting
- small group breakouts
- schedules
- leveraging visuals of tech
- seeking funding for tech
- listening to parent/family needs
- cell phone/smartphone use

Factors for technology use

- device access
- internet access
- software access
- platform accessibility
- SPED bureaucracy
- time
- teacher training
- institutional choices about tech
- gen ed collaborations
- reliability of technology
- resources
- student digital literacy
- student persistence
- home-school communication
- home factors for tech use
- teacher confidence with technology
- teacher beliefs about technology for teaching

Differences between SPED & general education (for technology)

Index

ableism 8, 15, 20
academic advisers 45–47, 56
accessibility 4, 36, 75, 77–80, 82, 84–86, 93, 98, 100–105, 125; checkers 103, 104; issues 78, 84, 103; practices 84–86; requirements 77, 79, 105; services 32, 33, 36, 81; tools 103, 125
accessible online learning 118, 131
accommodations 32, 34–37, 51–54, 76–78, 93, 115, 136
advisers 3, 45–57; experience 49; strategies 52
advising strategies 46, 56
agency 4, 68, 69, 99–101, 104
Alexander, R. J. 65
Angelaki, C. 35
anti-oppressive social work 29
Arksey, H. 10–11
article identification 64
assistive technologies 2, 4, 14, 16–19, 21, 92, 93, 125
asynchronous text-based interaction 47
Atkinson, R. 29

Barr, B. 37
Berger, R. 33
Biagiotti, G. 64
Brooks, C. 10

checklists 3, 66, 79, 80, 82–86
Chiwandire, D. 17
Clandinin, D. J. 29
co-agency 68
cognitive impairments 61
Cohen, L. 81
college students, advising 44–58
colonial logics 8
communication 29, 37, 44, 45, 47, 49–51, 55, 57, 117; strategies 48, 52, 55, 57
compliance 75–86, 103
composite scores 83
connections, building 31, 34
Connelly, F. M. 29
Cooke, A. 65

Cooper, S. 10
COVID-19 pandemic 2, 4, 27, 28, 35, 37, 76–78, 114, 115, 121, 135–137
critical disability studies 8

Daniel, J. 9
data analysis 49, 83, 96
database search 64
data collection 48, 96, 121, 131
data phase, charting 12
data sources 80, 81
democratic policies 21
dialogic feedback 66
digital environments 117, 122, 125
digital literacy development 127
digital technologies 2, 67, 116, 118, 122, 124, 126, 129
digital writing 125
Di Malta, G. 28
DiPlacito-DeRango, M. L. 36
disability-first language 95
disability policies 20
disabled students 67, 74, 76, 77, 92–95, 98, 108
disablism 8
distance learners 3, 61, 63–65, 69
distance student mental health 28
diverse learners 105, 107, 108, 126, 128, 130
diversity 13, 18, 56, 57, 61, 93, 98

education 2, 7, 9, 20, 21, 35, 62, 65, 75, 76, 95, 96, 98, 114, 115
educational delivery 9, 20, 22
educational technologies 117
emotional support 49, 53, 57
engagement 65, 67, 68, 108, 118, 122
enrollment 2, 4, 75, 76, 80–82, 84, 85, 92, 95; points 85
Equality Act 62
equity 13, 16, 17, 27, 29, 98
ethical considerations 48
exclusion criteria 63–64

INDEX

face-to-face meetings 52
faculty 10, 35, 51, 53, 55, 93, 94, 99–107;
    development offerings 103
feedback 62, 64–66, 68–70, 121, 124–126, 129;
    delivery 69
financial assistance 35, 36
flexibility 9, 13, 18, 31, 32, 37, 49, 55, 57, 92, 118
formative assessments 62, 69
free and appropriate education (FAPE) 114–116,
    129, 131
Friars, G. 27

higher education: institutions of 4, 7, 93, 95,
    104; leaders 92–108
home communities 37
humanitarian task 7

inaccessible digital content 116, 117
inclusion 2–4, 27, 29, 45–47, 49, 55, 56, 63,
    64, 85
inclusive approach 55, 56
inclusive online learning 92–94, 97–102, 104,
    105, 130
inclusive online practices 129
inclusivity 15, 17, 18, 98–108
institutional policies 20, 51, 100
institutions, barriers 105–106
instructional designers 4, 93–95, 99–101, 104,
    106–108
instructors 3, 33–36, 45, 47, 49–52, 82, 85, 86
intersection 31, 34
intervention strategies 52
interview protocol 96, 135–137
iron triangle 8–10

Johnson, G. M. 65

Kahu, E. R. 35
Kanuka, H. 10
Kinash, S. 2
Koutsouris, G. 62

learner inclusion 54, 74–86
legal precedence 77
Lieblich, A. 31
Linden, B. 28
Lister, K. 28
Lowenthal, P. R. 85

Maboe, M. J. 13, 16, 18, 19
MacDonald, J. E. 27
Madaus, J. W. 77
Mavroidis, I. 35
Mavropoulou, S. 2
McGuire, A. 20
McManus, D. 28, 32
medical documentation 33, 37

mental health 26–37; (dis)abilities 26–37;
    literacy 27
Miles, M. B. 96
Moriña, A. 64
Morven-Gould, A. 10
multiple case-study research design 119

narrative inquiry 3, 26, 29, 31
Ndeya-Ndereya, C.N. 17, 20
Ndlovu, S. 18
Ngubane-Mokiwa, S. A. 16, 18–19
noncompliance 78; potential costs of 78–79
nonmarginalization 18
nontraditional disabilities 56
Ntombela, S. 16, 19, 20

O'Malley, L. 10, 11
on-campus universities 44, 46
online accessibility 75, 77, 79, 80, 94, 106
online advisers 44, 46, 56, 57
online distance education programs 75, 77
online group work opportunities 64, 67, 69
online learners 44–46, 56
online learning 2, 3, 17, 49, 92–95, 108,
    116–118, 129–131; environments 28, 44, 46,
    49, 55, 115; leaders 93, 94, 96–98, 101–104,
    106, 108; materials 19
online program enrollment 4, 84, 85
online university 3, 46, 47, 49, 54–57; programs
    3, 74–86

pandemic-induced shifts 129
participants 29–35, 37, 48–50, 98–104, 106,
    107; recruitment 48; recruitment and
    selection 119
Paterson, T. 67
Patterson, Z. R. 37
Pavenkov, O. V. 2
peer assessment 62, 66, 69
Peters, O. 9
physical manipulatives 126, 129
positionality 95, 96
positive feedback 65, 69, 96
post-apartheid South Africa 7, 21
postsecondary student mental health 27–28
Potgieter, M. 17, 18
Power, T. M. 10
Prideaux, M. 67
proactive approach 56, 98, 106
professional development 35, 67, 94, 131, 137
psycho-emotional support 44
public educational institutions 76, 77

quality assurance frameworks 85

Rath, L. 36
reading experiences 124

recruit buy-in, senior leadership 106
relevant studies phase 11
reliability 96, 121, 128
research design 8, 47, 49, 94
research questions 10, 11, 49, 56, 63, 64, 79, 83, 84, 94, 97
Ribchester, C. 65
Richardson, J. T. E. 28
Riessman, C. K. 31

sanism 29, 34, 37
screencasting 122, 129
search strategy 64
self-assessment 62
semi-structured interviews 3, 48, 94, 96, 121
smartphones 126, 127
social media networks 46
social phobias 62
social service delivery 38
social work 30, 31, 34, 37; distance education 37; education 29, 30; student mental health 28–29; students 26–29, 36, 37
special education (SPED) services 114, 115, 119, 121, 125, 131, 135, 137; teacher practices 119, 121, 132; teachers 115, 118, 119, 121, 122, 124–129, 132
special educators 114–116, 118, 119, 121, 122, 124, 125, 127–131
specific online teaching strategies 117
Stentiford, L. 62
stereotypes 34, 37
storied lessons 35, 43
stories 29–31, 35, 37, 96; learning from 31; listening and hearing 30; telling and retelling 31–32
student agency 64, 67–70
student resources 128
students with disabilities (SWDs) 7–11, 14–22; in K-12 online learning 114–132; problems 116
study participants 119
study selection phase 11
sustainable development goals 2, 7
systematic review 10, 63

Tai, J. 68
teacher training 117, 128, 130, 135
technological skills 36
technological support 35, 36
technology infrastructure 128, 130, 131
Teixeira, A. M. 9
Tekane, R. 17–18
text-based communication 52
thematic analysis 15, 20, 49, 64
training 13, 18, 20, 21, 76, 100, 103, 105, 107, 116, 117, 128, 131
Tricco, A. C. 11
trustworthiness 11, 64, 96, 121
tutor feedback 62

Uleanya, C. 10
universal design (UD) approach 45
universal design for instruction (UDI) 45
universal design for learning (UDL) 45
universities 46–51, 53–55, 67, 77, 78, 80, 83–86; enrollment 82
usability 13–15, 17, 55, 85

validity 63, 96, 104, 121
Van Der Merwe, M. 19
Van Jaarsveldt, D. E. 17, 20
Vaughn, M. 68
videoconferencing 45, 48, 52, 53
Vincent, L. 17
virtual instruction 118, 126
virtual learning environment (VLE) 63

Wang, Y. 67
Waterhouse, P. 28
WCAG 2.0 79, 82, 83, 85
weak home-school partnerships 117
web and online interfaces 16
web content accessibility guidelines (WCAG) 76–80, 82, 83

Yin, R. K. 47

Zawacki-Richter, O. 9
Zongozzi, J. N. 16–20